309507

ISLE OF WIGHT COUNTY LIBRARY

BRITAIN SINCE 1945

GUY ARNOLD
Britain Since 1945
Choice, Conflict and Change

BLANDFORD

Blandford
An imprint of Cassell
Artillery House, Artillery Row, London, SW1P 1RT

Copyright © Guy Arnold 1989

All rights reserved. No part of this publication may be reproduced or transmitted in any form or by any means, electronic or mechanical including photocopying, recording or any information storage or retrieval system, without prior permission in writing from the publishers.

First published 1989

Distributed in the United States by
Sterling Publishing Co. Inc.
387 Park Avenue South, New York, NY 10016-8810

Distributed in Australia by
Capricorn Link (Australia) Pty Ltd.
PO Box 665, Lane Grove, NSW 2066

British Library Cataloguing in Publication Data
Arnold, Guy, *1932–*
Britain since 1945: choice, conflict and change.
1. Great Britain, 1945
I. Title
941.085

ISBN 0-7137-2124-3

Designed by Richard Earney

Typeset by Input Typesetting Ltd, London

Printed in Great Britain by Mackays of Chatham PLC

Contents

FOREWORD		1
INTRODUCTION	Fall from Power	7
PART ONE	COMPARISONS	13
1	Attlee and Post-War Purpose	15
2	Britain 1988	23
PART TWO	END OF EMPIRE	31
3	The Special Relationship and The Cold War	33
4	End of Empire	41
5	Immigration and Racism	50
6	Britain and Europe	57
7	Ulster	65
PART THREE	THE ECONOMY	75
8	An Economy in Decline?	77
9	The Unions	87
10	North Sea Oil	96
PART FOUR	THE STRUCTURE OF SOCIETY	105
11	The Welfare State	107
12	Education	115
13	The Political System	124
14	The Monarchy	133
15	The Church	141
16	Justice and the Law	149
PART FIVE	THE MEDIA	165
17	British Culture and the Media	167
18	Television in Every Home	180
19	The BBC	189

PART SIX	BRITAIN INTO THE 1990S	201
20	The Thatcher Years	203
21	Two Nations	218
22	Britain in 2000	229
Bibliography		236
Index		241

FOREWORD

From the end of World War Two until the start of the 1990s is as long a period as from the death of Queen Victoria to the end of that same war, and the changes since 1945 have been as momentous as were those from 1900 to 1945. If, as Mikhail Gorbachev declared in a well-publicized speech at the United Nations in 1988, the Cold War is over just where does that leave Britain and the West?

Following the Reykjavik summit of 1986, Margaret Thatcher's political antennae at once detected a possibility that the Superpowers might deal over the heads of their allies, hence her rapid visit to Washington to make certain that Europe is a part of any subsequent agreements; for if the Cold War really does come to an end Britain may once more find herself (in the famous words of Dean Acheson) without a role. Indeed, the bleak answer to where Britain would stand could well be: out in the cold from the special relationship whose justifications would at once fall away; and, if current attitudes towards the European Community continue, out in the cold in relation to Europe as well. By June 1989, quite suddenly, Britain's international standing appeared to have changed dramatically. The Prime Minister seemed to be increasingly marginalized and her attitudes old-fashioned or irrelevant to the disappearing Cold War, to Europe and to other political developments in a fast-moving era.

In Washington newly-installed President Bush clearly had no feeling, apart from politeness, for the special relationship, while a confident Gorbachev no longer needed to do business with the 'iron lady' after his ecstatic reception in West Germany where he could hint at the unthinkable: that the Berlin Wall might soon disappear. Even a reunited Germany began to creep back on to the political agenda. Such developments would spell an end to the role which has been attempted by every Prime Minister from Attlee to Thatcher: that of middle man or broker between the Superpowers.

During April 1989 newspapers, magazines and television celebrated ten years of Margaret Thatcher as Prime Minister (although she won her original victory at the beginning of May 1979). She played down the occasion but the media had a field day, defining Thatcherism and asking just what the Thatcher years had achieved, while a spate of books appeared to mark or analyse the event. Both at home and abroad there was a sense of *déjà vu*. In Britain there were unmistakable signs of a return to inflation and industrial unrest despite all the stringencies of a decade of monetarism and changes to the labour laws. And in international affairs, despite the dramas of *glasnost* and its worldwide repercussions, not much about the British approach had changed with the new times. Once her friend Ronald Reagan had ceased to be President, Mrs Thatcher had to work hard at the special relationship.

When President Bush visited London at the beginning of June, the Prime Minister stressed British loyalty to the United States and spoke of shared experience in two world wars and the 'great trials of strength which characterized the Cold War'. The timing for this nostalgia (just as the Euro-elections got underway) could hardly have been worse, emphasizing once more Britain's doubtful commitment to the European Community. And if Bush looked for a special relationship in Europe at all, it was one with Germany rather than with Britain.

The death threat against Salman Rushdie and the great furore which Rushdie's book *Satanic Verses* caused worldwide allowed the British to speak self-righteously of defending basic freedoms in a way far from borne out by behaviour over other matters, especially with regard to immigrants and freedom of speech. British meanness over refugees has become a matter of shame; all too frequently the authorities send such arrivals home to doubtful futures. This attitude was highlighted by the case of five Tamils deported to Sri Lanka last year. Under British law (the 1971 Immigration Act) a Catch-22 situation has been created under which refugees have no right of appeal against deportation while still in this country; they are free to appeal only from the country from which they have fled once they have been returned to it! Understandably, few are able to do so.

British attitudes were put to the test in June 1989 following the defeat of the student democracy movement in China, the massacre in Tiananmen Square and the subsequent public executions. This led to panic in Hong Kong and demands that the three and a quarter million British passport holders in the territory should be given the right to settle in Britain if necessary. While the Prime Minister and Foreign Secretary spoke of 'more flexibility' in handling the British Nationality Act 1981 and Sir Geoffrey Howe talked of hastening moves towards establishing democracy in Hong Kong 'to bolster confidence and serve as an example to the Chinese', the government and Tory Party together made plain their determination to prevent any major Hong Kong influx. Though quick to refer to China's 'regression to barbarity', Labour's foreign affairs spokesman, Gerald Kaufman, made plain that his party was as unwilling as the Tories to allow any major influx. The signs all pointed to another end of empire crisis, exacerbated by British racialism: attitudes exemplified by the acceptance figures for Hong Kong immigrants in 1988. Canada received 24,588, the USA 11,777, Australia 7846, while Britain (the responsible power) managed to allow in only 776.

Foreword

As the late 1980s witnessed a notable hardening of attitudes towards individual liberties – in particular the Criminal Justice Act in 1988 restricting the right to trial by jury and the removal of the 'public interest' defence in Official Secrets matters – so demands for a British written constitution or Bill of Rights became more insistent. The authors of Charter 88 presented a petition to Parliament in November of 1988; among other things they listed civil freedoms which they claimed had been eroded including 'the universal rights to habeas corpus, to peaceful assembly, to freedom of information, to freedom of expression, to membership of a trade union, to local government, to freedom of movement, even to the birth-right itself'. Lord Scarman has argued that Parliament should incorporate the European Convention on Human Rights into British law; Lord Hailsham has become a convert to the need for a Bill of Rights and has warned of the dangers of an 'elective dictatorship'. The British like to emphasize the principle of parliamentary supremacy which precludes one parliament from binding its successors by passing a Bill of Rights, but growing fears of elective dictatorship (made greater by a consistently poor Opposition) have been a feature of the 1980s so that demands for a Bill of Rights could become a fact of real political importance during the 1990s.

'No progress' appears to be the only possible description in relation to Ulster. During June Tony Benn called for the British to quit Ulster; he at least has shown a remarkable consistency on this sorest and most emotional of issues, but the government appear to have nothing new to say. However, Dr Garret FitzGerald, the former *Taoiseach* of the Republic of Ireland, made some forthright comments in an interview with a British newspaper. Among them was, 'The failure of the Irish to understand how stupidly the British can act is one of the major sources of misunderstanding between our countries ... because there's a Northern Ireland Secretary, people think there's a Northern Ireland policy – but there isn't.' That stands as the most accurate judgement on Britain's Irish performance over many years.

One has to dig back a long way to match the extraordinary political saga of the Prime Minister and a Chancellor so blatantly and publicly at odds with each other over such an extended period of time in 1988 and 1989. Following the 1988 budget, heavy hints from Downing Street suggested that Nigel Lawson's days as Chancellor were numbered. And yet, the more he appeared to lose Thatcher's confidence the more Lawson stubbornly proclaimed their differences. The Prime Minister has blamed the Chancellor's policy of shadowing the Deutschmark for the rise in inflation. The Chancellor (with the Foreign Secretary) wants Britain to belong to the Exchange-rate Mechanism of the European Monetary System; the Prime Minister does not. In a remarkable passage during an interview on the BBC's *On the Record* the Chancellor said the view expressed by Sir Alan Walters that the EMS was 'half-baked' was 'very difficult to reconcile with the facts of the matter'. He went on to say that whether he continued as Chancellor was a decision 'partly for the Prime Minister and partly for me, and it will be resolved in the fullness of time'. (Walters, generally seen as the architect of the 1981 budget, had been persuaded by Mrs Thatcher to return to London from the World Bank to take up once more the role of economic adviser at 10 Downing Street, which he did in May 1989.) Public differences between Prime Minister and Chancellor had become so obvious by mid-1989 that a clearly reluctant Mrs Thatcher had more than once to protest her support for her Chancellor even as inflation passed the 8 per cent level in May and the bank interest rate reached a high of 14 per cent. The government's monetary policy no longer even gave the appearance of being on course.

Perhaps ten years is too long for one person to remain at the top of a modern state in a period of great international change; certainly during 1989 there were a growing number of signs – from within the ranks of the Tory party as well – that many had had enough of Mrs Thatcher in Downing Street. The mood was not unlike that in 1963 when nothing seemed to go right for Macmillan. A social revolution – or any sort of revolution for that matter – must capture, inspire and keep a significant proportion of the young if it is to succeed; that seems to be exactly what Thatcherism has failed to do. The charity Shelter estimated in 1989 that there were 150,000 homeless young people in Britian and that homelessness among the young is growing faster than anywhere else in Western Europe. The teenagers sleeping rough or begging on the streets of London have become one of the capital's most depressing and notorious sights. The poorest four million people in Britian are now £2.30 a week worse off than they were a decade ago. There is also a bleak picture in education, with a growing shortage of teachers and a profession so demoralized that current estimates suggest that the state education system will be short of 12,000 maths teachers by 1995 (half its required total), 2300 physics and 3000 language teachers – at a time when technology and language are becoming ever more significant in the world market.

The government's official opposition to the proposed European Charter of Fundamental Social Rights was of a piece with the Prime Minister's Bruges speech of 1988, in which she said: 'We have not successfully rolled back the frontiers of the state in Britain only to see them reimposed at a European level, with a European superstate exercising a new dominance from Brussels,' yet an increasing number of her followers appeared to think otherwise. Thatcher might say, 'There is no such thing as society, only individual men and women and their families' but that assessment did not appear to be shared by a majority of people.

The policy of privatization began almost casually in the early 1980s. By 1987 some £24 billion of publicly-owned assets had been sold off, easing the Chancellor's tax-raising burden by approximately £3 billion a year and creating a new class of shareholder. The success of the early privatizations created a form of disinvestment euphoria which appeared increasingly bizarre if not dangerous; when suggestions are advanced, with all seriousness, that HM prisons and aspects of the public services might be better privatized, for many the time had come to call a halt.

The third Conservative government which came to power following the 1987 election announced that water and electricity were to be privatized during its term of office, and the Environment Secretary, Nicholas Ridley, began to exert pressures upon the Nature Conservancy Council to sell off some of its finest wildlife sites. But water raised the most complex problems. It is a natural monopoly; there is no obvious way that the public interest can be safeguarded once it is privatized; and within three months of the Queen's Speech announcing water privatization measures the news leaked out, in February 1989, that private water companies hoped to raise prices by 70 per cent. Another leaked memorandum indicated that the electricity industry was being fattened for privatization at the expense of the consumer by making the figures appear attractive to potential investors. Here, too, consumers will be faced with price increases to pay for the privatization process. Increasing Tory doubts have been expressed, especially about water privatization: there is a fundamental ideological contradiction when higher prices are imposed to pay for the benefits of privatization, whose principal *raison d'être* is the claim of greater efficiency and, therefore, lower prices.

During the years since 1945 a number of themes have dominated British public life – the Cold War, end of Empire, the special relationship with the United States, relations with Europe and the state of the economy. Underlying them all has been the problem British politicians have found hardest to come to grips with: the steady erosion of her power in relation to the Superpowers, and Japan and her principal European partners. This failure has been most marked in the determination to perpetuate the special relationship; as long as this illusion has been fostered it has deluded successive Prime Ministers into believing Britain has greater world influence than is the case. Mrs Thatcher's Conservative predecessor, Edward Heath, almost managed to end it by taking Britain into Europe. During the 1980s Thatcher worked to reverse that gain, helped by the particular metabolism which enabled her to work so closely with Reagan. Her innate 'little Englandism' put Britain back on to the edge of the European Community when the country might have played a central role in ensuring that a single Community without frontiers really does happen in 1992.

The European elections of June 1989 may turn out to be a watershed in British politics. The Conservatives ran a disastrous campaign, while Labour began to look more feasible as an alternative government, and the Greens emerged as a new third party. Labour increased its thirty-two seats to forty-five while the Conservatives were reduced by a similar number and failed to retain a seat in either Scotland or Wales. Even by her supporters, this defeat was seen to be the fault of the Prime Minister, whose attitudes towards Europe are regarded as too extreme by a majority of the electorate. It was also clear that the voters wanted to deliver a mid-term warning. Coming so soon after the celebration of her ten years in Downing Street, the results were a clear signal to the Prime Minister that her hold on the country is at risk.

The Labour Party had mild cause to celebrate for the first time in years: its organization had worked well, and it had gained seats at the expense of the Conservatives. Their policy review had apparently succeeded – to the disgust of the left-wingers – in eliminating 'negative' aspects of the party's image and presenting some alternative policies and images which might win the next election. Two and a quarter million people voted Green; in some constituencies the party polled 20 per cent of the vote. For the time being, the Green Party has replaced the other alternative parties which have been in total disarray since the 1987 election. As the main vehicle of protest against two-party dominance – and given the new world interest in conservation and the environment – the Greens will almost certainly be the most important alternative party at the next general election.

Guy Arnold

INTRODUCTION
Fall from Power

'We are a great nation, but if we continue to behave like a Great Power we shall soon cease to be a great nation.'

SIR HENRY TIZZARD

When Attlee came to power in 1945 the Empire was intact, Britain had 4.5m armed forces positioned round the globe and the Prime Minister could sit with Truman and Stalin as one of the Big Three. Forty years later the British government reached agreement with China for the handover of Hong Kong in 1997, and if British forces had been victorious in the Falklands War of 1982 it was a Pyrrhic victory: the Empire was dead. Brave words about Britain regaining her place in the world had a hollow ring. When the exiled Dalai Lama visited Britain in 1988, he did so under a Foreign Office injunction not to hold a press conference. The British government did not want any awkward questions raised about human rights in Chinese-occupied Tibet. Even some of Mrs Thatcher's normally loyal backbenchers expressed their disquiet at such pusillanimity, yet Britain's position in the world had changed out of all recognition since she emerged victorious but exhausted at the end of World War Two.

The period 1945 to the present has been one of momentous change by any standards and, perhaps, for Britain more than for any other major nation: it has witnessed her inexorable retreat from world power status. Several themes have dominated the period, no matter which party was in power: the end of Empire and transition into the modern Commonwealth; Britain's relations with Europe which she was forced to join, largely against her will; and the maintenance of the 'special relationship' with the United States. These three themes were overshadowed by Cold War considerations abroad, and at home by the seemingly inevitable deterioration of the economy in relation to those of her principal trade rivals.

After 1945 Britain realized rapidly just how much her power had dwindled, and though Europe remained the focus of attention it was as a focus of US-USSR rivalry while lines were drawn for the Cold War confrontation. The reality was that the USA and the USSR (soon to be referred to as the Superpowers) made all the running. Indeed, it was almost comforting to think of the Cold War in ideological terms for this gave to Britain a more important role to play than if the truth had been faced too soon: that it was a power struggle between the USA and the USSR, in which Britain could exert at best only a marginal influence. The dwindling extent of her power became apparent in 1947 when she found she could neither afford to run her zone of Germany nor continue to fund Greece and Turkey.

It is never easy to come to terms with loss of power. In Britain it was all the harder because of her performance in the war and the expectations that performance had engendered. The British had fought from the first to the last day – the only nation to do so – and had been victorious; they had a right to enjoy the peace and be an arbiter of the new world which was to emerge. But they did not have the means to play such a role. In the long period of economic decline following the traumas of 1947, the greatest problem was psychological. When the Attlee government gave independence to India in 1947, Britain's imperial story came to an end, although a long postscript was to follow. Winston Churchill's opposition to Indian independence had many causes, but at root he was concerned with power. As long as Britain held the subcontinent, she remained in the first rank; once India had gone she could never be a major power again.

In a speech to a Conservative meeting at Llandudno in October 1948 Churchill spoke of Britain's possible role in three circles:

> As I look upon the future of our country in the changing scene of human destiny I feel the existence of three great circles among the free nations and democracies ... the first circle for us is naturally the British Commonwealth and Empire, with all that that comprises. Then there is also the English-speaking world in which we, Canada, and the other British Dominions and the United States play so important a part. And finally there is United Europe ... now if you think of the three inter-linked circles you will see that we are the only country which has a great part in every one of them.

It was grand stuff and arguably one of the most disastrous passages in any of his speeches. For at least a generation following it, successive governments tried to do what Churchill had suggested Britain alone could do: play three roles. The only one Britain played with reasonable success was that of turning Empire into Commonwealth and in that Britain had no option: Britain could do it well or badly but empires were no longer in fashion. In the case of Europe, Britain missed the chance to take the lead, and by the time the Heath government took Britain into Europe entry was seen as a necessity that could no longer be avoided. In the case of the English-speaking world Britain fooled herself for years that she had a 'special relationship' with the United States when the 'special' part of the relationship was understood only in London. The disparity in power was too great to pretend any equality. But illusions and talk of a place at the top table played a significant role in Britain's decline at least until her entry into the European Community. Such illusions are not yet dead.

The most visible evidence of decline in world status came with the end of Empire. In the early stages, governments could present the change as something admirable, creating the myth that independence was what we had always had in mind. After Indian independence, there was a pause for ten years; when Churchill came back to power in 1951, he set his face against 'scuttle'. But Eden's disastrous Egyptian policy led him to embark upon Britain's last attempt at old-fashioned gun-boat diplomacy in 1956, which culminated in the humiliation of Suez. Perhaps nothing made the point about declining power more sharply than the fact that while Britain was forced to withdraw ignominiously from the Canal Zone the Russians invaded Hungary and the world did nothing to stop them. Suez marked the end of the first 'magisterial' phase of British post-war decline.

The second period of decolonization which did much to restore British self-confidence was conducted under a master politician, Harold Macmillan. It included the *annus mirabilis* of African independence in 1960, the year when Macmillan delivered his 'wind of change' speech in Cape Town and Britain's largest African colony, Nigeria, became independent. When the Prime Minister of the new state, Sir Abubakar Tafawa Balewa, paid tribute to the Colonial Service on Independence Day, 1 October 1960, he supported perfectly the myth Britain wished to create: 'We are grateful to the British officers whom we have known, first as masters and then as leaders and, finally, as partners but always as friends...' Five years later Sir Winston Churchill died: the funeral cortège marching in solemn grandeur through the streets of London could also be seen as the funeral of the British Empire.

The awkward problems had been pushed aside, only to rear their heads at the end of the story: Rhodesia, South Africa and Ireland – the first colonial problem and the last. In 1965 the white minority in Rhodesia made a unilateral declaration of independence (UDI), and for fifteen years successive British governments failed to bring an end to a rebellion which would have been resolved overnight in the heyday of the Empire. Troops were sent into Ulster in 1969 and direct rule was imposed in 1972 yet two decades later no solution is in sight. And in February 1988, for the first time in the history of the modern Commonwealth, many of its Foreign Ministers met in Lusaka to consider the South African crisis in the absence of the British Foreign Secretary. Meanwhile, Britain had contracted her world-wide commitments, withdrawing from East of Suez in 1968, ending her protective role in the Gulf in 1971, and slowly accepting that she had shrunk to the status of a European rather than a world power.

When Ernest Bevin was Foreign Secretary, the Cold War was just beginning. Winston Churchill delivered his Fulton, Missouri speech, in which he first used the phrase 'Iron Curtain', in 1946; the Berlin blockade and airlift followed in 1948; NATO was formed in 1949; the Korean War broke out in 1950 to usher in a decade of confrontation which included the beginnings of the US-USSR space race, where Britain did not even attempt to compete. By 1988 a confident Mr Gorbachev had introduced the age of 'glasnost'; the first US-USSR treaty to limit nuclear weapons had been signed, and Mrs Thatcher was in the vanguard of a European movement to prevent American-Soviet Superpower agreements which would leave Europe in the cold.

In 1948 the *Empire Windrush* docked at Tilbury and 500 West Indian immigrants became the forerunners of a steady stream from the 'New Commonwealth' (a euphemism for black or brown). Ten years later there were 'race' riots at Notting Hill Gate and Nottingham, and in the 1960s race became an electoral issue, with increasingly restrictive legislation to limit entry. By the 1980s strip searches were used by the immigration authorities to intimidate Asian women immigrants, a far cry from the 1948 Citizenship Act under which all Commonwealth citizens qualified for British passports.

The 1951 Festival of Britain was a brave end to the Attlee years, supposedly a signal that she was on her feet again. It ushered in consensus politics, full employment, government partnership with the trade union movement and rising prosperity. The 1960s saw the youth revolution, the pop culture of the Beatles and Rolling Stones and a sexually 'permissive society'. That decade also witnessed the end of the so-called 'special relationship' with the United States. President Kennedy dealt with the Cuban missile crisis of 1962 without feeling the need to consult his closest ally. At Nassau the following December he emphasized his lack of interest in the 'special relationship' by withdrawing from the agreement to provide Britain with Skybolt – as far as he was concerned she did not need an independent nuclear deterrent. In January 1963 President de Gaulle vetoed Britain's first application to join the EEC. Dean Acheson's much-quoted judgement that Britain had lost an empire and not yet found a role hurt the more because it came from an anglophile American.

Consensus was wearing thin by the end of the 1960s. In 1969 the Wilson government tried to curb the unions with the White Paper *In Place of Strife*, but the unions would not accept any diminution of their role and Labour abandoned the attempt. Then the Tories won the 1970 election and, unlike his predecessors Macmillan and Wilson, Heath was determined to take Britain into Europe. He succeeded and, with entry into the European Community in 1973, Britain admitted, however reluctantly, that her real future lay there. The Heath government also tried to curb union power. The attempt developed into a confrontation between the miners and the government, which led to the three-day week. A year later Heath went to the country with the challenge: 'Who runs the country, the unions or the government?' He lost. By 1975 unemployment was over one million for the first time since 1945. North Sea oil began to come onshore, but not until 1979 did it provide Britain's total needs and give a surplus for export. One of the worst of Britain's economic crises was in the mid-1970s when the Chancellor, Denis Healey, obtained the largest ever IMF loan up to that time.

What remained of consensus collapsed during the 1979 'winter of discontent' and in May 1979 Mrs Thatcher, the country's first woman Prime Minister, came to power. Two years later riots in Brixton and 30 other inner cities heralded the emergence of new divisions in British society of a kind not apparent in the affluent 1950s and 1960s. Mrs Thatcher's approach, soon to be dubbed 'Thatcherism', was a break with the past every bit as revolutionary as the era of welfare ushered in by the post-war Labour government. And though Britain faced a welter of problems in the 1980s, the lifestyle of her people had been transformed from the drab uniformity of the post-war period. Mrs Thatcher presided over a country where the average working man took home more than £200 a week, where television was the principal form of entertainment, where 20 million people owned cars and where debt (and the plastic card) had become a way of life.

The way Britain reacted to the outside world had also changed. Shortly after World War Two, the Guatemalan Ambassador, so the story goes, went to see Ernest Bevin, to advance his country's claims upon the colony of British Honduras. After listening for a few minutes Bevin is reputed to have said: 'Guatemala, where the 'ell is Guatemala?'. In 1980 British television screened 'Death of a Princess', a reconstruction of the public execution of a princess for adultery in Saudi Arabia. The Saudi government took exception and threatened to boycott British business. The Foreign Secretary, Lord Carrington, while protesting that the government had no control over the media (a claim Mrs Thatcher worked hard to reverse in subsequent years), made a sackcloth-and-ashes visit to Saudi Arabia, so that Britain could continue to enjoy her slice of the Saudi market.

But the habit of power dies hard and it was still far from clear in the 1980s whether Britain had come to terms with her altered state. C. P. Snow made a notable contribution to the debate in 1959 with his *The Two Cultures and the Scientific Revolution*. He likened the decline to that of the Venetian Republic, and is worth quoting at length:

> Like us, they had once been fabulously lucky. They had become rich, as we did, by accident. They had acquired immense political skill, just as we have. A good many of them were tough-minded, realistic, patriotic men. They knew, just as clearly as we know, that the current of history had begun to flow against them. Many of them gave their minds to working out ways to keep going. It would have meant breaking the pattern into which they had crystallized. They

were fond of the pattern, just as we are fond of ours. They never found the will to break it.

Whether Britain did in the 1980s what the Venetians failed to do is the question for the 1990s.

PART ONE: COMPARISONS

1
Attlee and Post-War Purpose

'When society requires to be rebuilt, there is no use attempting to rebuild it on the old plan.'
JOHN STUART MILL

'Why is it always the intelligent people who are socialists?'
ALAN BENNETT

Many myths have already been created to describe the post-war Attlee government: the only one this century to have translated its entire manifesto on to the statute books; one of the most efficient administrations ever; the government responsible for a revolution without tears (Attlee's personal description).

We can examine the myths later. The realities of 1945 were grim enough, and what was astounding at the time – and perhaps even more so measured against the performance of many subsequent administrations – was that so much was accomplished at home and abroad by a government which came to power when Britain had bankrupted herself in her last imperial war.

The Labour government which took office in 1945 had several major advantages. Its leading members had all played crucial roles in the War Cabinet and so had at their fingertips the machinery of government and a formidable array of wartime controls which they could deploy in peacetime. The Coalition government had been responsible for the Beveridge Report of 1942 on Social Security, a White Paper on full employment and the 1944 Butler Education Act, three of the foundations of the social policies the Attlee government was to put into effect. Moreover, while Churchill had concentrated upon fighting the war, social and home policies were left largely in the hands of the leading Labour ministers, so that no other group of men stepped into high office so well prepared to handle it as Attlee and his 1945 Cabinet. But if Labour came to office well prepared to deal with the tasks facing them after a sweeping electoral victory, they also found themselves in control of a Britain exhausted by its war effort and economically weaker than at any time in living memory.

The Labour manifesto of 1945, *Let Us Face the Future*, sets out clearly, without compromise, a programme which was breathtaking in its scope and revolutionary in its aims. Little wonder that few predicted a Labour victory, let alone one of such stunning dimension.

In the manifesto preamble there is a good deal about what happened between the wars, with tough anti-Tory talk of profiteers and racketeers. Then follows a short paragraph stamped with the Attlee hallmark of brevity and understatement: 'The Labour Party makes no baseless promises. The future will not be easy. But this time the peace must be won. The Labour Party offers the nation a plan which will win the Peace for the People.' The programme: jobs for all; public ownership of the Bank of England; public ownership of the fuel and power industries; public ownership of transport – rail, road, air and canal; public ownership of iron and steel; free or cheap milk for mothers and children; a housing policy; implementing the 1944 Education Act and raising the school-leaving age to 16 as soon as practicable. The social services section included a National Health Service, family allowances, social security. In retrospect the manifesto looks undramatic, but in one year seventy-five acts were placed on the statute books.

On 23 May 1945, Winston Churchill resigned as Prime Minister; King George VI invited him to form a caretaker government. Parliament was dissolved on 15 June and a general election called for 5 July. The Conservatives were seen as the strongest contenders but they relied upon Churchill's image as the country's wartime leader rather than presenting a tight policy like their opponents. Broadcasting at the beginning of the campaign, Attlee reminded the British people that the only time the country had experienced a political police force had been more than a century earlier under the Tory Prime Minister, Liverpool. He was answering Conservative accusations about socialist controls. He went on to say: 'I entirely agree that people should have the greatest freedom compatible with the freedom of others.' The *Daily Mirror* was unqualified in its support of Labour but otherwise – as in the 1980s – most of the press was Conservative or Conservative inclined.

The results were not made known until the end of July when the service votes had been brought home. Labour won a spectacular victory, with two million more votes than the Tories (Table 1.1).

Table 1.1: 1945 Election Results

PARTY	VOTES	MEMBERS
Conservative	9,972,010	210
Labour	11,967,746	393
Liberal	2,252,430	12
Others	903,009	25

Thus, with the largest majority of the century – 146 over all other parties – the

Attlee and Post-War Purpose

Labour Party came to power under Clement Attlee to implement a 'revolution without tears'.

The achievements of the Attlee government have to be measured against the legacy of the war years. Britain had been 'broke' in 1940 and in the five years since she had strained her resources to the limit. Her day-to-day economic survival depended upon American Lendlease which President Truman terminated abruptly at the end of the war. By 1945 Britain was not only the world's largest debtor nation – an estimated 28 per cent of the country's wealth had been wiped out during the war – but she was faced with huge imperial and other overseas commitments. Against such a background of national exhaustion, it would have been understandable had the government confined itself to national reconstruction, deferring promises of a socialist revolution to times when recovery had been achieved. It did no such thing, but embarked upon a comprehensive revolution of change which it carried out in addition to the enormous task of peacetime reconstruction.

Between the end of June and the end of November 1945 the forces, civil defence and munitions were reduced by 2.49m people. Yet industry faced desperate shortages of manpower and skills; following this first phase of demobilization Herbert Morrison reported in January 1946 that there would be a manpower shortage of 1.3m by the end of that year. Thus the administration began with a siege economy and much of its thought had to be given to the subject of raw materials, or their lack. As a consequence controls persisted: price controls; production controls, such as the continuation of utility furniture and design; food rationing not only continued but became more stringent than at any time during the war; there was control of trade and of labour.

As though these domestic problems were not sufficient, the Cold War descended upon a war-weary world within the first year of peace and huge resources had to be devoted to this new, unlooked-for confrontation. The costs of defence and the Cold War limited the rate of recovery and the scope for action of the Labour government almost from the beginning. A Labour Party paper of 1950 set out the defence burden (Table 1.2).

Table 1.2: Defence Expenditure

	USSR roubles bn	UK £m
1946	72	1,667
1947	66.4	899
1948	66.1	692
1949	79	760

With total budget expenditure in 1947 about £3000m, defence was costing an intolerable 30 per cent. The government compared British expenditure only with Russian, because NATO did not come into being until 1949, and the Foreign Secretary, Ernest Bevin, was deeply distrustful of American purpose and policy, although this changed when Marshall became Secretary of State.

Expectations were high; pressures for decent living conditions and the social programme were insistent, yet the country was virtually bankrupt. Despite this, the government set about implementing its programme of social reforms, and the years 1945 to 1948 were a time of almost non-stop legislation.

The implementation of Labour's social policies, of which the National Health Service is the most abiding monument, went side by side with the programme of nationalization. The Party adopted the Beveridge Report in its entirety and four Acts covered the most important aspects of the social revolution: Industrial Injuries, National Insurance, National Assistance and the National Health Service Act, which became law on 5 July 1948, the third anniversary of Labour's election victory. Dr Hugh Dalton, Chancellor during this period, has probably not received his due for the reforms which took place. The only post-war Chancellor who positively relished spending money, he infuriated the opposition with his quip that he did so 'with a song in my heart'. In 1948, at the end of this first hectic phase of post-war legislation, Dalton claimed: 'We have mounted without halt or hesitation the great social programme which the electors voted for when our majority was returned. We are entitled to say that the new Britain, represented by this House of Commons, has taken the cost of social security proudly in its stride.'

This claim was strongly contested by Winston Churchill, who said the programme had been made possibly only by spending the American loan. However, the social changes of the 1945–51 government were its greatest achievement, and at least the two main parties were in agreement on full employment. In 1949, the year before the first five-year mandate for Labour came to an end, unemployment stood at a low of 330,336.

During its first year in office the government nationalized the Bank of England, civil aviation, Cable & Wireless and coal. In 1947 the railways, electricity and long distance transport followed. Although these and other nationalization measures gave rise to fierce Conservative warnings about the evils of state control, the only measure which really caused opposition fury concerned iron and steel at the end of the period. As Attlee dryly remarked in his book *As It Happened*, this was because hopes of profit in that industry were far greater.

Coal was the most important of the nationalization measures and state takeover represented, as much as anything, the implementation of a series of social service measures for the miners, whose conditions over previous decades had been appalling. To read the 1947 National Coal Board Magazine, *Coal*, is to step back into a world of economic priorities and levels of social deprivation difficult to comprehend in the Britain of the 1980s. Then coal was 'king', the most important industry in Britain, and miners were solid in their support for the Labour Party. Nineteen forty-seven was the year of the great freeze, one of the coldest on record, and fuel shortages simply emphasized the place of coal on the British industrial scene. The official manpower target for that year was 730,000 men in the industry and the production target was 200m tons, with exports of 450,000 tons a month. *Coal* described the new programme to provide 71 pithead baths by the end of the year, and the NCB agreed an additional penny a ton levy for welfare over and above the penny already levied.

One of the most important developments in the industry was the introduction of the five-day week, much criticized by the opposition, which the editor described in the July 1947 edition of *Coal*: 'When the welfare and standard of living of every mineworker as well as every other person in the country depended on the maximum possible production of coal, to reduce the number of working hours was a brave, imaginative stroke which has already borne fruit.'

The magazine also set out a typical budget for a married miner with no children earning £6 10s a week (Table 1.3). It was calculated that £6 10s in 1947 was equivalent to £3 5s purchasing power the week before the war had begun, and at that time average mineworkers earned £6 a week.

At the 1947 Durham Miners' Gala Ernest Bevin, Foreign Secretary, Herbert Morrison, Lord President of the Council, and Hugh Dalton, Chancellor, were in attendance. In those days the Durham Gala was an annual affirmation of the miners' support for Labour.

It was a grim year for government and country, which began with the great freeze. Food rationing was at its most severe. In the summer, paying the price for the promised American loan (convertibility of sterling and opening up colonial markets), the government implemented convertibility under strong protest. It came into effect on 15 July and was preceded by a run on the pound. On 6 August Attlee presented further austerity measures, which set new targets for coal, steel, agriculture and exports, but so precarious did the position of sterling become that convertibility had to be suspended on 20 August. This economic crisis was the first of a monotonous series which recurred with biennial regularity in the years ahead, whether the government was Labour or Conservative.

During 1947 there was also a national debate on the subject of emigration to the Dominions. A reminder of its content shows what different priorities exercised the public interest then. Not only was the debate about Britons emigrating as opposed to the many later debates about New Commonwealth immigrants coming into Britain, but it was conducted in terms of imperial defence requirements: Britain would reduce her population to build up the empty spaces of Australia,

Comparisons

Table 1.3: Miner's Typical Budget (1947)

FIXED CHARGES

	£	s	d
Income tax		9	0
Rent		12	6
Husband's fare/bicycle		3	9
Electricity		1	0
Gas		2	6
Husband's canteen lunch		6	0
Insurance, hospital savings/club subscriptions		5	4
Shoe repairs		1	0
Household renewals		2	6
Washing and cleaning		2	0
Papers and wife's fares		2	4
	£2	7	11

FOOD BILL

	£	s	d
Groceries		14	0
Meat, tripe or sausages		5	9
Milk		2	7
Bread and cakes		3	9
Fish		5	6
Greengrocery		9	0
	£2	0	7

CASUAL EXPENSES

	£	s	d
Beer		4	8
Tobacco		5	0
Clothes		9	0
Furniture/hire purchase		2	6
Entertainment		3	6
Holiday allowance		5	0
Wife's sundries		4	4
Savings		7	6
	£2	1	6

New Zealand or Canada, so as to ensure they had large enough populations to make them better imperial partners in any future war. Part of the debate was conducted in the pages of *Picture Post*, Hulton's national weekly, then a national institution, now defunct.

The Australian Minister of Immigration, Arthur Caldwell, urged that Commonwealth needs in peace and war demanded the dispersal of 15m British emigrants throughout the Dominions and Colonies. Oliver Stanley, a former Colonial Secretary, replied that Britain should not denude herself of so much of her population. In *Picture Post* letter columns O. H. Dolley of Taunton said: 'I liken this country of ours at the moment to a sinking ship and anyone who leaves these shores is a patriot in as much as he is lightening the ship in order that she may sail again.' It was hardly a happy comparison and may have prompted one of

Winston Churchill's more extravagant political misjudgements when he referred in a radio broadcast to emigrants as 'rats leaving the sinking ship'.

Another letter writer said: 'I have five strong children and my husband would like to emigrate to Australia but cannot because we would need £300 to £400 to start with but as my husband only earns £6 a week we can never save such an amount.' But there were plenty of people who said the country was 'finished' and emigrated if they were able to do so.

The great bulk of social legislation had been completed by mid–1948. Sir Stafford Cripps had replaced Dalton as Chancellor (after a leak in October 1948, when Dalton was presenting an emergency budget), and Attlee, Bevin and Cripps became the dominant trio of a government increasingly concerned with foreign affairs. The administration at this time is conceded to have been remarkably efficient. In 1949, another financial crisis year, Cripps devalued the pound to $2.80 (from $4.03); this recognized the reality of Britain's financial weakness in relation to the USA.

Whatever the merits of arguments about what should have been done after 1945, the Attlee government went ahead on all fronts including massive and successful social reforms. By 1950 exports had risen to 175 per cent of their pre-war level; both production and productivity were up while the working week had been reduced: a remarkable economic recovery had been achieved. The government was highly efficient – perhaps none of its successors has approached its administrative competence.

One of the most appealing stories of this first Attlee administration concerns the Cripps-Attlee discussion about the timing of the 1950 general election: should it be before or after the budget? Cripps insisted it had to be before the budget so that his measures would not be seen as electioneering (Sir Stafford Cripps's conscience brought forth the Churchill quip: 'There, but for the grace of God, goes God.') As Attlee commented later: 'It is dangerous to play politics with the budget. It opens the way to every kind of stunt.' Cripps's view has not had any support since. So the election was held in February 1950. A Labour Party handout listed six social measures enacted during the first three years after the war: family allowances paid for the first time in 1946; social security for all ensured by the National Insurance Act 1946; real insurance against injuries at work guaranteed by the Industrial Injuries Act 1946; universal medical and hospital attention provided by the National Health Service Act 1946; the National Assistance Act (which abolished the old Poor Law) passed in 1948; and the Children Act 1948 (a charter for children). As James Griffiths described these measures, they provided 'a shield for every man, woman and child in the country against the ravages of poverty and adversity'.

Labour won the election but the Conservatives were closing the gap; their opponents had benefited from the redistribution of seats which the government had carried out to its own disadvantage before the election (Table 1.4).

Table 1.4: 1950 Election Results

PARTY	VOTES	MEMBERS
Conservatives	12.5	298
Labour	13.3	315
Liberal	2.6	9
Other	0.4	3

But the great post-war impetus was lost. Although Cripps was able to reduce taxes in his 1950 budget, shortly afterwards ill health forced him, as it did Bevin, to relinquish politics. His successor, Hugh Gaitskell, increased taxes in the 1951 budget to 3s in the £ on the first £50 taxable income, to 5s 6d on the next £200, and raised the upper limit to 9s 6d from 9s (47½ per cent). The profits tax was increased from 30 to 50 per cent and purchase tax from 33⅓ per cent to 66⅔ per cent. Food subsidies were to remain at £410m and the government aimed to keep National Health Service expenditure at £400m, with adults paying half the cost of dentures and spectacles.

Attlee's reputation has grown steadily with time and hindsight. He was honest with the electorate: in the February 1947 Economic Survey, he outlined the extent of the crisis and admitted the situation 'is beyond the power of any government machine'. His crisp, no-nonsense style as chairman is legendary, and made up for his lack of charisma. He had a curiously powerful appeal: when in 1947 Cripps, Morrison and Dalton wished to oust him and turned to Bevin to join them, Bevin's reply ('I'm sticking with little Clem') has about it a judgemental element which tells a good deal about both men.

Attlee thought that his government *had* carried out a revolution without tears. Its achievement was the establishment of the welfare state and a mixed economy, which became the hallmarks of 'consensus' for the following political generation. Mass poverty of the kind which had existed between the wars had been eliminated, full employment was set to last for 20 years and for most people a new range of opportunities had been opened up. In foreign affairs it was also a government of achievement: independence for India and the formation of NATO (Bevin's greatest accomplishment) would be enough to give it claim to greatness. As Kenneth Morgan claims in *Labour in Power* it 'was without doubt the most effective of all Labour governments, perhaps among the most effective of any British governments since the passage of the 1832 Reform Act'.

2
Britain 1988

'First define your objective; declare your need; say what you want. Then, and only then, consider the obstacles. But even then the obstacles must be subordinated to the objective. Never must the objective be renounced in favour of the obstacles.'

DAVID BEN-GURION

In 1988, after winning three elections in a row, Margaret Thatcher was at the height of her power. The extraordinary spectacle of a British Prime Minister picking up rubbish in St James's Park, which had been carefully scattered, and stuffing it into a black plastic bag which she trailed ostentatiously at her side – thus making a point about keeping Britain tidy – tells us a good deal about the essential vulgarity of Britain in 1988. One of the country's most powerful leaders was stooping to public relations gimmickry of a kind Attlee would have deplored.

After winning three general elections, Mrs Thatcher entered 1988 in an apparently unassailable position. Her back benches were so littered with former members of her Cabinets that her Cabinet has hardly anyone of stature left. So jealous is she of anyone who might try to outshine her that, even as Nigel Lawson presented his fifth budget (in Tory terms one of the most successful), the stories of a breach between the Chancellor and the Prime Minister were beginning to circulate. Within days of the budget, rumour had it that the Chancellor would quit politics for the City: Mrs Thatcher prefers to be surrounded by mediocrities.

The Conservative Party in the late 1980s is in a curious position. On the one hand a right-wing ginger group of MPs with business backing was pushing the frontiers of Thatcherism forward. The group wanted to privatize Job Centres and social services, abolish the postal monopoly, turn over the sale of council houses to private management, abolish rent control and introduce a voucher system to cover health, education and pensions. Mrs Thatcher's *guru* of the right, Sir Keith Joseph (now Lord Joseph of Portsoken), was behind this group, which is to be serviced by a Free Market Secretariat. In a private memorandum the group argues: 'Despite the Prime Minister's success in changing the climate of opinion in Britain, the first two Thatcher governments have failed to bring about many urgently needed reforms in the economy, particularly deregulation. In the field of welfare, things are much as they were eight years ago.' More ominously, the document suggests: 'There is a small group of Thatcherite backbenchers –

not more than about 20 – who could be extremely effective if their activities were co-ordinated and had back-up.' As one old-fashioned Tory backbencher remarked: 'We are at the beginning of the thousand-year Thatcherite Reich.'

On the other hand the alliance of two prominent former ministers now on the backbenches – Michael Heseltine and Norman Tebbit, not noted for their love for each other, but each ambitious to inherit the leadership of the party – highlighted how many able Tories are no longer in government and would like to see Mrs Thatcher go. Early in 1988 it seemed doubtful that the Prime Minister, despite an apparently unassailable position, would be able to survive another crisis such as the Westland affair.

Nigel Lawson's 1988 budget ended whatever vestige of consensus politics remained in Thatcher's Britain. Before Thatcher it was not credible that a Chancellor would have £4bn to distribute in tax cuts, and it took eight years of Thatcherism before he was in a position to do so. A rich man's budget, it was seen by economic commentators as being as radical in its way as Lloyd George's 1909 budget: a reversal from taxes on wealth to taxation neutrality. Predictably, it produced opposition outrage; for the first time in memory the budget sitting was suspended because of opposition rage, and one MP, Scottish Nationalist Alex Salmond, was suspended for a week. The outrage was because of the decision to cut the top rate of income tax to 40p in the pound (the basic rate was reduced to 25p).

The budget did nothing to assist the estimated 10 million of the population too poor to pay any income taxes. The Tory *Daily Mail* described it as 'the "best news" budget of the century: tax down to 25 per cent, soon to be 20 per cent'. In presenting it, Lawson argued that he did so against a transformed economy with Britain about to enter her eighth successive year of sustained growth.

According to Inland Revenue estimates, tax relief for a married man on average weekly earnings would be £4.83 on £244.70. Principal arguments against the budget were that it favoured the rich and better off, and that many people would have been prepared to forgo the 2p cut in the basic rate if the money were spent on the National Health Service. A week after the budget, public opinion polls showed that more than 60 per cent opposed the cuts in the upper rates of tax. Mr John Biffen, a former Treasury Minister and now one of the many ex-Cabinet ministers on the back benches, said: 'The government will have a challenging task to persuade the public that this is a budget in the tradition of mainstream conservatism.' What was fundamental was the fact that it did a great deal to reshape the political scene. The Labour Party will face great difficulty if it fights the next election on a platform of raising taxes again.

A major justification for Thatcherite economic policies has always been that they will make Britain more competitive in relation to her principal trading rivals: this claim requires careful examination. The coal industry, which held pride of place in Attlee's Britain, had changed out of all recognition. The year-long coal strike of 1984/5 witnessed a government-union confrontation unparalleled since 1926, including the 'most massive and sustained employment of the police ever experienced in Britain'. It was part of the government's policy to break the power of the unions – and it worked – but in 1986/7 the renamed NCB (the British Coal Corporation) produced 106.9m tons of coal (half the figure for 1947) and employed only one-seventh of the 1947 labour force to do so. North Sea oil and gas, as well as nuclear power, had revolutionized the energy picture and coal had long fallen from pride of place, although it remained one of the country's most important industries.

During the 1940s and 1950s Britain was the world's third largest producer of steel after the USA and the USSR. In 1945, at the end of the war, she produced 11.8m tons, and in 1946 the British Iron and Steel Federation drew up a post-war development plan to modernize and expand steel-making capacity to 16m tons by the early 1950s. By 1953 production reached 17.6m tons and rose to more than 25m during the next decade. Steel production was then regarded as the benchmark of an industrial society. By 1986, however, British production was down to 13.1m tons of finished steel, of which only 64 per cent was sold on the home market, and Britain had fallen to tenth place as a world steel producer.

Neither the decline of coal nor that of steel necessarily means an overall decline of British industry although both changes are indicative of radical shifts in emphasis. In the case of coal, modern methods of extraction – often bitterly contested by the NUM – meant that 100,000 men could produce in 1987 what it took 350,000 men to produce in 1947. More important was the growing dependence upon imports into a country which, as Nye Bevan once said, was built on coal. As for the decline in steel production, the relevant comparison concerns the difference in the contribution of manufacturing to total GDP. On average, for the years 1948 to 1952, manufacturing contributed 36 per cent, whereas in 1986 it accounted for only 24 per cent of GDP. This represents a formidable downward trend.

On the general industrial front, 1988 was depressingly familiar, although there were awkwardly insistent suggestions that British industry was becoming increasingly 'colonial' – hardly an advertisement for Thatcherite economics. Addressing the Institute of Directors in February 1988, the Japanese ambassador, Toshio Yamazaki, praised British workers for their 'loyalty, adaptability and energy', and suggested that the disease of low productivity, recurrent balance of payments crises and endless strikes was cured. He said that Britain was winning a larger share of Japanese investment than any other European nation, and the most significant encomium was his commendation: 'But it is also the upsurge of confidence felt by our managers, as well as your own, in the loyalty, adaptability and energy of the British workforce.' Japan appears to be discovering the benefits of a malleable British work force and Britain, apparently unable to create new industries, looks increasingly to the Japanese and the Americans to provide employment.

On the American front the story was very different: AWACS and Ford were the two names to note. In 1986 the British Ministry of Defence cancelled the £960m GEC Nimrod (British programme for early warning aircraft) and opted to buy American Boeing AWACS aircraft. Boeing pledged to create 4500 new jobs in Britain within the year by awarding high technology contracts to British firms. The Secretary of State for Defence, George Younger, told the House of Commons at the time of the switch: 'Our assessment is that job losses (2000) resulting from the cancellation of Nimrod will be equalled if not exceeded by job gains in firms all over the country resulting from Boeing's offset proposals.' Fifteen months later no such jobs had been created or could be identified. How the government can justify the cancellation of a British project to buy an American one which produces no jobs in Britain, as part of its general increase in British productivity, is difficult to see.

But the Ford case is even more illuminating. During the 1950s Britain produced about half the motor cars exported around the world; by 1988 almost the last remaining British company (Landrover) was being 'given away' to British Aerospace in a deal which, among other things, provided heavy subsidies to persuade it to take on the ailing car company.

The Ford Company of Detroit proposed to establish a new plant at Dundee in Scotland, but the Transport and General Workers' Union opposed the deal on the grounds that it did not comply with the agreed industrial relations covering other Ford plants in Britain. Ford wanted a single-union agreement as opposed to the twelve unions operating at its other British plants, and workers at the new plant would be paid less than workers elsewhere, reflecting the local average earnings. The press made much of the fact that the unions appeared to have learned nothing after eight years of Thatcherism; that the TGWU was selfishly opposing a single-union deal and that such behaviour played into the hands of Conservative hardliners who could say of the union movement, 'I told you so'.

TUC chiefs travelled to Detroit to persuade Ford to change its mind, but without success. Ford gave as its main reason for calling off the deal TGWU opposition to its originally secret deal with the AEU for a single-union structure at the plant. Ron Todd, general secretary of the TGWU, defended his stand: 'Any employer has only got to say to us they want to build a plant in Devon, with local pay rates and no national agreement. Do we have to acquiesce? If we don't,' he continued, 'the employer will use the moral blackmail argument and say we are stopping jobs from coming in. The trade union movement has got a responsibility to ensure that the agreements we have are adhered to.' Later Clive

Jenkins, joint general secretary of the white-collar Manufacturing, Scientific and Finance Union which also opposed the deal, put his finger on the problem when he said, 'We are not going to get into bizarre auctions of the British people, selling them and their jobs for the lowest rates.'

This episode highlights several aspects of the industrial scene in Thatcher's Britain, none particularly appealing. Companies – in this case Ford – see the current climate and the level of unemployment as a golden opportunity to divide and weaken union power further. The government is content that this should be so, and the unions fail to get their act together. Most disturbing of all, something few commentators touched upon, the story did not concern a failure of the British motor industry. What we were witnessing was the spectacle of a foreign company deciding whether or not to set up a plant to use British labour. If the Japanese ambassador was correct about the 'loyalty, adaptability and energy' of the workforce, of course Ford would be happy to set up a plant in Dundee on its own terms.

There has always been a strong tradition of overseas investment. In Thatcher's Britain the trend has accelerated from an estimated £12,000m of net external assets in 1979 to an estimated £114,000m at the end of 1986. The outflow of funds increased sharply following the abolition of exchange controls. Ironically, by 1988 British businesses in the USA were facing increasing hostility as they acquired more stakes in that country. If only half the £100,000m of investment which has gone overseas since Thatcher came to power in 1979 had been invested in British industry, there would be a stronger case for claiming growth in productivity. The British may have become the slickest takeover experts in the world but this is hardly the same as producing goods everyone wants to buy.

Another hallmark of the Thatcher years has been the programme of privatization: British Telecom, British Gas, British Airways – one by one the public monopolies have been sold off to become private monopolies in a reverse process to the Attlee government nationalization programme. In what turned out to be a near disaster, the government offloaded its huge stake in Britain's oil company, BP, ironically allowing a majority of the partly paid-up shares to be snapped up by the Kuwait Investment Office. Mrs Thatcher, who likes to refer to her dead predecessor as Winston, forgets that it was Churchill who insisted upon a government stake in the company as a vital safeguard of British interests.

Parallel with the return of publicly-owned industries to the private sector has been what the opposition sees as an attack upon the integrity and even the continued existence of the social services. Perhaps nothing symbolized the change of atmosphere in relation to the social services so much as a story in the *Observer* on Sunday 13 March (prior to the budget) that Labour's Shadow social security spokesman, Robin Cook, had told delegates at the party's Scottish Conference in Perth: 'All over Britain in DHSS offices they are putting up floor-to-ceiling screens to protect the staff against the wrath of desperate parents,' who he said would be the only people likely to qualify for aid under the new system. Following the budget, an Oxford University study of the new system suggested that losses for the poorest claimants would be larger than government estimates had suggested. What no one disputed was a significant change in the approach to benefits under the Thatcher government.

Money is the basis of power and, though Thatcher is seen as the most effective leader in the Western world, the British economic base remains fragile despite claims that an economic revolution has taken place. Sir Paul Gore-Booth, Permanent Secretary to the Foreign Office in the 1960s, wrote of Britain's declining position in world power terms: 'The object of policy had to be to ensure that a great nation could stop halfway down and establish itself as a second-level power with real tasks to perform and obligations to fulfil.' National decline, however defined, has been the preoccupation of the establishment ever since the end of World War Two. Ultimately, Mrs Thatcher's reputation will depend upon whether or not she is seen to have halted that decline. She and her government have certainly changed the climate of national thinking, but most of the problems the country faces have an entirely familiar feel.

Perhaps the greatest testimony to Thatcher's ability is the state of the opposition. As Britain entered the ninth year of policies which caused more bitter denunciations than a majority of the population could remember, the Labour Party continued in total disarray. The challenge to the leadership launched by Wedgwood Benn and Eric Heffer in 1988 was about where the Labour Party is to go. Despite a prolific offering of hostages to fortune presented by the Thatcher government – the sinking of the *Belgrano*, the Westland affair, three million unemployed, the assault upon the social services, endless spy absurdities, privatization and a City performance which makes Edward Heath's cry of 'the unacceptable face of capitalism' look like a Sunday School reprimand – the opposition continued to look unconvincing as an alternative government. The populist policies of Thatcherism have won enough adherents among former Labour supporters to convince the party that it must come up with radical new policies if it is ever again to achieve power. And by the beginning of 1988 the Liberal-SDP wing of the opposition had reduced itself to a pathetic joke. But opposition disarray does not mean that Thatcherism will solve the country's most acute problems. These add up to a formidable list: a nation increasingly divided between rich and poor; continuing unemployment; continuing deindustrialization; a growing sub-culture of young people who have never been employed and do not accept the mores of those in jobs or in control; a prison system which is the disgrace of Europe; the cancer of Ulster.

Perhaps no subject better reveals the differences between the Britain over which Attlee presided and that over which Mrs Thatcher presides than the game of cricket and how it is played and enjoyed. Attlee, so the story goes, was persuaded to have a ticker tape installed in Downing Street only because it would enable him to obtain the lunchtime cricket scores. In those days cricketers were divided into gentlemen and players, and there was a snobbish disparagement of Denis Compton, one of England's best all-rounders, because he not only used Brylcreem on his hair but appeared in the popular press advertising it. Possibly the best cricket all-rounder of the 1980s is Ian Botham, who has brought the game into international disrepute by his vulgarity, swearing, disputes with umpires and loutish behaviour of a kind that selectors in the 1940s would simply not have tolerated. Despite this, he is probably one of the most popular sporting figures in the country. He would not have been forty years ago for the simple reason he would not have been allowed to continue playing.

In May 1960 Attlee delivered the Chichele lectures at Oxford and these were published as a small book, *Empire into Commonwealth*. The very last paragraph begins: 'One further rather curious link in the Commonwealth must be mentioned, and that is the game of cricket.' Later he says: 'Everywhere this very distinctive British game evokes enthusiasm. Perhaps this last point may serve to emphasize the very peculiar character of the British Commonwealth ... perhaps also it illustrates the difficulty to the foreigner of understanding its nature.' Those sentiments belong to an age which admirers of Ian Botham would simply not understand.

PART TWO: END OF EMPIRE

3
The Special Relationship and the Cold War

'He who wants a defender is naturally a subject to him who can defend.'
PLUTARCH

'No question, now, what had happened to the faces of the pigs. The creatures outside looked from pig to man, and from man to pig, and from pig to man again: but already it was impossible to say which was which.'
GEORGE ORWELL

The special relationship between Britain and the United States was a natural product of World War Two and it would have died a natural death in the years after victory had it not been for the Cold War. Even then it was always Britain which pushed a relationship seen by successive Prime Ministers as crucial to British power; it was never more than peripheral to American interests. The importance of the special relationship to Britain was in direct proportion to her real decline in power after 1945 and it became a constant of post-war politics to persuade Washington of Britain's unique value as a peacetime ally.

There was nothing inevitable about this and immediately after the war there were signs that the United States was prepared to withdraw from involvement in Europe and, more particularly, adopt policies harmful to British interests. Truman's decision to end Lendlease and the American refusal to share nuclear secrets despite wartime collaboration were immediate indications of this, as were early American pressures to decolonize the Empire and open it up to US economic penetration. It was not until December 1962, 17 years after the end of the war, that Dean Acheson made his remark that 'Great Britain has lost an empire and not yet found a role.' He was a perceptive man, sympathetic to Britain, and it was almost as though he were saying: Stop pretending to be still a great power; you must come to terms with your new status. He might have added that the new status should not include the special relationship since this was based upon a fundamental fallacy: that Britain had enough power to affect American international decisions. She did not.

During the five years between the end of World War Two and the Korean

War the basis of the Western response to the Soviet threat was established and in that early period Britain rather than the United States acted as the Western peacemaker. Ernest Bevin was the architect of the European system of treaties and alliances which culminated in NATO. Only in March 1947, when Marshall replaced Byrnes as US Secretary of State, did he get on better with his American counterpart, for in the first years after the war the US was reluctant to accept that a major confrontation with the USSR was inevitable, nor did Washington trust British motives.

In a series of treaties – the Dunkirk Treaty between Britain and France, the Brussels Treaty of 1948, which extended to Belgium, the Netherlands and Luxembourg the collective defence envisaged in the Dunkirk Treaty; and finally the North Atlantic Treaty Organization of April 1949 – Bevin provided the framework of the Atlantic Alliance, a political legacy in foreign affairs which was to be largely intact down to the 1980s. When he signed the NATO treaty on 4 April 1949, Bevin said: 'I am doing so on behalf of a free and ancient parliamentary nation and I am satisfied that the step we are taking has the almost unanimous approval of the British people.'

When Britain and the United States merged their zones of Germany the Soviet response was to blockade Berlin; this led to the Berlin Airlift from June 1948 to May 1949, when the Russians lifted the blockade. This was the first joint British-American action since the war had ended, and Britain alone of the Western allies was in a position to assist the USA – a fact which gave point to the special relationship.

In 1949 Mao Zedong and the communists came to power in China. The USA did not recognize the new regime; Britain did. But already the power inequalities were apparent because American pressure ensured that recognition never went beyond exchanging consuls rather than full ambassadors, so that, in effect, Britain got the worst of both worlds. Her 'half recognition' of communist China was scorned in Beijing and gave her no practical advantage. Bevin's oft-quoted remark that if the miners would produce an extra million tons of coal he could give Britain a new foreign policy went to the heart of the matter. Britain no longer had the power to pursue an independent foreign policy and this ensured that every Prime Minister put relations with Washington before anything else. None the less, under Attlee Bevin had more freedom of manoeuvre than any of his successors: the country saw itself and was still seen to be a great power.

Bevin was acutely aware of the limitations that a weak economy placed upon his action. In 1947 he said

> You cannot carry out – as I want to do – a completely independent British policy dovetailed in with other people, until we can get out of this economic morass we are in. . . I should hate to think that we are going to become a sort

of financial colony of someone else, whoever it was, for one cannot have that without one begins to be told what to do.

By then, Britain was being told what to do – by the United States.

Between 1948 and December 1950 Britain received $2700m in Marshall Aid. Lord Keynes had warned that Britain would face a financial Dunkirk if she failed to secure a post-war American loan. She obtained $3.75bn and a further $1.25bn from Canada. Only a few voices were raised against such dependence. In December 1945 the Conservative MP Bob Boothby warned: 'But there is one mandate which His Majesty's Government never got from the people of this country and that was to sell the British Empire for a packet of cigarettes.'

In his biography of Bevin Alan Bullock claims: 'There is no period, except during World War Two, when the special relationship between the two countries has been stronger than in 1947-49.' Yet during 1945 and 1946 the US government showed every sign of disengaging from both the special relationship and Europe, and altered its approach only when Cold War pressures made disengagement impossible, and then Britain was the only possible European partner. Bevin made sure that Britain was an effective partner and, to quote Bullock again, 'the strong lead which Bevin gave in foreign affairs in 1947 steadily gathered support to the point, in 1947/9, when it came as near consensus as any British Foreign Secretary has been able to count on in time of peace.'

In the ten years from the end of the war to his retirement as Prime Minister, Churchill's foremost priority was the maintenance and strengthening of the special relationship in the face of what he saw as the growing Soviet menace. When he said that an 'iron curtain' had descended across Europe 'from Stettin in the Baltic to Trieste in the Adriatic' he was defining what he saw as the framework of the coming Cold War; and he was doing so in the USA to make sure that Washington saw the coming struggle in alliance rather than in American terms. As long as he was the leader of the Conservative Party or Prime Minister it was just possible to pretend that the special relationship was one between equals. During his last two years in office (1953/5), he was obsessed with the idea of a summit to resolve Cold War differences; he can claim credit for the later habit of summits, although the United States was extremely dubious at the time.

Of the three options which he had advanced in his 1948 speech Churchill's clear preference was for the Atlantic Alliance. He might tell Europe to unite but he never seriously pushed Britain to be a part of it; he might pay lip service to the Dominions and Commonwealth, but by comparison with the USA he found them a bore. He returned repeatedly to the theme of the special relationship and gave it an importance in British political thinking which it could not have achieved without him. On 8 June 1954, in a speech in honour of General Gruenther, NATO Supreme Commander, Churchill said:

We are entitled to fix our thoughts on the might, and I think I may say majesty, of the unwritten alliance which binds the British Commonwealth and Empire to the great Republic of the United States. It is an alliance far closer in fact than many which exist in writing. It is a treaty with more enduring elements than clauses and protocols. We have history, law, philosophy and literature; we have sentiment and common interest; we have language. We are often in agreement on current events and we stand on the same foundation of the supreme realities of the modern world.

Later in June Churchill and Eisenhower issued the Potomac Charter, a declaration on foreign policy. With Churchill at the helm there was a certain reality about the special relationship; when he had gone this at once appeared hollow.

As British power contracted the United States stepped in to fill the gaps. The Truman Doctrine of 1947 provided economic aid to countries deemed under threat of subversion (by the USSR), and came into being when Britain could no longer provide economic support for Turkey and Greece. In 1951 the US entered into a treaty with Australia and New Zealand (ANZUS) for mutual military support – a treaty which did not include Britain.

When the Iranian Prime Minister, Mossadeq, tried to nationalize British oil interests and sparked off the oil crisis of 1951/5, the role of Britain's 'special ally' was ambivalent to say the least. Washington was less concerned to help Britain hold on to her oil stakes than to ensure American penetration of what had been an all-British preserve. When a settlement was reached and the Shah restored (with help from the CIA), the US had gained a large share in the international consortium which replaced the Anglo-Iranian Oil Company.

Colonel Nasser's nationalization of the Suez Canal in July 1956 makes sense only within the context of the Cold War. Nasser had concluded an arms agreement with Czechoslovakia. John Foster Dulles, the US Secretary of State, approached the Cold War in simplistic terms of 'with us or against us' – the concept of non-alignment was anathema to him – so his response to Nasser's move was to withdraw the offer of American aid for the Aswan High Dam and put pressure upon the World Bank to do the same. Britain followed suit and this Western withdrawal gave the Russians the opportunity to build the dam in their stead. In retaliation for the Western withdrawal, Nasser nationalized the Suez Canal, giving Britain and France the excuse to invade Egypt, which they did in collusion with Israel.

The 'special relationship' broke down. Anglo-American relations at the time were made more difficult because the Prime Minister, Anthony Eden, and Foster Dulles could not stand each other. When the combined Anglo-French forces invaded the Suez Canal Zone in November 1956, they found themselves opposed by both Superpowers. Nikita Khrushchev spoke of raining rockets on London and Paris, and Eisenhower refused to speak to Eden on the hot line between London and Washington. By 15 November United Nations' forces were moving into Egypt and the British and French had agreed to withdraw.

A special relationship was clearly of little use if it fell into abeyance during a crisis. It was partly a question of personalities, but also a failure adequately to consult the more powerful partner. Another important factor was that Eden was attempting to hold back the advance of the Third World to preserve British interests, while the USA was not interested in propping up British power, except where she was seen as an ally in Cold War terms. Perhaps nothing illustrated the collapse of British power worldwide so painfully as Suez. She could no longer discipline a weak state which had decided to nationalize her 42 per cent of Canal shares; she had failed to obtain the support of her special ally; she had to retreat ignominiously at a time when the USSR marched half a million troops into Hungary and sat out world condemnation with contempt.

During the late 1950s and the 1960s Britain found herself under pressure from the United States to join the European Economic Community, which she had so far resisted joining. This was a clear message from Washington that the special relationship was at an end and that from an American point of view it made more sense to create a strong European partner rather than have Britain try any longer to go it alone as Washington's special ally.

Britain's pretensions to great power status have always been closely related to her defence expenditure. In the decade following World War Two it made sense that Britain spent more than either France or West Germany on defence, because she still had her imperial and global commitments. Yet long after both countries had passed Britain in terms of economic performance (and size of GNP) and Britain had abandoned her east of Suez role, she still devoted a higher proportion of her national income to defence. Defence expenditure of the leading military powers at the beginning of the 1980s is shown in Table 3.1:

Table 3.1: Defence Expenditure (beginning 1980s)

COUNTRY	US$ bn
USA	171.00
USSR	185.00
UK	28.66
France	26.00
West Germany	25.00

Source: The Military Balance 1981–2 (IISS).

Britain's planned expenditure for 1987/8 included £18.8bn for defence, a figure exceeded only by the £42bn for health and social security. Britain's determination to be at the 'top table' as a nuclear power illustrates the dilemma of her decline since 1945. On the one hand possession of the bomb and the means to deliver it placed her in the major power league; on the other, she became increasingly dependent upon the USA for the means of delivery, so that her nuclear independence is a myth.

Political instinct made Britain develop her nuclear arsenal; as long as she had a deterrent she was not entirely subservient to decisions taken in Washington – the unspoken theory throughout the years of the special relationship. If Britain was to enjoy a special status in Washington she would do so only from a position of strength. Similarly, scrapping her nuclear deterrent would have to be for reasons other than a belief that the USA would protect her. As Ernest Bevin said in 1946, 'We have got to have this thing over here whatever it costs . . . we've got to have the bloody Union Jack on top of it.' He was reacting to the bitter experience of being lectured by the Americans and did not wish any other Foreign Secretary to be treated the same way. On 8 June 1947, a Cabinet committee decided to go ahead with the British bomb and Bevin said: 'We could not afford to acquiesce in an American monopoloy of this new development.' Britain tested her first bomb in 1952 and entered the nuclear club.

In 1954, when the United States detonated its first hydrogen bomb, Churchill, who was again Prime Minister, supported the decision to develop a British one because he took the view that Britain had to be able to bargain with the Russians from a position of strength. (The Treasury was more interested in cutting costs by substituting bombs for troops on the ground.) The UK Atomic Energy Authority was formed that year and Britain manufactured her own hydrogen bombs; on 15 May 1957, her first hydrogen bomb was exploded at Christmas Island. In June the US Congress gave approval for the exchange of nuclear information with Britain – a triumph for Macmillan and the readmission to a nuclear special relationship with the USA. The 1957 Defence White Paper explicitly committed the country to a policy of nuclear deterrence, and an immediate result of the new accord was the February 1958 Anglo-American agreement to site US missile bases there. Britain's V-bombers entered service in 1955 and the Polaris submarines in the 1960s, after the Americans had reneged on the Skybolt agreement. Polaris turned out to be a highly cost effective system; capital outlay was £350m and by the 1970s it cost only £32m a year in upkeep. By the 1980s the nuclear argument revolved round the question of whether to prolong the life of the British deterrent by switching from the ageing Polaris system to Trident. The Thatcher government determined to do so although the Trident agreement included servicing in the USA, a support which can always be withdrawn or refused, so that it is not a truly independent deterrent.

It is strange how that most subtle of British politicians, Harold Macmillan, pursued the American alliance with such determination; like Churchill, he saw it as the first priority of policy and when he became Prime Minister on 10 January 1957 he set about repairing the damage Eden's Suez adventure had done. Macmillan coined the term 'interdependence' which he applied to the alliance; the term allowed a blurring of the edges and suggested a greater role for Britain than was the case. He cultivated Eisenhower and Kennedy, with each of whom he developed close relations: he had the advantage of wartime collaboration with Eisenhower, and he flattered Kennedy, using his elder statesman role as an entrée to the counsels of the young President.

The decision by Congress to share nuclear secrets with Britain after the success of the British hydrogen bomb was something of a Macmillan triumph. Later in 1957 the two powers made a Declaration of Common Purpose, followed in 1958 by the Amendment to the McMahon Act which gave Britain access to US nuclear secrets. Under Macmillan she was clearly recognized as the third nuclear power, a political achievement which, among other things, ensured de Gaulle's veto of her application to join the EEC at the beginning of 1963. But her lack of real power was revealed during the 1962 Cuban missile crisis when US-USSR confrontation threatened nuclear war: whether or not there was to be such a war was a Washington decision which Britain's deterrent capacity would not alter. Thus, the argument for a separate deterrent – that it gave us a voice in Washington – looked hollow when a Superpower confrontation occurred.

There is sadness in the spectacle of Macmillan using his persuasive skills with ever greater insistence to less and less effect from 1961 onwards when Washington no longer saw any need for the special relationship. When the US Secretary of Defence, Robert Macnamara, reneged on the Skybolt agreement, Macmillan had to pull out all the stops at Nassau (December 1962) to persuade Kennedy to provide Polaris as a substitute. Britain had become the suppliant and that was the time when the special relationship concept should have been dropped. None the less, the culmination of Macmillan's policy was the 1962 tripartite talks between the USA, the USSR and Britain on non-proliferation which led to the 1970 Non-Proliferation Treaty.

The advantages of the special relationship for Britain were tangible enough: it linked her to the greatest power in the world during the dangerous years of the Cold War and permitted her to decline in the least painful fashion. It was the easiest to pursue of Churchill's three options and was seen to be so by every Prime Minister until Heath.

The disadvantages were less obvious but more dangerous. The special relationship tied Britain to American policies, sometimes against her interests and her political instincts; it prolonged an illusion of power which had vanished, and it aided American economic expansion at her expense. Since it was never possible for Britain to be an equal partner, she would have done better to pursue an independent 'gaullist' path and not try to be a partner at all.

The habit of dependence is hard to break. In post-Macmillan years Britain witnessed the depressing spectacle of her Prime Ministers flying off to Washington to make their 'number' with the American President, something French Presidents saw no need to do. Wilson's maintenance of the special relationship included support for Johnson's Vietnam policy in 1966. Only Heath broke the pattern when he took the country into the European Community in 1973, but both Wilson and Callaghan were determined to restore the special relationship. Twenty years later Thatcher allowed American planes to take off from Britain to bomb Gaddafi's Libya.

By October 1986, when President Reagan and Mr Gorbachev met in Iceland for the Reykjavik Summit, the special relationship had worn very thin indeed, so in November Mrs Thatcher went to meet Reagan at Camp David to be informed what had happened. The INF Treaty between the USA and the USSR signalled the end of 40 years of Atlantic Alliance and the beginning of direct US-USSR diplomacy which will be over the heads of the US's European allies. The Europeans are correct to be wary of a Superpower agreement which leaves them in the cold. If there were ever political justification for Britain's independent deterrent, now would be the time. (The French, logically, always insisted upon complete development and control of their independent deterrent). That Trident is leased from the USA and will be serviced by it makes nonsense of its independent nature. It is one of the ironies of the special relationship story that under Thatcher, who made great play of her friendship with Reagan, Britain found herself trying to keep Europe nuclear in case the United States, ignoring the special relationship and the Atlantic Alliance, did a deal with the USSR regardless of its European allies.

4
End of Empire

'We join the Commonwealth obviously because we think it is beneficial to us and to certain causes in the world that we wish to advance.'

PANDIT NEHRU

'I do not know how long it will take the British to notice that the Commonwealth is no longer anything more than an Old Boys' Association which meets every year...'

P. DELOUVRIER

In 1939 Britain had gone to war as an Empire. Despite Churchill's rhetoric about standing alone, Britain did no such thing for the Dominions and Colonies stood with her – more or less. Hitler had plenty of admirers among the whites in South Africa and Smuts only just carried the day. In India Congress was bitterly offended at the way war was declared on its behalf by the Viceroy. Even so, when the war came to an end the Empire was intact, if battered, and Britain had survived the last great war she would fight as an imperial power.

There was, therefore, an understandable desire to return to business as usual. It was assumed that the British could pick up where they had been interrupted, that as victors they had a right to a peace of their own ordering, which meant a resumption of the status quo prior to 1939. But the realities of a changed world situation and the limitations of British power made such a possibility remote. It took time for the lesson to be learned and in the retrospect of history, once India had achieved independence, there was already something anachronistic about the assumptions of the Attlee government concerning the rest of the Empire.

Although rapid solution of the India question by the grant of independence in 1947 has been seen as Attlee's greatest achievement, he was by no means anti-imperialist and thought in terms of the Empire as a whole with Britain the hub. It was a Victorian concept. Bevin saw it as a single unit for defence and he and Cripps wished to defend an imperial sterling area which the Americans wanted to break down. A new imperial momentum was signalled by Labour's concern with development. The notorious groundnut scheme in East Africa, which never got off the ground, was sound in concept if not in planning: Tanganyika would obtain development aid and an assured market for groundnuts, which were required by the United Kingdom. The logic of Indian independence – that every

Colony would sooner or later demand the same right – had yet to be understood in London.

Less than a year after Indian independence the British quit Palestine. It might be argued that this was a special case, but the retreat had set in. Churchill found it impossible to come to terms with this retreat from Empire – partly for sentimental reasons and partly because he saw that there was no end to the process and that it signalled the downgrading of Britain's worldwide power. He talked of 'a steady and remorseless process of divesting ourselves of what has been gained by so many generations of toil, administration and sacrifice.' In subsequent years various Conservative ministers and backbenchers were to argue that certain places could never be abandoned – Cyprus or Malta for example – because of their strategic value, but each became independent in turn and the Empire shrunk inexorably. Those who had always been sceptical of imperialism watched its dissolution with approval or equanimity but many found it hard to swallow the visible dwindling of British power. The debate about emigration to the Dominions was based upon imperial assumptions: that Britons should emigrate to make the white Dominions stronger and better able to come to the mother country's assistance when the Empire was again threatened.

In *The End of Empire* John Strachey accurately summed up national feeling when he wrote: 'The morale, the spirit, the mental health even, of all of us in Britain are deeply involved in the question of the dissolution of our Empire.' No other question over this period roused such strong emotions, but the Empire had to pass and the danger was of a Britain permanently mouthing its glorious past instead of getting on with the future.

The post-war world faced immense nationalist pressures, especially in Asia. These heralded an assault upon the European-centred empires which war-weary Britain was unable to resist. She had no option after 1945 but to come to terms with Asian nationalism. Also, when Britain disbanded her armies she sent home about 250,000 black African troops who had fought as far afield as Burma and had been taught that they were defending freedom and democracy. Back home, they discovered themselves to be still second-class citizens; from among their ranks arose a new breed of nationalist such as the young Waruhiu Itote in Kenya, known as General China during the Mau Mau uprising. Then the United Nations came into being; its Charter proclaimed equal freedom for all people so that it exercised particular attraction for the subject peoples of the old empires. It became a forum where imperialism could be denounced.

Britain also had to face the antagonism of the two Superpowers to old style European imperialism. Finally, and most importantly, European imperialism had run its course. In the years following the war the demand for independence, for freedom, for an end to European domination became overwhelming. The dismantling of empires grew apace.

The Cold War led Britain into alliances with European countries which were a new departure, an admission that her aloofness from European entanglements had passed for ever. The Dunkirk, Brussels and North Atlantic treaties and the permanent commitment of a British army to the Continent as part of the European Defence Community in 1954 all signalled a fundamental change from a policy which, in theory if not in practice, had seen the Empire as a self-sufficient entity. Moreover, other members of the Commonwealth were entering into defence agreements: Britain and Pakistan joined the Baghdad Pact in 1954; Britain, Pakistan, Australia and New Zealand the South East Asia Treaty Organization in 1954. And earlier, in a traumatic break with the past, Australia and New Zealand had entered into the ANZUS Pact with the United States – without Britain – in 1951. The world was splintering into power blocs, a process complicated by the emergence of non-alignment. India, which had elected to remain in the Commonwealth, was opposed to both the Baghdad Pact and SEATO.

In the middle of this period of realignment Attlee told the House of Commons (5 May 1948) that he was disturbed by the suggestion that Britain might be getting closer to Europe than to the Commonwealth: 'The Commonwealth nations are our closest friends. While I want to get as close as we can with the other nations, we have to bear in mind that we are not solely a European power but a member of a great Commonwealth and Empire.' But the signs of changed orientation were unmistakable.

Other different factors were at work. One was the drying up of Britain as the main source of investment capital for the Dominions and Empire. The principal *raison d'être* for the Empire had been British power and this was demonstrably on the wane. In 1951 the Persian oil crisis illustrated the point. Iran, like the Arab Gulf states, was within the British imperial sphere of influence. At an earlier time we would have despatched gunboats and resolved the crisis swiftly. A fire-eating Herbert Morrison as Foreign Secretary did despatch HMS *Mauritius* to the Gulf, but force was not used and the eventual solution saw an international consortium replace a British monopoly. It was all part of the worldwide shrinking of British power.

The end of Empire was accomplished in phases: India; the Suez Crisis; Cyprus; the Wind of Change; South Africa leaving the Commonwealth; UDI in Rhodesia; the Falklands War. Each phase called forth new regrets or last moment jingoism, but the process went on.

Attlee regarded Indian independence as his greatest achievement. When on 3 September 1939 the Viceroy, Lord Linlithgow, declared war on Germany in India's name without any consultation, he set off a chain reaction of Congress opposition. Congress wanted British recognition of India's right to self-determination as one of the conditions of its co-operation. By the end of the war the question was not whether but when and how India would achieve independence. It was the key to the break-up of the European empires, not just Britain's. The subcontinent had long been regarded as the centrepiece, the 'brightest jewel in the crown' and much imperial policy – the acquisition of Aden and the control of the Suez Canal – had been designed to protect India and the lifeline to it. Other aspects of imperialism – her role in Persia and the Gulf, expansion into the Malay Peninsula and the opium wars with China which led to the acquisition of Hong Kong – had been mounted from India rather than London. While Britain held India she was in the superpower bracket, but when India went she fell forever from the top rank. The Labour Party was committed to Indian independence and brought it about in 1947 under the last Viceroy, Earl Mountbatten. India and Pakistan emerged as the successor states and their independence was followed a year later by that of Burma (which did not stay in the Commonwealth) and Ceylon (later Sri Lanka), which did.

Its loss represented the real end of Empire but, traumatic as that was for the generation which supported Churchill's vehement opposition, the coming storm over Suez was even more damaging to the national psyche. The Suez Crisis was deeply entangled in Cold War considerations, but it also represented a convulsive effort to reverse the process of decolonization. There were powerful racial overtones in the British contempt for Nasser and the Egyptians whom Britain had 'managed' for so long and there was deep anger at the nationalization of Britain's 42 per cent of Suez Canal shares, a holding which went back to Disraeli and the beginning of the great imperial period during the last quarter of the nineteenth century.

When Nasser nationalized the Canal on 26 July 1956, Britain was unable to mount an immediate military operation – itself a mark of her declining power – and by the time she had assembled enough forces to invade the Canal Zone world opinion was so mobilized against intervention that it had to be aborted almost as soon as it was begun. The action split the British public deeply, and the inability to discipline a weak Middle East state was a far greater insult to national pride than withdrawal from India, which could at least be represented as a voluntary decision.

Two years later when revolutionary ferment swept away the monarchy in Iraq (finally ending Britain's semi-imperial influence there) and threatened stability in Lebanon and Jordan, Britain had recovered sufficient international self-assurance to intervene again, but British troops went into Jordan (at the request of King Hussein) only after American marines had arrived in Lebanon. This recovery was due to Harold Macmillan; perhaps his greatest achievement, an impossibly difficult one to quantify, was to make the British come to terms with their diminished power and begin to accept an altered place in the world.

The traumas of decolonization continued, and Cyprus brought out another aspect of rearguard regret. The Greek majority on the island, led by Archbishop Makarios, wanted *enosis* (union with Greece) and though many argued that Britain had to hold on to Cyprus for strategic reasons (her huge military base had been transferred there from the Canal Zone) there was anger that Greek Cypriots wanted union with another country instead of opting either for independence or membership of the Commonwealth. Later, Cyprus abandoned *enosis* and did join the Commonwealth, but many of the difficulties in ending Empire were less to do with problems on the spot than with British pride and regret at inevitable loss of power.

During Macmillan's premiership the pace of decolonization quickened markedly, with the focus on Africa. His choice of the young Macleod to succeed Lennox Boyd as Colonial Secretary in 1959 was inspired. Macleod fell into the category of radical Tory and was indifferent to the clamour of the party's right wing – a fact which enabled him to push through remarkably unpopular measures leading to independence in Tanganyika, Uganda and then Kenya, where the Mau Mau rebellion had focused attention upon white fears of black rule.

The Macmillan years witnessed the flood of independence: two crucial countries – Malaya and Ghana – became independent in 1957; Nigeria, British Somaliland and Cyprus in 1960; Sierra Leone and Tanganyika in 1961; Jamaica, Trinidad and Tobago, Uganda and Western Samoa in 1962; and Kenya and Zanzibar at the end of 1963 (when Sir Alec Douglas-Home had succeeded Macmillan as Prime Minister). These years also saw the groundwork laid for the dismantling of the Central African Federation of the Rhodesias and Nyasaland, and South Africa left the Commonwealth in 1961.

At the beginning of 1960 Macmillan went on a long tour of Commonwealth Africa and in Capetown gave the speech in which he said that a 'wind of change' was blowing through the continent. White South Africa set its face against the wind, but elsewhere the message was clear: Britain was determined to decolonize, and hoped to achieve the goodwill of her former subjects in the process.

In West Africa Britain's largest African colony, Nigeria, became independent in 1960, to be followed by Sierra Leone in 1961. The transition was smooth mainly because of the absence of white settler minorities. This was not the case in East Africa. Two events in 1959 focused attention on Kenya and the Central African Federation: in Kenya eleven Kikuyu prisoners were killed as a result of brutal treatment by guards in Hola camp; and the report of the Devlin Commission discribed Nyasaland as a 'police state'. Macmillan's appointment of Macleod signalled a speed-up of the independence process. Macleod believed that though it might be dangerous to go too fast it was even more dangerous to go slowly. As he wrote some years later in the *Spectator:*

> It has been said that after I became Colonial Secretary there was a deliberate speeding-up of the movement towards independence. I agree. There was. And in my view any other policy would have led to terrible bloodshed in Africa. This is the heart of the argument.

In January 1960 Macleod presided over the crucial conference which recognized that majority rule had to be established in Kenya. In the following year he persuaded the Conservative Party to accept the wind of change. The government managed to prevent serious white rebellion in Kenya, but more formidable opposition to majority rule was developing in Central Africa where the whites of Southern Rhodesia were to make their unilateral declaration in 1965. At home the backlash to the wind of change was led by the Marquess of Salisbury.

In 1961 Macleod presided over another conference, to do with constitutional advance for Northern Rhodesia (Zambia), and it was in the middle of long-drawn-out negotiations that Lord Salisbury denounced Macleod in the House of Lords as 'too clever by half'. Lord Salisbury claimed that he spoke for the white communities and this went to the nub of the whole imperial problem. It was one thing to give independence to Nigeria or another Colony where there was no resident white minority; it was something quite different when there was such a minority. The lengths to which successive British governments went to safeguard white minority interests emphasized the racial element of the imperial story. Racial sympathies with whites were evident in Kenya, during the long years of UDI in Rhodesia and finally over sanctions against South Africa. Recognizing the limits to which he could push the Conservative Party, Macmillan moved Macleod from the Colonial Office in October 1961 and replaced him with Reginald Maudling, although the thrust of policy was not abandoned.

In 1965 Ian Smith and the Rhodesia Front made their unilateral declaration of independence (UDI), defying the wind of change and attempting to perpetuate white minority rule indefinitely. Having committed their treason, the white leaders of the Rhodesia Front asserted their loyalty to the Queen. In the years which followed successive British governments showed pusillanimity in their handling of Rhodesia, an issue which bedevilled Britain's relations with the Commonwealth, while vociferous racists inside and outside Parliament espoused the cause of the white minority. Rhodesia became the focus for the backlash against the end of Empire. Few people in Britain or Rhodesia believed that had Joshua Nkomo and the African majority seized power in November 1965 the British government would have argued as it did for Smith – that it was powerless to do more than apply limited sanctions. Troops would have been sent to Central Africa within a week; that this did not happen was testimony to loss of will and political weariness with the problems of ending Empire. Wilson, who was Prime Minister when UDI occurred, was not a man to take decisive action; his responses were not those of the Prime Minister of an imperial power, even one in decline, but the manipulations of a party manager who appeared to enjoy the endless rounds of talks about talks which he initiated. As late as 1971, in defiance of all the evidence, Ian Smith claimed: 'We have the happiest Africans in the world.' Nine years were to pass and much blood shed before he was proved wrong.

Britain's reactions to UDI were among the least heroic of her dealings with the final phases of Empire. When Mrs Thatcher did her first U-turn at Lusaka in 1979 and accepted a formula which led to the Lancaster House Conference and the end of white rule in 1980, she was able to solve the problem only because the whites had lost the guerrilla war which had lasted 15 years.

Independent Zimbabwe under Robert Mugabe joined the Commonwealth in April 1980, and the process of decolonization had been all but completed. A few anomalies and loose ends – the Falklands, Hong Kong, Gibraltar – remained, and two of the most difficult and dangerous leftovers of empire – Ulster and South Africa – still threatened major difficulties. The New Commonwealth had emerged in place of the old Empire.

In the 1940s one still spoke of the *British* Commonwealth and Empire; the adjective was dropped in deference to the newly independent Asian members. When India became a republic in 1949 and elected to stay in the Commonwealth, a formula was devised which allowed the British monarch to be head of the Commonwealth though not necessarily head of state of a Commonwealth country. Nehru's decision to stay in the Commonwealth ensured that the association subsequently flourished; had he taken India out it is doubtful whether Colonies which came to independence later would have sought to join, and the Commonwealth would have become little more than an association of the old white Dominions. Instead, almost every British Colony became a member on achieving independence, so that by 1980, when Zimbabwe joined, membership had reached a total of 45.

The difficulty facing the generation of Britain's leaders who presided over the end of the Empire was always to come to terms with a Commonwealth where Britain was one among equals rather than the imperial power which controlled the whole. In exact proportion as the Empire was dismantled, so membership of the New Commonwealth expanded. There was always the danger that the British would treat the Commonwealth as a surrogate for Empire. This was brought out clearly during the 1966 Commonwealth conference in London, which was dominated by Rhodesia. After seven days when British policy – or lack of it – was constantly under attack, Harold Wilson, in the chair, lost his temper and said he was adjourning the conference. In the interval which followed the Vice-

End of Empire

President of Kenya, Joe Murumbi, told Wilson that the conference was not his to adjourn. The same week a former Conservative Commonwealth Secretary, Duncan Sandys, appearing on television said under pressure 'but I thought the Commonwealth was British'. The reactions of these two able politicians to Commonwealth pressures over Rhodesia revealed a failure to come to terms with a changed world.

Macmillan played a major role in the conversion of Empire into Commonwealth: not only did he preside over the most important concentrated phase of decolonization since Indian independence, but he made the Commonwealth conferences of 1960, 1961 and 1962 into major events of consultation between partners. The issue of South Africa dominated the first two and in 1962 he consulted his Commonwealth colleagues about Britain's proposed entry into the European Community. He saw the need to change the emphasis and did so with great skill.

This is not the place to discuss the potential of the Commonwealth as an international association except to say that it contains within its membership a microcosm of the world's main problems in the second half of the twentieth century, which may be summed up as the North-South relationship. How it contributes to solutions will depend upon the extent to which Britain is willing to be a part of the whole and does not attempt to dominate or, as over South Africa, to block actions which the majority wish to take.

When the Commonwealth heads of government met in Melbourne in 1981, there was a collective sigh of relief that Rhodesia was out the way and they could devote their attention to questions of development. Yet only a year later the world was treated to the spectacle of a British war fleet sailing halfway across the world to fight an old-fashioned campaign to recapture the Falklands, which Argentina had invaded. Britain's victory was Pyrrhic: it solved nothing and called forth another wave of post-imperial jingoism. As the Argentinian writer, Jorge Luis Borges, said ironically: 'The Falklands thing was a fight between two bald men over a comb.'

One of the last stories of the end of Empire concerned Hong Kong, and was especially shabby. The 1988 Hong Kong White Paper found that the people of the Colony were sharply divided about whether or not they wanted direct elections, which were deferred to 1991. For future trade advantage with China, Britain was unwilling to bequeath to the last of her major Colonies the democratic structure which she had insisted upon giving to all the rest. As Empire began so it ended: dominated by greed. But Britain was not to be allowed to shuffle off her responsibilities quite so easily. The students-for-democracy protests that focused world attention upon Beijing, and ended in the June 1989 massacres in Tiananmen Square and the subsequent public executions, produced panic in Hong Kong and renewed demands for the *right* of its 3.25m British passport holders to come to Britain. Under a spotlight of world concern the British government made deliberately vague statements about relaxing immigration requirements; yet it neither condemned in forthright terms what had happened in China nor gave any clear commitments to the people of Hong Kong. It was plain that no real change of policy was contemplated.

Speaking in 1988, two disparate British politicians saw its end as perhaps Britain's greatest achievement in the period since 1945. John Biffen argues: 'To have extricated ourselves from Empire and on the whole to have done it without too much bloodshed ... although we have landed ourselves with the absurdity of the Commonwealth which really can have no long term value ... is nonetheless a great achievement ... we have buried Empire and at least provided ourselves with the option of returning to a nation state.' But, as Biffen wryly remarks, we have jumped out of the frying pan of Empire into the fire of the European Community.

The second judgement comes from Tony Benn: 'The greatest achievement might be [seen as] realism in the end of Empire. There could have been a sort of Vietnam war or an Algerian war in which Britain tried to prevent itself losing its imperial possessions.' Mr Benn went on to say: 'I was born at the heart of an Empire; I live in an American colony. When I was born twenty per cent of the surface of the globe and a population of 475 million people was governed from London. Now I live in a country where there are 30,000 troops controlled by a President for whom I haven't even got a vote.'

5
Immigration and Racism

'Civis Britannicus sum.'
LORD PALMERSTON

'This is a white man's country, and I want it to remain so.'
SIR CYRIL OSBORNE

In 1850 the Foreign Secretary, Lord Palmerston, threatened Greece with bombardment by the Royal Navy unless compensation was paid to one, Don Pacifico, whose house had been burnt down by a Greek mob. Don Pacifico was a Maltese-born Jew living in Greece; his birthplace gave him the right of appeal to British protection. In his inimitable way Palmerston provided it and the Greek government caved in and paid £7000 compensation. In the last great speech of his parliamentary career Sir Robert Peel attacked Palmerston for his swashbuckling approach to foreign policy, but in what even his opponents conceded was one of his finest performances Palmerston replied that any British subject anywhere in the world had the right to expect protection and, like the Romans, should be able to say, *'Civis Britannicus sum.'* The principle of a worldwide imperial citizenship was abandoned only with the passing of the Immigrants Act in 1962.

The public approved of immigration as long as it was the immigration of British people into other lands; once the situation was reversed and immigrants wished to come into Britain (mainly from those lands which had been incorporated into the Empire), tolerance was replaced by racial nationalism.

Between 1815 and 1930 24 million people (nearly two-fifths of all the world's emigrants) left British shores to settle in other parts of the world. An opinion poll of 1948 indicated that 42 in every 100 Englishmen favoured emigrating and it was always seen as an important aspect of imperial policy that Britons settled the Empire. It should not have come as a surprise that when the Empire became the Commonwealth many of its citizens decided to reverse the traffic and come to Britain, which offered better economic opportunities than their own countries.

The 'open door' policy was maintained for 10 years after World War Two without serious thought about the consequences, but by the mid-1950s pressures were increasing to control immigration. By 1988 it was controlled by the Immigration Act 1971 (as amended by the British Nationality Act 1981) and the rules made in accordance with that act. These were the successors to a number of increasingly restrictive acts or amendments passed since 1962. So great had been the changes of policy that, unlike most Commonwealth citizens, European Community nationals did not require entry clearance or permission to seek work in Britain. Even so, of the 46,800 people who were accepted for settlement in 1986 a third came from the Indian subcontinent and half were the wives and children of men already settled there.

In June 1948, the *Empire Windrush* docked unannounced at Tilbury bearing 500 immigrants from Kingston, Jamaica, an event which marked the beginning of large-scale immigration of West Indians, to be followed by Asians, Africans, Cypriots and others. The Colonial Secretary of the day, Creech Jones, said they would stay for only one British winter. Of the 500, about 300 had jobs or addresses to go to, and the government provided temporary accommodation for the remainder in Clapham underground shelter. The event marked the beginning of racially motivated legislation, bitter political controversy, job and other forms of discrimination and fundamental changes of British outlook. Ministers in Attlee's government became nervous at this new phenomenon of coloured Commonwealth immigration. Attlee set up a Cabinet committee in 1950 under the Home Secretary and in 1951 Chuter Ede came near to recommending controls but these were not to be applied for another 10 years.

One comment upon the country those Jamaicans came to in 1948 was made by one of their number, Vidal 'Des' Dezonie, in an article which appeared in the *Standard* of 25 April 1988: 'It's a pity that social values have changed. One of the outstanding things about Britain after the war was that everyone was friendly and inclined to let you get on with the job. Now the general attitude is "me first, me second and me last".'

The Home Office began to collect figures for 'coloured' Commonwealth immigrants in 1953 and the estimates for the years 1953 to 1961 (from the West Indies, India and Pakistan) are shown in Table 5.1.

Table 5.1. 'Coloured' Commonwealth Immigration 1953–61

1953	2,000
1954	11,000
1955	42,700
1956	46,850
1957	42,400
1958	27,450
1959	21,550
1960	58,300
1961	125,400

Following the 1955 election MPs began to support Tory Sir Cyril Osborne, who called regularly for controls on Commonwealth (coloured) immigration. Such calls were resisted during the 1950s, but they stimulated countrywide opposition to such immigration, which increased markedly by 1960 and 1961 so as to beat any restrictive legislation. As early as February 1954 Churchill had said in Cabinet that the pressure of these immigrants 'sooner or later would come to be resented by large sections of the British people' and by November 1955 the Cabinet was divided on the issue: the Colonial Secretary, Lennox Boyd, was against any curbs; Lord Salisbury, in his role as defender of the white race, in favour. Lord Home then held the post of Commonwealth Relations Secretary and he showed clearly that the dilemma was a racial one: legislation would have to be non-discriminatory yet no one wanted to keep citizens of the old Commonwealth out – that is Australians, Canadians, New Zealanders or white South Africans.

The pressures for restrictions were increased by the race riots in the summer of 1958 at Notting Hill Gate in London and at Nottingham, but the Macmillan government resisted demands for legislation. Since the riots were not repeated they could be dismissed as one-off affairs but they had broken the myth of British tolerance. After the furore attending the 1962 Immigrants Act but before Enoch Powell's 'rivers of blood' speech in 1968, racial discrimination received increasing attention. A PEP Report was published as a Penguin Special – *Racial Discrimination in England* by W. W. Daniel. It contains a number of succinct quotes, such as that from a local authority transport officer: 'We're very lucky here, we've managed to keep the buses white.'

The end of Empire and the growth of immigration controls went together. As Empire receded into the past so concern about former subjects now classified as Commonwealth citizens became part of a growing determination to keep them out. Finally in 1961 the government of Harold Macmillan introduced a Bill to restrict Commonwealth immigrants. The Bill was primarily concerned with 'coloured' immigrants, not those from the old white Dominions. It is amazing how politicians who were responsible over the years for restricting the flow of Commonwealth immigrants into Britain always did so reluctantly. Writing with unctuous blandness in his autobiography, *Time and Chance*, James Callaghan, careful to bring both parties into the act, says of the 1961 Bill: 'The immigration of large numbers of coloured people arouses particular passion, and every Home Secretary since Rab Butler has been scorched by the flame. It was he, no less, despite his childhood in India, who decided with great reluctance in 1961 that he must bring forward the first Act in our history to control immigration from the Commonwealth.'

That fine radical Tory, Iain Macleod, claimed to have been the last member of Macmillan's Cabinet to be persuaded of the necessity for the 1961 Bill, and he was passionately opposed to the 1968 Act. At the Conservative Party Conference of 1961 Macleod spoke of the brotherhood of man but later when challenged by Hugh Gaitskell about his support for Butler's Bill he replied: 'I detest the necessity for it...' Gaitskell described the measure as a 'miserable, shameful and shabby Bill'. It empowered immigration officers to refuse entry to anyone who could not support himself without working or did not hold a labour voucher. Students and visitors were excepted but courts could recommend deportation and there had to be a five-year period before a Commonwealth citizen could be registered as a British citizen. Irish immigrants were excluded from the Bill on the grounds that it would be too difficult to police the hundred-mile border between Ireland and Ulster, and this exclusion emphasized its racial nature. When Barbara Castle expressed the fear that it would destroy the Commonwealth Sir Cyril Osborne said: 'The Honourable Lady the Member for Blackburn said that the Bill would destroy the Commonwealth. That is irresponsible and untrue. It will not affect Australia, Canada and New Zealand.'

The next landmark in the saga of British racialism came with the Smethwick election in 1964. The sitting member was Patrick Gordon Walker, an undistinguished former Labour Commonwealth Minister whose principal claim to fame was banning Seretse Khama from returning to Bechuanaland because he had married an Englishwoman. He had what was considered a safe majority of 7000 but was opposed by a young Tory councillor, Peter Griffiths. Immigration was a major issue in Smethwick, where a higher number of immigrants than the national average had gone to work. In 1962 Gordon Walker had already made one reactionary statement: 'This is a British country with British standards of behaviour. The British must come first.' Then in the run up to the poll the Labour Party issued an election leaflet which said: 'Be fair: Immigrants only arrived in Smethwick in large numbers during the past ten years – while the Tory government was in power. You can't blame Labour or Gordon Walker for that.'

Griffiths fought the election on the immigration issue. When Gordon Walker announced that during the municipal elections children had been organized to chant: 'If you want a nigger neighbour, vote Labour,' Griffiths replied: 'We can't stop children reflecting the views of their parents. The people of Smethwick certainly don't want integration.' In his election address he said:

> I shall press for the strictest control of immigration. We British must decide who shall or shall not enter our country. So vital a matter cannot be left to other governments. Over-crowding and dirty conditions must be ended. There must be no entry permits for criminals, the unhealthy or those unwilling to work. Our streets must once again be safe at night.

The election was fought in dirty fashion but while Griffiths openly demanded restrictions Gordon Walker tried to pretend that the presence of immigrants was the fault of the Tories, a line in its way more contemptible. The Tory won and, though Harold Wilson made headlines by calling him a 'parliamentary leper', both parties realized how many votes were tied to the race issue.

Whatever they had said in opposition, once in power the new Labour government behaved much as had their predecessors. In 1965, when the 1962 Act had either to be renewed or let lapse, the government used its provisions to cut the number of immigration vouchers from 20,800 to 8,500 a year. This time a special case was made for white Maltese, for whom 1000 of the vouchers were reserved. Thus both parties accepted a policy of control.

Next came the question of the Kenya Asians. When Kenya became independent at the end of 1963, the British government had deliberately created ambiguities about those subjects of Kenya – whites and Asians – who could retain British citizenship. The object was to ensure that white settlers could return to Britain later if they wished. At the end of 1967 the Kenyatta government announced that residents who were not citizens would have to apply for 'entry certificates' to remain in the country. This produced a panic among the Asians, many of whom had not taken out citizenship after independence, and there was an exodus to Britain of those who qualified for citizenship. This heralded the year which marked the nadir of British attitudes to race. Enoch Powell and Duncan Sandys called attention to the fact that 200,000 Asians in Kenya had the right of entry into Britain – a figure grossly exaggerated – and the Home Secretary, James Callaghan, introduced a measure on 22 February 1968 to restrict Asian entry. Apart from tightening up existing legislation, the new Bill prevented Asians in Kenya from entering Britain even though they possessed British citizenship. With the active connivance of the opposition this was rushed through both Houses in record time. In *Time and Chance* Callaghan describes the passage of the Bill:

> David Ennals, who was responsible for carrying the legislation through the House, took it on the chin and the Bill passed through all its stages with a large majority in both Houses of Parliament in seven days and became law on 1 March 1968. While the Bill was going through Parliament I was given a difficult time, and was upset at the harsh tone of some of the personal criticism, which was extremely bitter. But although this was an unwelcome task, I do not regret the decision we took.

It would have been easier to admire our 'liberal' politicians if they had enacted this and other racially biased legislation without so often protesting how much it upset them to do so.

At Birmingham on 20 April Enoch Powell made the first of his notorious speeches attacking the personal habits and hygiene of immigrants and calling for their repatriation, in which he said: 'As I look ahead, I am filled with foreboding. Like the Roman, I seem to see "the River Tiber foaming with much blood".'

Immigration and Racism

Edward Heath dismissed him at once from the Shadow Cabinet. Three days later, on St George's Day and Shakespeare's birthday, London dockers staged a march on Parliament in support of Enoch Powell. The International Commission of Jurists said simply: 'There is no doubt that the United Kingdom's reputation as a bastion of civil liberties has been seriously shaken.' In *The Times* Ruth Glass said of the British passport holders, white or Asian, living in Kenya: 'If you are white your British passport is valid; if you are brown, it is not.'

In November Enoch Powell returned to the attack with another speech. He spoke of the 'key significance of repatriation or re-emigration'. Plenty of people were happy he had made the speech and though Heath condemned it as 'character assassination of one racial group' the Conservatives were moving sharply to the right on the race issue. Later, in a speech at Walsall, Heath called for fresh legislation by the government to prevent new immigrants being allowed permanent settlement and suggested that they should be admitted for specific jobs for a specific time. Heath, for all his sacking of Powell, was moving in pursuit of him; one of his audience said: 'May I say how delighted we are that Mr Heath appears to have adopted many of the views expressed by Enoch Powell.'

Many of the Kenyan Asians, joined by those from Uganda, went on to become exemplars of those Victorian values of thrift and hard work which Britain's Prime Minister of the 1980s was to praise as the background for a better Britain.

What these arguments about immigration and race made clear was the sameness of approach by the major political parties. Enoch Powell did a service to both by propounding such extreme views that he could be used as everybody's whipping boy. Middle-of-the-road and 'radical' politicians could deplore his statements and then regret the necessity for more severe restrictions. Few aspects of the story redounded to Britain's credit. The closing of the doors to all but a handful of Commonwealth immigrants was one of the last, least honourable chapters in her long imperial story.

Parallel to the immigration story were reactions to UDI in Rhodesia and to the growing crisis in South Africa. Fierce defence of the Smith regime in Rhodesia came mainly, though not exclusively, from the political right. Only when it was clear that the whites had lost the guerrilla war did the British government do a U-Turn and call the Lancaster House Conference at the end of 1979, which led to Zimbabwean independence in April 1980.

The story of white South Africa still has a long way to go, but for years on the international stage Britain has shielded it from growing world pressures. The racialism of the British attitude can be tested simply by playing a political 'game': let us suppose that a political miracle occurs and the position in South Africa is reversed. President Mandela and the blacks have control (including the weaponry of the armed forces) and announce that they will impose apartheid on whites as it has been applied to blacks since 1948. Can anyone imagine that for the succeeding 40 years Britain would argue as it has since 1948: these things take time; we do not believe in violence; you must understand the black point of view? Were the situation in South Africa reversed British and Western pressures upon a black government would be so great that apartheid would be ended overnight.

Speaking on the subject of South Africa at the Royal Commonwealth Society in May 1988 the Foreign Secretary, Sir Geoffrey Howe, reminded his audience that perhaps a million South Africans (he meant white South Africans) qualified as British citizens. He did not suggest that the legislation rushed through Parliament to keep out Kenyan Asian passport holders would be passed to keep out white South Africans who qualified for citizenship, should a racial explosion take place in that unhappy country.

The twentieth anniversary of Powell's Birmingham speech – 1988 – saw a good deal of discussion in the press about race. The playground murder of an Asian boy in Manchester called in question the way the community education department within the school approached the subject of racial behaviour. After the Prince of Wales voiced his concern at the absence of black or Asian Guardsmen the Commons Defence Select Committee suggested that the army should monitor its black and Asian recruits by regiment. The Runnymede Trust reported that black workers were no better off in 1988 than they had been twenty years earlier.

The Home Secretary, Douglas Hurd, claimed that the Conservative government and Conservative Party shared an absolute, unquestioned and unqualified opposition to racial discrimination. Indeed, there appeared to be a government propaganda campaign to suggest that all was well on the race relations front. It was not; the laws governing immigrants left much to be desired. The government dragged its feet for two years before agreeing to use a DNA test to decide paternity, yet even then wanted to deport a 26-year-old Indian despite the DNA evidence that he was related to his parents. Britain had a very long way to go before she could claim to have eradicated racialism at official levels.

Lord Whitelaw, retired from a long career in the mainstream of Toryism, told me in May 1988: 'Considering the inevitable feelings in any country, I think we have actually been more tolerant over race despite a great deal of pressures the other way. I think nationally we have worked very hard to be tolerant and are just winning.' That judgement may be reasonably applied to the Britain of 1988 but that Britain was the product of twenty years' activity, much of which had been blatant in its racial intent.

6
Britain and Europe

'We are part of the community of Europe and we must do our duty as such.'
GLADSTONE

'We are not a continental nation but an island power with a Colonial Empire and unique relations with the independent members of the Commonwealth. Though we might maintain a close association with the continental nations of Europe, we could never merge our interests wholly with theirs. We must be with, but not in, any combination of European powers.'
LORD SALISBURY

The psychology which led to the emergence of the European Community has been inadequately examined. Most of the reasons for its formation were negative rather than positive. The rise of the Superpowers after 1945 meant that the individual nation states of Europe were pushed to the sidelines of world decisions after centuries originating them: if Europe were to regain a position centre stage it had to act as a major power.

Fear of German power and ambitions which twice in the space of thirty years had devastated Europe led to the demand for a structure which could contain and control a renascent Germany. The end of empires produced a Europe weaker in terms of power and worldwide influence; policies formulated under the Yaounde and Lomé Conventions, whereby European aid could be channelled into former colonial fiefs was colonialism under a different guise. Fear of Soviet expansion and resentment of American domination could be effectively countered only by a united Europe. There were idealists – Spaak, Monnet and Schuman for example – spurred on by the horrors they had witnessed who hoped to ensure that war would never happen again. But much of the subconscious psychology behind the European Community might be summed up thus: if the nation states of Europe could not go it alone as big powers, it was better to work together than forgo big power status altogether.

Britain was not affected in the same way as her continental neighbours. She had not been defeated, she had not been devastated, she emerged from World War Two with much glory and her Empire intact. In consequence she managed to delude herself for a generation that she was in a special category, different from other European states and able to play a unique role in the Atlantic Alliance (the 'special relationship'); to be of but not in Europe; and to exercise worldwide influence through her Commonwealth – in other words, playing a special part in each of Churchill's three circles.

Germany's Professor Hallstein put the purpose of the European Community succinctly: 'We are not in business at all; we are in politics.' Reflecting the greatest fear of Western Europe at that time he also said: 'The European Community is a guarantee that none of its members can be picked off, extracted out of the orbit of the free world by political threats or economic promises from the East.' There has been so much discussion of the economics of the European Community that many people have forgotten its political intent. The eventual aim of the Treaty of Rome is 'an ever closer union'. A summary of the aims set out in its 240 articles is as follows:

> The establishment of a Common Market and co-ordination of the economic policies of the member states.
> The establishment of a common agricultural policy.
> The right of free movement of workers throughout the Community.
> The right of establishment both for individual nationals or for their agencies, subsidiaries or branches in any part of the Community.
> Free movement of capital; a common transport system; common rules governing competition.
> The approximation of laws where these relate directly to the working of the Common Market.

Other provisions ranged over economic, commercial and social problems and aimed to produce common policies. Thirty years have passed since the Treaty came into effect and no one can delude themselves any longer that it is not a political organization.

As with so many other post-war policies, Winston Churchill's influence upon this country's approach to Europe was profound. In his immediate post-war speeches, such as that in Zurich in 1946 calling upon France and Germany to forgive the past and 'build a kind of United States of Europe', he gave the impression that Britain would be willing to play a major part in any moves towards continental unity. Addressing a United Europe meeting at the Albert Hall in May 1947, Churchill said: 'If European unity is to be made an effective reality before it is too late, the whole-hearted efforts both of France and Britain will be needed from the outset. They must go forward hand in hand. They must in fact be founder-partners in this movement.' The irony is that Britain left West Germany to be the founder-partner with France.

Such statements were meant at the time more for European than British consumption, and the tragedy is that Europeans did not pay enough attention to

Churchill's reservations and particularly to his idea that Britain had a special role to play in the Atlantic Alliance, Europe and the Commonwealth. Had they done so they might have been less disappointed when Churchill resumed power in 1951. Britain's refusal in 1952 to join the Schuman Plan – to pool coal and steel resources – was a real beginning for Europe and a major rejection by Britain which from then on was not involved in the early building of a united Europe. Nine years later when Britain did apply to join the Community *The Times* of 1 August 1961 said: 'What is contemplated may well be a turning point for the Western world.' The arrogance of this statement – that a turning point would be achieved only when Britain joined the Community – was belied when de Gaulle vetoed the British application to join.

De Gaulle's veto highlighted another political aspect of the growing Community: the extent to which one nation could use the whole for political purposes. Many years later Mrs Thatcher tried to use de Gaulle's tactics to get her way. De Gaulle always made clear his intention to mould the Common Market as an instrument of French policy.

Britain's post-war obsession with the American Alliance which she wished to maintain as an exclusive relationship ensured that no close ties with Europe were possible until Macmillan learned that President Kennedy did not see Anglo-American relations in remotely the same light as they were viewed from London. But by then Britain was excluded from the Community and more than a decade had to pass before she joined, still relatively unwillingly and not on her own terms.

The Commonwealth represented the other major obstacle to membership. Many British politicians expend a great deal of rhetoric upon the subject of the Commonwealth; in relation to the debate about Britain and Europe many die-hard imperialists talked Commonwealth when they meant only the white Dominions. Even so, at the beginning of the 1960s the Commonwealth was the world's largest preferential trading organization, accounting for 25 per cent of total world exports (excluding the Soviet bloc) and 30 per cent of imports. Much emotion was expended upon Britain's ties with the Commonwealth and much of the concern was part of the psychological difficulty of coming to terms with end of Empire.

Churchill's failures were as great as his successes. Had he determined in 1951, when he led the Conservatives to electoral victory, that he would put into practice his rhetoric and make Britain play her full part as a member of the European family advancing 'hand in hand' with France, the story of the Community would have been very different. Instead he was concerned with larger concepts: the Atlantic Alliance, our global role, summits as a means of reversing the Cold War. European anglophiles learned with dismay that a benevolent Britain expected them to proceed towards unity without her, which in the end is what they did.

It was under Macmillan that Britain first turned down the chance to become part of the European Community from its inception. She then tried to combat its impact by proposing alternatives, finally realized that she ought not to remain excluded and applied to join. These three phases could well be interpreted as the learning process by which Macmillan and the British people came to terms with the European-centred nature of the country's future. It was a reluctant process. While Macmillan made a great positive contribution to British acceptance of declining power, it might be argued that a negative achievement – because he had to learn first – was to prepare them for later entry into Europe. Macmillan, like Churchill before him, put the American Alliance first and worked ceaselessly to maintain Britain's 'big power' status as the broker between the two Super-powers. This infuriated de Gaulle and was probably the most important reason for his veto.

The Messina Conference which began in 1955 was not taken sufficiently seriously by the Foreign Office and the British were absent from the crucial negotiations which hammered out the Treaty of Rome. Britain did not believe that anything concrete would emerge from the discussions, and a Foreign Office official is recorded as saying: 'If it works we can always join it later.' At the time of the Conference real unity looked unlikely and Britain's concern with the American Alliance was based upon the fear that the USA might retreat into isolation again; her survival had twice depended upon the United States entering a world war on her side.

The miscalculations of this time were great if understandable. What Britain found in 1958 was that she was excluded by her own choice from a Europe of the Six which was potentially immensely powerful in economic and political terms. Over the preceding four centuries she had pursued the balance of power in Europe and had fought Spain, France and Germany in turn to prevent any of the major nation states from becoming too powerful and dominating the Continent. Now, by default, she had allowed a powerful European union to form over which she had no control; her exclusion from the Six could be seen as the failure of 400 years of policy.

Between 1957 when the Treaty of Rome was signed and 1961 when Britain applied to join the Common Market the Conservative government with Labour support tried to establish alternatives: first the European Free Trade Area and then the European Free Trade Association. A White Paper set out a Free Trade Area plan which emphasized increased specialization, the pooling of technical and industrial development and the benefits of large-scale production. The tone of the Paper was to suggest an alternative to the Common Market rather than a supplement to the Six; it received a cold reception in Europe, where it was seen as a deliberate attempt to undermine the Common Market. The White Paper was published during the last stages of the debate on the Treaty of Rome and Spaak scuppered it when he said that the signature of the Treaty of Rome should 'not be delayed a single day'. If a Free Trade Area was to come into being it must be after the establishment of the Common Market and as an addition to it, not as an alternative. In May 1958 a constitutional crisis in France led to the return to power of de Gaulle; by November France curtly dismissed the idea of a Free Trade Area and the first effort at sabotaging the Common Market had been defeated.

Britain now fell back on her second idea of a European Free Trade Association (EFTA or the Outer Seven as it became known), consisting of Britain, Norway, Sweden, Denmark, Austria, Switzerland and Portugal. This was designed to counterbalance the Six but the United Kingdom was its only major industrial-economic power, so it stood little chance of becoming an effective rival to the Six. In a sense it was too obviously a device to undermine the cohesiveness of the Common Market. By 1960 its failure compared with the growing success of the EEC made plain that Britain would have to think again. Through a painful process of indifference, opposition and floating alternatives Britain came to accept that a European force had been born from which she had excluded herself when she might have been its leader.

So finally Britain applied to join the Common Market but from a position of weakness rather than strength. There was a financial crisis but this was less important than that she appeared to be approaching Europe not from conviction but because everything else had failed. Moreover, for Europe and especially for a confident France under de Gaulle, there was no indication that Britain intended to identify fully with Europe. Her negotiations were conducted largely in terms of the exceptions which should be made on behalf of Commonwealth countries; nor was there any indication that she intended to surrender her 'special relationship' with the USA. She appeared to want the advantages of membership without surrendering her place as a great power, the centre still of Churchill's three circles. This was too much for de Gaulle.

Britain made her application to join the European Economic Community on 31 July 1961. Much of the argument in favour of joining was in terms of the stimulation to our industry and the psychological fillip this would provide when Britain's broker role between the Superpowers was becoming increasingly hollow.

A majority of Conservatives were in favour with a substantial minority against; a majority of Labour were against with a substantial minority in favour. By the time of the 1962 Conservative Conference Macmillan had convinced himself that the country should go all out for membership: 'Now is the opportunity and we must seize it,' he said although this after four years when Britain tried just about everything else might be regarded as a somewhat belated recognition of Europe's importance. But as Nigel Fisher argues in his biography of Iain Macleod: '. . . as the fortunes of the party declined throughout 1961 and 1962, most members, and certainly most Ministers, looked increasingly to the Common Market to relieve the administration of some of its more intractable problems. It was hoped that the vitality of the Six would help Britain's sagging performance...' Such a negative approach hardly deserved success. There was little conviction that Britain should be a part of the Community for her own sake.

On 14 January 1963 de Gaulle vetoed the British application and the first attempt to join the European Community came to nothing. There were a number of reasons for de Gaulle's attitude: his dislike of the 'special relationship', from which he felt excluded, played a vital part but perhaps the most important reason concerned power – who would control the Community. As Nigel Fisher reports in his book, the French President explained privately: 'If Britain was in the Community, there would, at best, be two cocks in the hen run. At worst there would be only one and it would not be France. And that is not interesting to me.'

A majority of the Labour Party were pleased that Britain had failed to get into the Community – not just for party political reasons but from ideological opposition to what they believed the Common Market to represent. Renewed rhetoric was expended upon the Commonwealth. Then, in 1964, Labour came to power under Harold Wilson. From his accession until his defeat in 1970 Wilson was faced constantly with the problems presented by UDI in Rhodesia, which plunged the Commonwealth into crisis. The tensions it produced at the 1966 Commonwealth Conference soured Wilson's faith in it and in the autumn he announced that the Labour Party was to approach the EEC.

In January 1967 Wilson and his Foreign Secretary, George Brown, toured the capitals of the Six exploring the chances of entry. In May Britain applied to join and in November, predictably, de Gaulle again vetoed the application. Nothing had changed since Macmillan's attempt; de Gaulle's suspicions were the same as ever, and the British were divided on the issue, two-thirds of the Labour Party being anti- rather than pro-marketeers. Above all, it still appeared that entry was seen in London more as a solution to current problems than as a statement of faith in the European idea.

When the Conservatives returned to power in 1970 there was no doubt about their intention to take the country into Europe. Edward Heath had always been pro-Common Market and had been the principal negotiator in Brussels in 1961/3. De Gaulle had been replaced by Pompidou, who was far more amenable to an expanded Community. Though protracted, negotiations were completed and Britain joined the Community in January 1973, the Six becoming the Nine because Ireland and Denmark joined at the same time. Yet it was not a popular decision. A vociferous Tory minority, led by Enoch Powell, was against entry as was the majority of the Labour Party. Moreover, argument about the pros and cons had by then gone on for so long that many people were bored, and few advantages became apparent as a result of joining.

Harold Wilson led the Labour Party to victory in 1974, and pledged to renegotiate terms of membership. The object was to appease the anti-marketeers, not to take Britain out, and this process led to the referendum of 1975 – the first in British history – adroitly handled to ensure that Britain stayed in the Community. James Callaghan, who became Foreign Secretary in the new administration and had overall responsibility for the renegotiation, was at best lukewarm about Europe. In *Time and Chance* he says that Heath's concentration upon Europe had meant diminished concern with the Commonwealth, and later he says: 'Membership of the Community was only marginal to our economic success or failure.' In that at least he was correct.

After the referendum there was no further question of leaving, although acceptance of membership was a lukewarm fact of economic life rather than a fundamental tenet of political faith. Periodic rows – the waste of the Common Agricultural Policy (CAP), anger that Britain is seen to be paying more than her share of expenses, interference in British sovereignty by the European Court, or a wrangle over what are to be the approved contents of sausages – add spice to the political scene and bring out some underlying anti-European prejudices. Psychologically Britain continues to have problems about Europe and not simply in terms of yearning for a Commonwealth connection or the 'special relationship'. There is also the problem of unfulfilled expectations.

Entry in 1973 did not solve Britain's economic problems; like the rest of Europe, she found herself facing recession and the oil crisis. The referendum of 1975 did not put doubts to rest. The 1984 Fontainebleau meeting which agreed a more equitable British contribution to the Community budget did not make her a better participant. The early opposition and late entry ensured a continuing European suspicion of her wholehearted wish to be a part, a suspicion which is justified in part.

Although there will be rows along the way, the next major development will come in 1992 when it is intended to create a frontier-free Community. In mid–1988 it did not seem that many British businessmen had grasped just how big were the opportunities this would present for them or for their European rivals if they were not ready to grasp them. In 1993 the Channel Tunnel may have been completed and there should no longer exist an administrative border with France or other members. If there is to be a single, border-free European market, other changes are also inevitable but Britain appears to be dragging her feet.

One major difficulty is that while Community advantages can be described in macro terms – it offers great opportunities to successful businesses – its disadvantages can be presented far more concretely: the average British family pays £11.50 a week to help store and destroy the CAP food mountains. The future of the European Community is far from clear, and Britain's relations with it, despite those who believe that the tunnel will make all the difference, are even more obscure. The real problem is easy enough to identify: continuing British suspicion about the concept.

Lord Whitelaw represents the middle ground of the Conservative Party, which has always been more in favour than Labour, and he said in 1988: 'I don't think the hearts of the British people are ever really quite in Europe.' That may well be the eventual epitaph of Britain's relations with Europe.

7
Ulster

'This country's planted thick with laws from coast to coast – man's laws, not God's – and if you cut them down . . . do you really think you could stand upright in the winds that would blow then? Yes, I'd give the Devil benefit of law, for my own safety's sake.'
ROBERT BOLT
(*From* A Man for all Seasons)

'But there is no precedent in our history to teach us that political measures can conjure away hereditary antipathies which are fed by constant agitation.'
THIRD MARQUESS OF SALISBURY

'One of the proudest bastions of liberty is that the rule of law is inviolate. That is what is at stake.'
MARGARET THATCHER

'Thatcher will now realize that Britain cannot occupy our country, torture our prisoners and shoot our people in their own streets and get away with it. Today we were unlucky. But remember, we have only to be lucky once. You will have to be lucky always.'
ANONYMOUS TELEPHONE CALL TO A DUBLIN RADIO STATION AFTER THE IRA BRIGHTON BOMBING

Ireland was Britain's first colonial problem as Ulster undoubtedly is her last, and three centuries of a Protestant minority planted in Ulster does not alter the colonial nature of the problem. Henry II landed in Ireland in 1171 to claim suzerainty of the whole island. One of his motives was to provide a fief for his youngest son, John, then only three years old.

In 1185 young Prince John was sent to try ruling the land intended as his appanage or province. He insulted the Irish chiefs – one account says he pulled their beards as they knelt to swear fealty – and was promptly recalled by Henry. It was an inauspicious beginning to 800 years of Anglo-Irish relations. These have been turbulent and bitter, fraught with endless misunderstandings and violence. They have gone through many stages whose culminating high or low points (depending upon attitude) were the plantation of Ulster in the seventeenth century by lowland Scots (the ancestors of today's Ulster Protestants), Roman Catholic Emancipation in 1829, the potato famine of the mid-nineteenth century and the long campaign for Home Rule which ended only after World War 1 with partition and the emergence of the Irish Free State (Eire) in 1921.

Between 1921 and 1949 Eire enjoyed an ambiguous relationship with what was then very much the *British* Commonwealth. In 1933 de Valera told the Dominion Secretary, J. H. Thomas, that he envisaged a united Ireland as a republic in some form of association with the Commonwealth and recognizing the King as head, a formula rejected out of hand at the time, although it was used 16 years later when India became a republic. By the Ireland Act of 1949 Eire ceased to be a Dominion in the Commonwealth and became instead the Republic of Ireland. As Winston Churchill remarked: before Eire's secession from the Commonwealth it was both 'in and out'; after the 1949 Act it was 'out and in'. There was a short period of relative calm in Britain's relations with both Ireland and Ulster.

During the 1950s there was an IRA campaign of violence in the North, but this had petered out by 1962, after which reconciliation between Protestant and Catholic might have been possible. Lord Brookeborough retired after twenty years as Prime Minister of Ulster, to be succeeded by Captain Terence O'Neill who took the brave, almost revolutionary step of inviting the Irish Prime Minister, Sean Lemass, to visit him in Belfast. O'Neill tried to lessen sectarian bitterness but was increasingly opposed within the Unionist Party. Discrimination against Catholics continued in employment, housing and civil rights as did the gerrymandering of ward boundaries in the Protestant interest. Only in April 1969 did the Ulster Unionists concede universal adult suffrage, but this led to O'Neill's being forced out and saw the rise of the extremists led by Ian Paisley.

Britain appeared to think that partition had solved the Irish problem, with Northern Ireland returning Unionist MPs to support the Conservative Party in apparent perpetuity. Only in 1969 did a dramatic change occur. The Catholic civil rights campaign had been launched, clashes between Catholics and Protestants were more violent and in April 1969 Bernadette Devlin took her seat in the House of Commons after beating the Ulster Unionist candidate at the Mid-Ulster by-election. Once more the passions of Ireland moved centre stage in British politics: 60 per cent of the people of Ulster are Protestants and almost all are also Unionists; 40 per cent are Catholic and Nationalist and look for an eventual united Ireland.

On 14 August 1969 troops were despatched to Ulster. It was the signal that one-party rule and blatant sectarian discrimination had come to an end although few predicted that it would be followed by so long a period of bitter civil and sectarian strife. In 1970 the Home Secretary in Heath's new government, Reginald Maudling, introduced internment as a weapon against sectarian violence but this further alienated the Catholics and produced greater violence. Then on 30 March 1972, following the refusal of the Ulster Premier, Brian Faulkner, to accept London control of law and order, Heath suspended the Parliament, Stormont, and put Whitelaw in charge of the province as Secretary of State. This was the beginning of direct rule from London.

A year later Whitelaw put forward his proposals for elections to an 80-seat assembly by proportional representation. Executive powers would be devolved to this assembly as long as they were shared between the representatives of the two communities. Control of law and order and justice was to remain with the government in London and the emergency powers were to stay in force. There was provision for a Council of Ireland on which Dublin would be represented. The proposals were rejected by the Unionists led by Craig and Paisley although Faulkner accepted them as did the Social Democratic and Labour Party (SDLP). This was the background to the Sunningdale Conference held at the end of the year.

The Sunningdale Conference was an attempt to agree a new formula which would satisfy Dublin and London and get the Faulkner Unionists and the SDLP to work together. In the final agreement the Irish Government made a declaration 'that there could be no change in the status of Northern Ireland until a majority of the people of Northern Ireland desired a change in that status' while the British government reaffirmed that Ulster was a part of the United Kingdom. Sunningdale was a unique departure for no matter how obliquely it had associated the Republic of Ireland (a foreign country) with the affairs of a British province, it implied that sovereignty for this part of the United Kingdom was less than absolute. That was certainly how the Unionists saw the agreement which their council rejected in January 1974. In February, when Heath was fighting the general election on the issue of the miners, Paisley fought on an anti-Sunningdale platform and 10 of the 11 Unionist MPs returned were anti-Sunningdale.

When Harold Wilson returned in February 1974 to lead a minority government, he was too busy manipulating factions to pay much attention to power sharing in Northern Ireland, which in other circumstances he might have been able to save. According to Phillip Whitehead in *Ruling Performance*: 'Whereas Wilson had put his public support behind calls for an ultimately united Ireland, Callaghan relied on tough proconsuls with military backgrounds in Belfast.' The years 1974 to 1979 saw little movement, no real initiatives and a continuing growth of violence.

Steadily, from 1969 onwards, the Dublin dimension became more important in London. There are parallels between the search for a settlement in Northern Ireland and those in Israel and South Africa. Just as it will be impossible to have a lasting peace in the Middle East without the PLO, or in South Africa unless the ANC is involved, so no lasting settlement here can ignore the wishes of Dublin and no assertions of Westminster sovereignty alter that fact.

On the eve of the 1979 election Margaret Thatcher's close adviser and ally,

Airey Neave, was assassinated by the IRA, an event which directed her attention to the Irish problem. Her instinctive sympathies were with the Unionists but Thatcher was moved by the logic of the situation towards gradual accommodation with Dublin. She had two meetings with Jack Lynch in 1979 before he resigned as Taoiseach and then had to deal with Charles Haughey who in 1980 announced his new policy for the North. As he said that February:

> We must face the reality that Northern Ireland, as a political entity, has failed and that a new beginning is needed. The time has surely come for the two sovereign governments to work together to find a formula and lift the situation on to a new plane, that will bring permanent peace and stability to the people of these islands.

Haughey and Thatcher got on well together; in December there were suggestions that a 'sellout' by Thatcher was contemplated, but their apparently close relationship disintegrated and in March 1981 Margaret Thatcher made it plain there would be no sellout and that none had been contemplated. Those Thatcher-Haughey meetings were the beginnings of a process of London-Dublin exchanges which, despite fitful ups and downs, were to continue.

In *A Balance of Power*, James Prior – one of the most successful Secretaries of State for Northern Ireland – writes a revealing paragraph:

> What also made my job different from that of any other Secretary of State, apart from the Foreign Secretary, was the importance of establishing close relations with another government, the Republic of Ireland. This was essential, because of the strength of the Irish tradition in the North, where around 40 per cent of the population identify with Dublin and because any Dublin Government is bound to be concerned with their interests.

As even the right-wing Thatcher government came increasingly to recognize, a solution had to be acceptable to Dublin if it was to work.

In politics attitudes and perceptions are at least as important as and often far more important than facts, and Northern Ireland is predominantly about attitudes. In January 1969, at the outset of the troubles, James Callaghan told his Cabinet colleagues: 'The cardinal aim of our policy must be to influence Northern Ireland to solve its own problems.' It must have seemed a commonsense approach at the time. Twelve years later, he expressed the same view to the House of Commons which, he records in his memoirs, was not well received. The great difficulty about such an approach is that it ignores several centuries of ingrained bigotry between Protestant and Catholic and between North and South which defy commonsense solutions. As Enoch Powell, who had sat as a Unionist MP since 1974, told James Prior, shortly after the latter became Secretary of State, he should never use the word 'reconciliation' because it meant reconciliation between the two parts of Ireland as well as between the two factions in the North.

There are those in Ulster and in the Conservative Party who argue for full integration in the United Kingdom. This approach has now been ruled out as impracticable. It is also clear that the majority of people in Britain are bored by or indifferent to Ireland. They get angry when the violence spills over into England or when soldiers are killed in the province but they are not deeply engaged by its sectarian bitterness or religious bigotry. That indifference will ultimately make it easier to reach a solution.

One of the principal problems faced by any Secretary of State, and especially a Tory one like Prior, lies in the division within the Conservative Party between a right wing which emotionally backs the Unionists and those in the centre of the party who are indifferent or prepared to support any reasonable attempt to find an equitable solution. As James Prior found, his efforts towards a power-sharing formula were undermined by his own right wing, while Thatcher relied for advice upon the hard-line pro-Unionist Ian Gow.

Yet, despite the right, it was the Thatcher goverment which reached the Anglo-Irish Agreement signed at Hillsborough in November 1985. This represented a turning point: it established an inter-government conference (Britain and Ireland) on Ulster, whose object is to convince Northern Catholics that their nationalist aspirations are seen as serious, in the hope that they will turn to constitutional means rather than para-military groups such as the IRA. Seen in this light, the agreement is designed to help London fight terrorism. It is also to bring peace to Ulster by recognizing equally the rights and aspirations of both communities, but in the course of lessening Catholic alienation the agreement has increased the sense of betrayal among Protestants.

Prime Minister Garret Fitzgerald signed the agreement for Ireland. This was a courageous act for it required co-operation with London, which did not recognize a united Ireland unless a majority in Ulster voted for it. By the agreement, Britain acknowledged that Ulster is not simply a part of the United Kingdom but has a wider dimension. That admission was the most important aspect of the agreement and the reason why it was condemned by the Ulster Protestants, but giving Dublin a consultative role represents a small but real step towards a solution. Predictably the Unionists opposed Hillsborough and there followed increased violence, non-co-operation, refusal to set rates, the resignation of 11 Ulster MPs and, in April 1986, the severing of Unionist ties with the Tory Party.

By 1988 the Anglo-Irish Agreement was under strain. Early in the year the Home Secretary decided to abandon the requirement to redraft the Prevention of Terrorism Act every five years, and the Attorney-General, Sir Patrick Mayhew, who played a key role in the decision not to prosecute RUC officers involved in the shoot-to-kill policy (the Stalker affair), was accused by Dublin of refusing to comply with the new Irish legal requirements for extradition warrants. This subject had already caused much ill-will since it was the habit of the British Attorney-General simply to enclose a note which said he was satisfied that enough evidence of terrorism existed to justify an extradition, a practice which hardly satisfied Dublin. The Anglo-Irish Agreement requires careful nurturing and, as was often the case, Westminster arrogance had surfaced once more.

Speaking in New York towards the end of April 1988, Charles Haughey (once more Taoiseach of Ireland) said that only a new structure embracing both Ulster and the Republic could accommodate Protestants and Catholics in Ireland. In London Thatcher demanded an assurance that Haughey was not backing away from the Anglo-Irish Agreement and though Foreign Secretary Howe made a conciliatory speech London-Dublin suspicions were rampant once more. Haughey was correct: the Anglo-Irish Agreement was a step not a solution, and by moving a stage further he was forcing the pace faster than London wished, but which it will have to follow in the end.

From 1969 onwards an awful catalogue of violence formed the backdrop to every decision about Northern Ireland. In October 1969 the first policeman, Victor Arbuckle, was killed while the Home Secretary, James Callaghan, was visiting the province. In February 1971 the first soldier was killed in Belfast. In January 1972 13 people died in Londonderry on 'Bloody Sunday'. In 1974 21 people were killed by two bombs which exploded in Birmingham pubs.

The always brutal nature of terrorism – whether individual sectarian killings or indiscriminate bomb outrages – added to the bitterness on both sides and contributed to the despair of those trying to find solutions. On 1 March 1981, Bobby Sands began the hunger strike from which he died, and by August 10 others had followed him. On 12 October 1984 a bomb at the Tory Party Conference in Brighton narrowly missed the Prime Minister.

Violence breeds insensitivity and this has surely become true of Ulster. Dublin complained that a young soldier, Ian Thain, sentenced to life imprisonment for the murder of a Catholic in Belfast in 1983, had been released and allowed back to his regiment. The nationalists argued that double standards applied to members of the security forces. Another young man, Aidan McAnespie, was shot dead from a security post near the Irish border; the inquiry instituted by Dublin suggested that the RUC claim that he was killed by a ricochet bullet was a cover-up. His family insisted that it was murder. This was followed less than a month later by the IRA funeral at which the crowd attacked and killed two British soldiers. This violence, which has become part of the daily agony of Northern Ireland, has achieved another quite different result: it has perverted, brutalized and corrupted British standards of justice. From the erosion of civil liberties through the lies and smear tactics of the Stalker affair to the shoot-to-kill tactics of the SAS in Gibraltar, violence has brought something horrific in terms of long-held standards of behaviour. In essence British governments have come to accept that a different set of rules applies to the Irish problem than elsewhere in the United Kingdom.

The erosion of civil liberties in Northern Ireland has its roots in the long-standing Unionist ascendancy, which led to the civil rights campaign and the introduction of troops. Since then successive British governments have followed a classic colonial pattern of repression. By 1970 the army was conducting extensive searches for arms in Catholic areas; in 1971 internment was introduced. Detention without trial was accompanied by brutalities such as hooding, subjection to electronic noise, spread-eagling against walls for hours at a time, deprivation of sleep and beatings. When the Compton Commission investigated and substantiated complaints, two of its members supported the use of in-depth interrogations although the third, Lord Gardiner (a former Lord Chancellor), condemned them as 'illegal, not morally justifiable and alien to the traditions of what I still believe to be the greatest democracy in the world'. Juries were abolished on the grounds that their members allowed themselves to be swayed by sectarian bias (a claim never substantiated) and though a 1980 public opinion survey revealed a majority of both communities in favour of restoring trial by jury nothing was done. The Diplock Courts – special no-jury courts 'designed to obtain convictions which might not be obtainable otherwise' – led to demands by the Provisional IRA for the status of special category prisoners.

The catalogue of special or different laws has grown steadily. The Prevention of Terrorism Act, passed in November 1974 (replaced in 1976), banned the IRA, allowed the Home Secretary to ban other organizations and gave the police powers to detain those 'reasonably' suspected of terrorism. The Act also gave the Home Secretary and the Secretary of State the right to exclude citizens of Northern Ireland from other parts of the United Kingdom. This amounts to a form of internal exile, a practice we are ready enough to condemn in the Soviet Union. It is an essential denial of the principle of the rule of law, and denial of the rule of law – as applied to the rest of Britain – has become a feature of Britain's policy in Ulster.

The Stalker affair illustrates the extent to which cover-up on behalf of one side has become a way of life. John Stalker was the Deputy Chief Constable of the Greater Manchester police. In May 1984 he was asked to investigate cases of possible murder and conspiracy by members of the Royal Ulster Constabulary to pervert the course of justice. He spent two years on his investigations and when these were almost complete and he appeared to be close to answers which would have shown the existence of a shoot-to-kill policy by the RUC he was removed from the job. Subsequently attempts were made to smear him and he resigned from the police. As Stalker says in his book, 'The way in which my removal was handled has left the firm conviction in many people's minds that I was getting too close to the truth about the activities of policemen operating under cover and without proper control in Northern Ireland.'

The evidence he amassed, circumstantial and precise, points overwhelmingly to a shoot-to-kill policy operated by the RUC and that this is known and connived at by the British government. The Stalker story is disgraceful. He was removed from the job on a spurious charge, never proved, that he had some criminal connection with a man against whom no charges were brought. He was not allowed back to finish his investigation, which was completed by Colin Sampson, the Chief Constable of West Yorkshire. Despite the fact that RUC Special Branch officers lied about incidents in which five unarmed men and one boy were shot dead in 1982, the Attorney-General announced in February 1988 that legal proceedings had been ruled out. That a cover-up has taken place is evident.

On Sunday 6 March 1988, three members of the IRA – Daniel McCann, Mairead Farrell and Sean Savage – were shot dead in Gibraltar by members of the SAS. In the House of Commons the next day Eric Heffer asked Sir Geoffrey Howe: 'Why were those three people, although accepted as an active service unit of the IRA, killed and shot when it was admitted they did not have guns on them and they had not actually planted any bombs in Gibraltar?' To this and subsequent questions the government gave less than precise answers. The damning evidence of the Gibraltar witness, Carmen Proetta, that two of the three had their hands up when they were shot, would not go away. And Thames Television's programme *Death on the Rock* had other witnesses whose evidence suggested a summary execution. When she was questioned about her attitude to 'trial by television', Margaret Thatcher said: 'One of the proudest bastions of liberty is that the rule of law is inviolate.'

Government anger at the showing of the Thames Television programme was then turned on the BBC when it, too, produced a programme about the shooting a week later. By May, when for no obvious reason the Gibraltar coroner postponed the inquest, evidence of a government cover-up for the SAS appeared overwhelming. Attempts to prevent public discussion were of a pattern that had gone on for years, but as Lord Scarman wrote in *The Times*: 'The right to be informed and to comment upon matters of public interest is vital to the working of a democratic society.' The Gibraltar killings were one more episode in a long and increasingly perverted story. It was a story, moreover, that would not go away. Bits and pieces of evidence kept cropping up to reinforce claims that a cover-up for a shoot-to-kill policy had taken place. In June 1989 the families of the three IRA members shot dead by the SAS launched an international petition calling on the Irish government to take legal action against the British government in the European Court of Human Rights.

Tony Benn, whose comments on constitutional matters often possess a precision and clarity of thought lacking in others, said in 1988:

> I don't believe there is an Irish problem but a British problem and it is very interesting to reflect on why British troops are there ... the United States and Britain, for military reasons, don't want a neutral Ireland because that would intervene between the power of the USA and Europe – any more than the White House or the Pentagon would want a neutral Britain... If the Republic were to join NATO ... I think British troops would be out in a year or two.

Benn concluded his judgement with a thought that is undoubtedly shared by an increasing number of people, though many are not yet prepared to voice it publicly. He said quite simply: 'I think by the end of the century we will be out.'

PART THREE: THE ECONOMY

8
An Economy in Decline?

'Not since Marie Antoinette milked cows in the Trianon has there been a ruling class in Europe with such an urge to play the peasant!'

MICHAEL SHANKS

'Like a horse dragged unwillingly to the water, a distrustful public has repeatedly balked at policies designed to cajole or force it into adaptation against its will.'

DAVID MARQUAND

After they had got their five-day week during the crisis days of 1947 the miners were accused of holding the country to ransom as they made the most of overtime opportunities. Ernest Bevin made plain that he could not blame them for using their chance to redress a balance which had been tilted against them for so long.

The title of David Marquand's book *The Unprincipled Society* from which the above quote comes presupposes that individuals or groups should have principles which they apply to the workings of the national economy. As a matter of fact, an abiding principle has long operated in Britain as far as the economy is concerned: it is the simple one that a group which has the advantage uses it for all it is worth to further its own ends. In the years since World War Two the operation of this principle has been most evident: first, in the heyday of union power when the 'fifth estate' used its muscle to get what it wanted no matter what the effect upon the economy as a whole; and, second, during the Thatcher years when, at the other end of the political spectrum, we have witnessed greed raised to the status of principle in the City of London.

The economy has provided subject matter for endless discussion since 1945: why have we under-performed in comparison with our principal trading rivals? What death wish has made us accept options which have reduced us to one of the lowest performances of all major economies? We have blamed the unions, we have blamed bad management, we have blamed the class system, we have argued that Germany had an advantage at the end of the war because her industry had been flattened and she could build it up from scratch, while we had to make do with old machinery. We have blamed Empire and the cosy possession of closed markets instead of having to fight for them like our principal competitors.

One school of thought has even wallowed in our decline, claiming that it is better to be less materialistic since this has allowed us to be one of the most tolerant and pleasant societies to live in, as though the object of the exercise were to turn the country into a gigantic rest home for Americans who laud the 'quality of life' here. Rarely, as we have tried to explain our decline, have we remembered that the USA, Germany, France and Japan have had as many (albeit different) problems to face as ourselves. One of the best-selling books of the 1960s was Michael Shanks's *The Stagnant Society* which attempted to ask what had gone wrong and why Britain performed so badly. It was one of the first and best of a long line of such books.

The theme of selfish workers pushing their claims through the unions has been a constant of post-war years although there has been no equivalent attack upon management for giving itself higher rewards while arguing for restraint elsewhere. The curiously one-sided argument has been advanced that if you want the best management you have to offer top salaries (which is fair enough). It appears to have slipped the attention of those who put forward this proposition that it applies equally to those who work on the shop floor.

In the period immediately after the war, when Europe had yet to recover, the British performance was not at all bad, or seemed not bad because her major rivals were not yet ready for comparisons. But by the beginning of the 1950s the position had changed and in the period 1952 to 1956 her national output increased by 15 per cent while that of France increased by 20 per cent, Italy 26 per cent, the Netherlands 27 per cent and West Germany 38 per cent. Wages did not rise much faster than those of her rivals, but the output of goods and services to match the wage increases rose much more slowly. This point has been made again and again: the rate of growth since the war has as a rule been below that of her main rivals. Why this should be so has never been adequately explained.

In *The Stagnant Society* Shanks demonstrates that between 1953 and 1960 industrial production in the USSR rose by 91 per cent, in the USA by 16 per cent and in Britain by 21 per cent. The world average was 30 per cent, so on that showing she was not doing too badly until we look at figures for Japan (108 per cent), Germany (62 per cent), Italy (58 per cent), France (52 per cent) and the Netherlands (39 per cent). A claim of those years was that Britain was one of the highest taxed countries in the world; in fact, West Germany and France, as well as Norway and Sweden, paid more in taxes than we did.

If the British economy declined in relation to its main rivals, no one could argue that the public were unaware of it. Few countries could have been so busy examining their performance and searching for reasons to explain it. The general fall continued in the 1960s and 1970s so that, according to the Select Committee on Overseas Trade of 1985, by the early 1980s Britain's trade in manufactures was in deficit for the first time since the Industrial Revolution.

In his book *British Economic Policy since the War*, published in 1958, Andrew Shonfield posed the question: 'Must we ... accept it as a fact of life in the middle of the twentieth century that Britain has become an "undynamic society"?' After examining a variety of possible explanations Shonfield quotes a British engineer who had made a close study of attitudes in the USA: 'Most important of the reasons for higher productivity ... is the general atmosphere there that nothing is impossible and most things are worth trying. In contrast, the attitude here seems to me to be that most things are impossible and not worth trying.' Over the years, the theme has remained broadly the same: that British productivity is stultified by outmoded attitudes, whether of unions, management, reliance upon dwindling imperial or Commonwealth markets, or lack of drive. Perhaps one of the most important explanations has been Empire and the consequent determination to behave as a major world power. In 1987 British military expenditure came to a total of $27.6bn only slightly below that of West Germany at $28bn, yet her GNP was $505bn compared with West Germany's $736bn.

Britain's determination to be a nuclear power, the 'special relationship' with the USA, reluctance to join the EEC because of her position at the centre of an Empire and Commonwealth, the maintenance of military 'policeman' roles east of Suez add up to a familiar litany repeatedly trotted out over the years when West Germany, Japan and, to a lesser extent, France concentrated upon markets. Britain's pretensions to great power status had to be paid for; in effect she decided to live beyond her means and pay for big power grandeur when it would have been more sensible to bother about humdrum things like productivity. As Shonfield wrote in the aftermath of Suez: 'The economic hazards of fighting even quite a small war, in which Britain does not have the immediate and visible support of the United States, are now overwhelming.' Though many reasons have been advanced in explanation of this poor performance, one explanation is undoubtedly the constant hankering after big power status out of a medium power's purse.

The inability of the economy to match international pretensions was demonstrated by the endless sterling crises. At one stage it seemed that a financial crisis was part of a biennial pattern. The crises of 1947 and 1949 (when sterling was devalued from $4.03 to $2.80) could at least be seen as part of the process of postwar readjustment, but they continued: after the inflation following the outbreak of the Korean War; after Suez (indeed the run on the pound was given as one of the main reasons for abandoning Suez), and on into the 1960s.

Callaghan, much of whose period as Chancellor was spent grappling with sterling crises, records, 'Throughout the whole of the post-war era of fixed exchange rates, the stability of sterling had been a never-ending source of concern to successive Chancellors.' The nub of the problem was that the role of sterling as a worldwide currency had been established when Britain dominated world trade; after 1945 she no longer did so but insisted upon maintaining sterling's role long after it made economic sense to do so. Callaghan had to introduce a second post-war devaluation in November 1967, reducing sterling from $2.80 to $2.40. As he explained in his biography: 'The fundamental reason was that the world was not convinced that Britain could establish a long-term equilibrium in its balance of payments.'

A major world currency must be able to withstand international disruptions, and this sterling was increasingly unable to do. The 1967 devaluation followed the Six Day War in the Middle East and the closing of the Canal. The next really big crisis came in the mid-1970s following the oil shock of 1973. Sterling once more came under massive pressure and though the new Wilson government took deflationary measures they were not enough; in 1976 the pound fell from $2.00 to $1.60 in six months and Britain was forced to seek a massive loan from the IMF.

By the 1980s consensus was a dirty word, and yet the search for it was arguably the most important principle of home policy for every government from Attlee to Heath. A high proportion of the economic and social policies pursued by the Attlee administration had been agreed during the war in the coalition government. Broadly, the post-war consensus embraced a commitment to a mixed economy, full employment and the welfare state; for these three commitments to be achieved there was the need for wider educational opportunities and an acceptance of the place of the unions in national decisions. Consensus included the attempts by both Wilson and then Heath to curb the over-powerful unions. For three decades both parties had believed in government interventions, various forms of controls, in effect management of the economy. Following the fall of Heath's government, consensus collapsed. Management of the economy by government was manifestly not working as unemployment and inflation rose and industrial conflicts became less controllable until they produced the awful 'winter of discontent'. Even so, right up to 1979, the last three 'consensus' Prime Ministers – Wilson, Heath and Callaghan – did try to mobilize support for their economic policies across class and party lines. When Thatcher came to power, consensus was no longer an object of policy.

Whatever the judgements of hindsight, the post-war Attlee government did battle with enormous determination to get the economy back on a peacetime basis and to capture overseas markets. Indeed, it was part of the austere post-war culture that when goods were in short supply or not available in the shops they had gone for export. The terrible winter of 1946/7, with is desperate fuel and food shortages, brought home to the government just how fragile the economy had become. Industrial production was virtually halted for three weeks because there was not enough coal for the power stations.

The close liaison between government and unions was a vital ingredient in the post-war recovery; the key figure in this relationship was Ernest Bevin. Alan Bullock summarized Bevin's role:

> Only a man as completely trusted as Bevin by the Prime Minister and the Cabinet on the one hand and by the union leaders on the other could have maintained such a link without disaster. Bevin managed to do it until his death without either side feeling that its long-term interests were being sacrificed to the other's, a feat in which he has had no successor and one of the keys to understanding the history of the 1940s.

Defence crops up again and again as the economic stumbling block which prevented deployment of resources elsewhere. By 1948 defence expenditure was proportionately greater than that of the USA and more than France and the Benelux countries combined. For decades British defence expenditure exceeded that of all other nations except the USA and the USSR. While a renascent West Germany and, still more, Japan devoted small proportions of GDP to defence (in the case of Japan a derisory figure even today) and concentrated resources upon industrial recovery, Britain continued as the second military power of the Western Alliance.

Even so, following the setbacks of 1947, the industrial recovery under Cripps went ahead and by 1948 exports were at 150 per cent of their pre-war (1938) level. From 1948 to 1950 output increased by 4 per cent a year. Rigid controls (strikes were illegal) and Marshall Aid helped this process and output per man increased faster than in the USA. As a result Cripps could provide tax incentives in 1949 to stimulate private sector investment, although by mid-1949 recession in the USA and a run on the pound led to the devaluation crisis of September.

By 1951 when the Conservatives returned to power the Attlee government had presided over a major economic recovery. Debate will continue as to whether the priorities chosen were the correct ones but given those commitments – the establishment of the welfare state, NATO and the Western Alliance, and the determination to continue acting as a world power – it is difficult to see that economic performance could have been much better than was the case.

The Churchill government of 1951/5 was not notably successful at economics. Although it 'set the people free' by bringing an end to wartime controls and finally ended rationing to provide them, in Lord Woolton's phrase, with 'good red meat' it did not tackle productivity or the rising costs of the welfare state. When Churchill did turn his attention to home affairs it was to insist upon consensus politics. R. A. Butler, like his predecessor at the Exchequer, Hugh Gaitskell, followed a middle course so that the word 'Butskellism' entered the language to describe what would later be called consensus politics. The Conservatives were as anxious as Labour to preserve full employment and building 300,000 houses a year, the Conservative Party's most obvious success on the home front, was more of a social welfare than an economic achievement and reflected the priorities of a government which was liberal, middle-of-the-road and social democrat in at least as many respects as it was Tory.

Churchill finally retired in April 1955. Two weeks later Butler introduced a budget in which he took sixpence off income tax and raised personal allowances while speaking of doubling the standard of living in 25 years. Eden appeared to have inherited a buoyant economy. Yet as early as July difficulties over the balance of payments and inflation led him to say 'we must put the battle of inflation before anything else' and once more Britain was facing an economic crisis. As the *Daily Telegraph* said in an editorial in January 1956: 'Most Conservatives, and almost certainly some of the wiser trade union leaders, are waiting to feel the smack of firm government.' They waited, largely, in vain.

Describing how his government faced the growing economic pressures in *Full Circle*, Eden descends to bathos when he excuses raising purchase tax: 'It is difficult to advocate a property-owning democracy to the tune of "Your kettles will cost you more".' Later he puts his finger on the problem (without suggesting any solution) when he says: 'The most disturbing feature of our economy is that the Americans' cost of living and that of many other countries has remained about stable over the last four years, while ours has climbed steadily, and of late sharply.'

Harold Macmillan was Chancellor in 1956 and he tackled two of the country's economic weaknesses: low savings and high government spending. Macmillan introduced cuts of £100m in government expenditure and incentives for personal savings including premium bonds which appealed to the gambling instinct of the people. Whatever else the Eden government might have achieved in the economic field was lost in the Suez crisis. Sterling could not stand the strain of Suez and the economic crisis ensured an end to the Suez intervention, hastened Eden's resignation and brought Macmillan in as Prime Minister in January 1957.

During the remainder of the 1950s industry stagnated. Basic wages rose by 14 per cent (1955/8) and industrial earnings still more, but the index of industrial production rose only one per cent. Very little capital investment went into the manufacturing sector. It was as though the primary economic function of government was to keep the people quiet if not happy. In Macmillan's first period in office, as John Barnes explains in *Ruling Performance*, 'The government had

An Economy in Decline?

achieved a unique double in postwar politics, a sharp rise in living standards coupled with eighteen months of stable prices.'

Macmillan, perhaps the consensus politician par excellence of the post-war period, was determined not to retrench on the social services. In 1958 he accepted the resignation of his Treasury team headed by Peter Thorneycroft, who did want to retrench, and in the autumn went for a policy of reflation. The economic boom which followed lasted until 1960, but then produced an increasing trade deficit which developed into another major crisis in 1961. The Chancellor, Selwyn Lloyd, was forced to introduce an emergency July budget. He also introduced a pay pause, which became part of the stop-go policies of the 1960s and 1970s.

During this economic crisis Macmillan applied to join the European Common Market, giving rise to the accusation that we regarded membership as a solution to internal problems rather than as anything more positive. By 1962 disaffection with the economy and the attractions of a resurgent Labour Party contributed to the slide in support for the government. De Gaulle's veto was the final blow to an economic performance which had gone sour; Table 8.1 shows how growth lagged behind that of the European Community:

Table 8.1: Economic Growth Rates 1959–1964

Britain	18%
Belgium	29%
Netherlands	31%
France	32%
West Germany	32%
Italy	32%

The performance of the Macmillan years was good in comparison with that of the next two decades and at the time gave rise to reasonable expectations of steady if unspectacular growth. As James Prior says in *A Balance of Power*: 'His period as Prime Minister was the most prosperous and settled this nation had known since the war and it is some justice that he has come to be recognized as a great elder statesman.'

In an article in the *Independent* on the day of Lord Stockton's funeral (5 January 1987) Peter Kellner listed some economic statistics covering Macmillan's period of office; by comparison with 1987 they make impressive reading. Prices rose by no more than 2 per cent a year and inflation never exceeded 5 per cent; unemployment at its highest was 480,000; the bank rate went up to 7 per cent in a crisis; public spending was only 33 per cent of GDP; and economic growth averaged 3 per cent a year. By way of comparison: 'If Mrs Thatcher's tenure had enjoyed the same record, Britain would now be £1500 a year per family better off.'

Harold Wilson became leader of the Labour Party in 1963 when the fortunes of the Conservatives were in steady decline. He pushed the idea of technological change and spoke scathingly of 'Tory amateurs in the boardrooms of Britain who were unable to think or speak the language of our scientific revolution.' By 1964, after 13 years of Tory rule, the country was ready for a change and prepared to give a chance to Wilson's ideas. In fact, the Wilson approach to the economy was remarkably similar to that of his predecessors. There was a sterling crisis in 1964, another in 1966 and the second post-war devaluation in 1967. Unemployment was kept low, public expenditure rose sharply, taxation increased; various attempts at economic management were introduced between 1964 and 1970, including a Department of Economic Affairs and a Ministry of Technology, the Prices and Incomes Board, the introduction of a corporation tax, the publication of a National Plan. But his government seemed no more able than its predecessors to break the mould of high wage increases and low productivity; Britain's main rivals still performed better in terms of growth and world market share.

Like Macmillan, whom he greatly admired, Wilson also tried to take Britain into the European Community, and towards the end of his first period in office he faced up to union power and tried to curb it by legislation. When he lost the election to Edward Heath in June 1970, the economic problems which faced the new government were not remarkably different from those Wilson had inherited.

Like every Prime Minister since 1945 Edward Heath saw the country in economic decline and wished to make it dynamic again. Unlike Macmillan and Wilson, he succeeded in taking Britain into Europe, his one great achievement, and he believed passionately that Britain should be part of the Community. Otherwise his prescriptions were little different from those that had gone before: government intervention in the infrastructure to increase efficiency; the abolition of controls and an end to restrictive practices in the unions. He also aimed to reduce taxes and go for new markets, especially in Europe, as opposed to relying upon old imperial outlets. He was a consensus politician who accepted the goal of full employment and the maintenance and expansion of the welfare state.

Heath didn't have much luck. Almost from the beginning of the administration labour disputes dominated economic and social affairs: the electricity workers' go-slow in the winter of 1970/1, the miners' strike the next winter. By early 1972 the unemployed were nearly one million, the worst figure since the war (apart from the crisis winter of 1947). In the autumn of 1972 the government introduced a statutory prices and incomes policy which met with bitter resistance. Another confrontation with the miners followed and in December 1973 the government put industry on a three-day week. This confrontation coincided with the oil crisis following the Yom Kippur War, so it was not possible to switch to oil from coal. In February 1974 Heath went to the country – and lost.

The 1970s witnessed endless economic problems and few solutions. It marked the messy end of the consensus era though it is unlikely that politicians recognized

An Economy in Decline?

this at the time. The trade unions had become so powerful that they had to be curbed, but since both Wilson and Heath had tried and failed no one was willing to try again. The cost of the social services rose constantly as did the proportion of the population who were old age pensioners. Ingrained attitudes of 'them' and 'us' continued to inform almost every labour dispute and if the unions were arrogant and intransigent management was old-fashioned and unimaginative. Entry to the EEC had not stimulated the economy as its advocates had expected. The 1970s were unglamorous years when the British finally realized that the days of their worldwide influence were over.

Yet the men principally responsible for economic policy over these years were on the whole exceptionally able. It is not that Wilson, Healey, Jenkins or Callaghan did not have the ability to deal with the problems – they were as able as any politicians of the preceding decades – but they lacked the psychological drive to break the existing mould. It became increasingly obvious during the 1970s that the ingredients of consensus were being abandoned: unemployment rose steadily and its continued rise was tacitly accepted by politicians of all parties. Low productivity coupled with low investment in industry continued parallel with high wage demands. The pound continued to fall.

When Wilson returned in February 1974 to lead a minority government during the worst economic crisis since the war, the 1973 oil price rise was having its full impact. After a second general election in October Labour had an overall majority – but only just. By the end of the year wages had increased by 29 per cent. As usual, productivity had not kept pace. The next year saw the implementation of the voluntary pay policy and unemployment was more than one million, and 1976 marked economic disaster: the pound reached an all-time low of \$1.56 by October; unemployment was more than one and a half million; Chancellor Healey called in the IMF; and inflation reached 17 per cent.

In May 1976 Wilson was succeeded by Callaghan, who survived on the Lib-Lab pact because by-election defeats had deprived Labour of its majority. At the beginning of 1978 Callaghan suggested a pay limit target of 5 per cent which was incorporated in an incomes policy White Paper. This was challenged by striking car workers and rejected by the Labour Party Conference in October. The new year began with the lorry drivers' strike and went from bad to worse. Callaghan returned from the economic summit in Guadeloupe to a deteriorating economic situation and was misquoted as saying 'Crisis, what crisis?' At the end of March the government lost a no-confidence vote and an election was called. That winter tolled the final death knell of consensus.

The Thatcher government which came to power in 1979 knew what it did not want; it is far from certain that it knew what policies it would adopt. The term 'Thatcherism' came to mean all aspects of economic and social policy associated

The Economy

with her government: in a sense, the quality of unyielding toughness, especially in face of the unions, which had been so markedly absent in her predecessors. Perhaps in the end Thatcherism will be seen as the replacement of consensus by the creed of exalting individual opportunities, which has led to the growth of personal greed and lack of concern for those less able or less fortunate.

The policies of the Thatcher years are dealt with later. The claim, repeatedly advanced, is of a reversal of Britain's economic decline. Her rate of growth became the best in Europe in the 1980s and by 1986 productivity had risen to 4.4 per cent. Moreover, for the years 1982/6 GNP growth rate averaged 3 per cent and though this was below that of the USA and Japan it was above West Germany at 2.5 per cent and France at only 1.4 per cent. If, as Thatcher supporters claim, this performance owed a great deal to the breaking of union power, it was also achieved at great social cost. The government inherited more than a million unemployed but by the end of 1980 the figure was more than two million and by mid-1986 was touching three and a half million.

Thatcher made the fight against inflation the top economic priority – from 22 per cent in 1980 it was brought down to 3.7 per cent just before the 1983 election and thereafter has ranged between 3 and 6 per cent. Yet, if comparisons are to be made with trade rivals, in 1988 the rate was only 1 per cent in West Germany, Japan, Belgium and Holland and 2.5 per cent in France, so on this front where so much effort has been concentrated Britain was doing less well than her principal trade rivals. By June 1989 inflation had passed 8 per cent.

The central question remains: why is Britain less able to grapple with the economic problems it faces – inflation, management-union relations and productivity – than its competitors? The 1980s have witnessed a scramble for wealth, but not a comparable creation of wealth. During the eight years to 1988, to give just one example, the British merchant fleet declined from 44 million to 12 million deadweight tons.

Education may well be the key. Britain does not keep pace in terms of training skilled people. Whereas industrial training in the USA is estimated to cost $40bn a year, the comparable figure here is £2bn. While nine-tenths of German school leavers go for further training before taking jobs, only a tiny proportion of Britain's one million school leavers each year will be apprenticed, approximately 40,000. In 1988 the Secretary of State for Education, Kenneth Baker, turned down the headmasters' proposal that the school-leaving age should be raised to 18, which it has been for many years in most EEC countries. Neglect of education, or the right sort of education, for a modern industrial society is perhaps the most important reason behind years of poor industrial performance and low productivity.

9
The Unions

'*During our inquiry we found a widespread conviction, which we share, that the problem of Britain as an industrialized nation is not a lack of native capacity in its working population so much as a failure to draw out their energies and skill to anything like their full potential.*'

ALAN BULLOCK

'*... our Conservative belief that all employees have a right to be involved in the way that their enterprises are run, that they have a positive contribution to make, and that their full participation will not only bring greater satisfaction to their work, but will also make for more efficient management and a healthier economy.*'

MARGARET THATCHER

'*We are redefining and we are restating socialism in terms of the scientific revolution ... the Britain that is going to be forged in the white heat of this revolution will be no place for restrictive practices or outdated methods on either side of industry.*'

HAROLD WILSON

The triumph of the trade union movement came with Labour's electoral victory in 1945. Their acceptance as part of the consensus society followed in the 1950s when Churchill invited their leaders to Downing Street, a practice which was to last until Thatcher.

Churchill's Minister of Labour, Sir Walter Monckton, had a brief to avoid industrial strife and build trust between the Tory party and organized labour. From then until 1979 and the 'winter of discontent' successive governments approached the unions — more or less — as a part of a corporatist state which had to be included in all major economic decision-making. They became more powerful and more arrogant until, predictably, governments tried to curb their power and failed. The unions then behaved as though consensus did not apply to them until they met a government which was determined to reduce their power.

Commenting in 1988 Lord Whitelaw said: 'The trade union leaders are not so powerful as they were; therefore, inevitably, because they are not so powerful so they are not so prominent. You don't hear so much about them. How many people who would always have been able to tell you of Jack Jones, Carron or Cousins — now if you ask them who is General Secretary of the NUR, how many would know?' In the late 1980s media projection of the union image fell off; they were simply less important, less relevant to national economic decisions.

The unions came into being to protect their members from exploitation; they were opposed to capitalism. In essence they are conservative, not radical, and they are reactive, bargaining for the best deal they can obtain from the existing system rather than trying to change it.

The movement was brought fully into the decison-making process under Bevin and Churchill during World War Two, and much of the bitterness against Thatcher governments since 1979 has been because of their exclusion from that role. The best incomes policy was devised during World War Two when the government stabilized living costs by subsidies and controls in return for restraint in wage claims. Collective bargaining dominated the post-war industrial scene until the 1980s, when a combination of government policy, unemployment and union weakness led to a growth of individual, local deals rather than nationwide settlements.

During the years of consensus and full employment in the 1950s the trade union movement went into decline: in 1950 44.1 per cent of the workforce were members, but 10 years later the figure had dropped to 43.1 per cent in 183 unions affiliated to the TUC, with a total membership of 8.3m. The size and power of unions also changed according to adjustments in the national industrial pattern. Thus the NUM (the National Union of Mineworkers), which had 638,988 members in 1960, had shrunk to 261,871 members by 1976. NUPE (the National Union of Public Employees), which claimed a membership of 240,000 in 1964, had almost tripled its membership by 1977 to 670,000.

The spearhead of union strength in the 1970s was 300,000 shop stewards who led the movement. The Donovan Commission in 1968 pinpointed the problem of industrial relations as the failure to control the power of the shop stewards. This was still more true 10 years later. By 1980 there were 109 unions affiliated to the TUC and more than 12m members nationwide. By 1985, however, battered by years of high unemployment, government assaults upon union power and disaffection among segments of the movement, membership had dropped to 10.8m and 81 per cent of these were in the 24 largest unions with over 100,000 members each. The largest were the Transport and General Workers' Union (1.4m members), the Amalgamated Engineering Union (975,000) and the General, Municipal, Boilermakers' and Allied Trades' Union (827,000); of non-manual unions the National and Local Government Officers' Association had 752,000 members and NUPE 664,000.

The TUC itself has comparatively little power: during the heyday of the 1970s the big unions were far too jealous of their power to surrender real decision-

The Unions

making authority to the centre, and by the 1980s, when a strong TUC might have made a difference, it was too late.

The 1950s were the years of Butskellism and consensus yet Frank Cousins's remark in 1957 that if there was to be a free-for-all then the Transport and General Workers' Union wanted to be part of the all gave a foretaste of how the big unions were likely to behave in the future. On the other hand, though a scramble for as large a slice as possible of the economic cake came to be regarded as the norm of behaviour, little attention was paid to increasing pay through greater productivity in the manner of Sweden or Germany. In a majority of cases unions were wary of change and seemed concerned to safeguard what they had rather than experiment with modernization. Multi-unionism – as opposed to single-industry unions – meant that the movement remained backward looking and tended to chaos.

Since 1945 the union movement has been subject to enormous shifts of power. The Attlee government, despite close ties, did not for a moment contemplate the sort of relationship which emerged in the Wilson days of the social contract. The Emergency Powers Act was extended for five years in 1945, troops were used to break dock strikes in 1945 and 1949, and in the London power stations in 1950. Attlee always made plain that a Labour government would transcend the claims of organized labour because its concerns were national, not sectional, and Cripps operated a successful policy of wage restraint from 1948 to 1950. Labour's ability to handle the unions after the war was due in part to the circumstances of the time: the prestige of the first Labour government with a huge majority; the nationally accepted need to rebuild; and the presence in the government of such major union figures as Ernest Bevin and George Isaacs, whom Attlee appointed Minister of Labour. In part it derived simply from the firmness of the government, its assumption that it was there to run the country – an assumption in relation to union affairs not always obvious in the 1960s and 1970s.

The period of Tory ascendancy from 1951 to 1964 coincided with the most prosperous post-war years when consensus was broadly unchallenged. But when Labour returned with a small majority in 1964 it faced a series of financial crises which dominated the middle of that decade. Frank Cousins was persuaded to join the government as Minister of Technology, a new department, and left his job as General Secretary of the Transport and General Workers' Union to do so but he was not happy and left the government in 1966. He had been brought into the government in an effort to improve government-union relations, but when he returned to the TGWU he made it plain that his union would not cooperate with the wage freeze. It was becoming clear that the relationship between the Labour Party in office and organized labour was growing more strained; by 1968 the strains persuaded Wilson to attempt to curb union power.

In Place of Strife, which Barbara Castle introduced in 1969, marked the end of consensus, certainly as far as governments and unions were concerned. For a quarter of a century – more if the harmony of the war years is taken ino account – no government had seen the need to introduce legislation to control the unions. Now a government sought to diminish and regulate their powers. Even more remarkable, the legislation was proposed by a Labour government: the party which had been created by the unions was to attempt to control them.

The main thrust of the Donovan Report of the Royal Commission on Trade Unions and Employers' Associations, which was presented to the government in 1968, was the need for modernization of the system of collective bargaining which was described as primitive and outmoded. A bitter row developed in Cabinet between Barbara Castle and James Callaghan, because Castle wanted to find remedies for unofficial strikes and bypass the Industrial Relations Committee of the Cabinet on which Callaghan sat. He was then excluded from the inner Cabinet and accused of plotting against Wilson.

The nub of the argument about *In Place of Strife* was the attempt to impose obligations on the unions in relation to unofficial strikes, and the right of the Secretary of State to require a secret ballot before a strike which he saw as posing a threat to the economy or the public interest. Two measures in particular were seen by unions as unacceptable (and unworkable). The government was to have powers to order a 28-day conciliation pause when unofficial strikes were threatened and to fine workers who continued to strike; and it would have the power to enforce settlements in inter-union disputes. The government tried to get the most controversial points through by means of a 'short Bill' in April 1969 which the Chancellor described as 'an essential component in ensuring the economic success of the Government'. It was bitterly opposed by the TUC and by backbench Labour MPs and the government was forced to abandon it in return for a 'solemn and binding undertaking' by the TUC General Council that it would deal with unconstitutional disputes.

The government's retreat in 1969 was the beginning of a five-year period, culminating in Heath's electoral defeat in 1974, when both Labour and Tory governments were perceived by the public to be battling with the unions and losing. Whatever the rights and wrongs of the arguments, in those years they came to be regarded as capable of defying governments of both political complexions and winning.

Robert Carr was Secretary of State for Employment in the 1970 Heath government and introduced the Industrial Relations Bill which became law at the end of 1971. He tried to strike a balance between restrictions on union powers and encouragement for recognition by employers, but suspicion between unions and government was by then so great that the unions did not believe Carr when he said part of the government's purpose was to strengthen collective bargaining.

The Unions

The Heath government became so embroiled in industrial strife that the Act never had a chance; it was repealed in 1974 when Labour returned.

James Prior, who had responsibility for labour relations 10 years later, provides an insight into the Carr Act in *A Balance of Power*:

> We tried to do far too much at once, putting our faith in the idea that sweeping changes in the law would rapidly change behaviour on the shop floor.... We rewrote the entire framework of the law on industrial relations, and had our Industrial Relations Act on the statute book by the end of our first parliamentary session, in 1971. We would have been better advised to put our own proposals into abeyance and take up the reforms which the Labour government had proposed in 1969 in their White Paper, *In Place of Strife*. But apart from Robert Carr ... scarcely anyone in the Party understood industrial relations or knew industrialists, let alone any trade unionists.

That last damning admission could have been repeated with equal truth 15 years later. Prior continues, 'Ted was determined that a better balance had to be restored in collective bargaining by reducing union power. He had given Geoffrey Howe the task of seeing how the legal framework could be amended. Geoffrey's approach was legalistic in the extreme, with no appreciation of what made the unions tick on ... the shop floor.'

In 1972 the coalminers went on strike to support their wage claims which were twice as much as the maximum being offered by the Coal Board, under government pressure to keep the offer minimal. The strike lasted eight weeks, then the government caved in. It was a total union victory. Joe Gormley, president of the NUM, was one of the toughest, most able leaders, (when Arthur Scargill replaced him as president, he was remembered as a moderate). The victory had two momentous consequences: it heralded ten years of union militancy culminating in the year-long miners' strike of 1984; and it had a deep psychological impact upon many Tories, who could neither forgive nor forget their defeat at the hands of the NUM.

The government had already faced on damaging industrial dispute in the winter of 1970/1 when the electricity power workers operated a go-slow. This was settled by an inquiry under Lord Wilberforce which had satisfied both sides. Wilberforce was called in again when the miners struck – and found wholly in their favour. Government determined not to 'do another Wilberforce' and opted for a statutory prices and incomes policy, which went ahead after the TUC had rejected a tripartite (government, CBI and TUC) agreement on wages restraint. The miners were due for another pay award in November 1973 and this time the NUM operated an overtime ban (the Yom Kippur War had just precipitated the oil crisis). Determined not to be caught out a second time by the miners, the government put industry on a three-day week. The miners decided to strike and were backed by the TUC. Heath, supported by increasingly militant backbenchers, determined not to back down a second time, called a general election, which he lost.

The double victory of the miners set the tone for government-union relations when Wilson returned as Prime Minister. In his presidential address to the Yorkshire miners in 1975, prematurely as he was to discover, Arthur Scargill said: 'The capitalist society belongs to the dustbin of history. The ideal of a socialist society belongs to the youth of today and to the future. I have seen the vision of the socialist tomorrow and it works.'

The concept of the social contract has been ascribed to Jack Jones who floated the idea at a Fabian meeting in 1971. Certainly it was time for a new approach, for Labour-union relations had deteriorated so much that their backing for Labour in the 1970 election had been less than wholehearted. Essentially, in return for the repeal of the Heath legislation and the promise of a programme of social change, the unions agreed to restrict pay settlements voluntarily in line with rises in the cost of living. It was not a policy likely to succeed.

By 1977 Jack Jones and Hugh Scanlon were becoming pessimistic as their members urged a return to free collective bargaining. In *Time and Chance*, Callaghan provides a picture of the frantic desperation of the government to persuade the unions to go along with the social contract against a steadily deteriorating economic background. There is a sense of doom about the relationship, an acknowledgement that it could not last. By 1978 Moss Evans, who had succeeded Jack Jones as General Secretary of the giant TGWU, was telling the government to 'back off' and leave the unions to secure the best deals they could. The TGWU was claiming a 30 per cent rise for Ford car workers and a 40 per cent increase for the road haulage industry. By the autumn of 1978, when Callaghan decided not to go to the country, the social contract had collapsed and the pay policy was in a shambles.

There is a kind of logic in the behaviour of groups (or nations) which achieve great power; they almost always overreach themselves. Overweening pride or *hubris* makes them unable to resist the temptation to push their power and their luck to the limit. Inevitably, they create counter-forces determined to reduce their pride.

The trade union movement had fought long and hard to improve conditions for its members since the repression following the Napoleonic Wars. In the emergency conditions of World War Two, they were accepted as national partners, represented in the Cabinet by the towering political figure of Ernest Bevin. It is ironic that the Heath government which Norman Tebbit describes as the most corporatist ever was destroyed largely by them. For the remainder of the

1970s, they used their industrial muscle with less and less concern for the impact upon the rest of the country.

In a poll carried out in 1976 for Granada Television's *World in Action* more people (23 per cent) blamed the unions for high unemployment than employers or the international situation. It was a sign of the times. At the 1977 Tory Party Conference James Prior, Shadow Spokesman for Employment, was viciously attacked by the right for his moderate views. It was the year of the Grunwick dispute in North London and MP John Gorst described Prior as a 'Quisling' and Tebbit said some Conservatives had the morals of Petain or Laval for adhering to 'the doctrine of appeasement'. By the end of the 1970s trade unions were highly unpopular with the public generally. Their shortcomings were highlighted by the media; they were made scapegoats for Britain's poor industrial performance, and people were more likely to blame them for forcing up wages as the explanation for the country's industrial ills than prices, bad management, lack of investment or any other cause.

As the Callaghan government failed to deliver its part of the social contract, while the Prime Minister tried to make the unions stick to a 5 per cent rise over the winter of 1978/9, the country was treated to the disruptions of the 'winter of discontent'. While some of the more moderate union leaders like Sid Weighell of the NUR tried to exercise restraint at the Blackpool Labour Party Conference: 'If ... you now believe in the philosophy of the pig trough – those with the biggest snouts get the largest share – I reject it', others did little to restrain their militant members. Labour supporters argued subsequently that 'the winter of discontent' lost them the election of May 1979.

In any case, disillusionment with Labour policies of the Callaghan-Healey variety was growing in the ranks of the Party as a number of unions became markedly more militant. NUPE's members spearheaded the 'winter of discontent' when hospitals were picketed, the dead went unburied (providing the media with perfect anti-union copy) and the fabric of an orderly society appeared under threat. Writing of the refusal of the Liverpool grave-diggers to bury the dead, Callaghan said: 'Such heartlessness and cold-blooded indifference to the feelings of families at moments of intense grief rightly aroused deep revulsion and did further untold harm to the cause of trade unionism that I, like many others, had been proud to defend throughout my life. What would the men of Tolpuddle have said?'

Mrs Thatcher's initial approach was one of caution: in 1981 she gave in to the demands of the NUM. But the issue of union power was highly charged and the Tories argued in 'constitutional' terms against their overwhelming power. The reforms introduced by James Prior in 1979 came against a background of continuing recession and rapidly rising unemployment, which were powerful factors weakening union effectiveness and making the task of the new government easier.

Prior's bill had four principal planks: government money to fund secret ballots for strike calls, elections or amendment of union rules; the limitation of picketing to a person's workplace; changes in the operation of the closed shop; making coercive recruitment unlawful. Prior found his task made easier by the attacks upon him from his own right wing but immeasurably more difficult when the steelworkers went on strike at the beginning of 1980, leading to fresh demands in the Tory Party for tougher anti-union action. This came from the Prime Minister who announced without any prior Cabinet discussion that strikers claiming social security benefits would be deemed to be receiving strike pay and would have an amount docked from their claims each week.

After the 1983 election Thatcher was much more prepared for a tough stand. The Employment Acts of 1980 and 1982 had weakened the position of the unions substantially. The Trade Union Act of 1984 aimed to ensure basic democracy in them ('give trade unions back to the members' in the government phrase) by requiring that members of the principal executive committee of a union should be elected by secret, direct ballots once every five years. But in the words of a TUC consultative document, 'The presentation of much of the present Government's ... legislation has been consciously designed to foster and exploit anti-union prejudice.' This would be hotly denied but there is a strong ring of truth to it; by 1984 the wheel had indeed come full circle since 1979, helped by the coal strike of 1983/4.

This was the longest and most bitter since the 1920s. Scargill made plain that he wanted to confront a government whose policies he totally opposed. Prior says:

> In this case, Arthur Scargill's motives seemed to be concerned with inflicting defeat on the democratically elected government as much as they were with the issue of pit closures. Neither the National Coal Board nor the government was left with any alternative but to fight it through to the bitter end.

This is the view of a Tory centrist. Tam Dalyell, a Labour centrist, in his book *Misrule* records the role of a millionaire supporter of Thatcher, David Hart, who said on television in 1986 that he had advised the Prime Minister that 'it was politically undesirable to settle' the miners' strike. Dalyell argues that for Mrs Thatcher the miners' strike was not about the national interest but about domestic politics: 'Mrs Thatcher revealed volumes about her own attitude of mind when she saw fit to draw a comparison between the Argentines during the Falklands War as "the enemy without" and the National Union of Mineworkers as "the enemy within".' Many opponents of Thatcher would agree with Dalyell; more were happy that the government had taken on the miners and won.

The Unions

Writing in 1978 Labour's Giles Radice said: 'The strength of open unionism means that, short of a major cataclysm, the construction of British trade unions on industrial lines is not a practical possibility.' By 1988, as a result of the Thatcher assault, the cataclysm had come – at least in part. The leader of the power workers, Eric Hammond, was at last being listened to as he pressed for single-union agreements as the way forward. The TUC was beginning to look at a code to control single-union deals in the aftermath of the aborted Ford plant in Dundee. Despite bitter disputes it was clear that the more progressive part of the labour movement was moving cautiously towards single-union deals.

Writing in the *Independent* in April 1988, Eric Hammond, General Secretary of the Electrical, Electronic, Telecommunication and Plumbing Union (EETPU) said: 'There is a wilful reluctance by too many trade union leaders to come to terms with the often harsh realities of modern industrial life. Worse, there is a dangerous determination by some to turn back the clock, to revive the sorry image of a Britain torn by industrial strife.' Battered by a decade of high unemployment, confronted by a government determined to limit their power, and threatened by harsh international competition, some trade unions had come to accept reality and were prepared to modernize.

10
North Sea Oil

'God has given Britain her best opportunity for one hundred years in the shape of North Sea oil.'

JAMES CALLAGHAN

'The North Sea oil opportunity should be used to bring about two revolutions in British society: the regeneration of British industry so that the country will continue to prosper long after the oil runs out, and a sustained attack upon poverty and squalor and the scars which are still to be seen, particularly in our great cities.'

PETER WALKER

Until the coming of North Sea oil Britain, like the rest of Europe, was almost totally dependent upon imports from the Middle East where she controlled huge stakes through British-owned BP and the partially British-owned Shell (Netherlands 60 per cent, Britain 40 per cent). Coal was the basis of her energy supplies and though Middle East oil was cheap for 20 years from the early 1950s to early 1970s it had to be imported into what was an energy deficient country. The importance of the Iran crisis of 1951/4 did not lie simply in the threat to nationalize a British asset – Peron had already done that with British-owned railways in Argentina – but in the nature of the asset. Even in the early 1970s, when oil had been discovered in the North Sea, the country was exceptionally vulnerable to external pressures. Following the Yom Kippur War in October 1973 the Arab oil-producing states quadrupled its price and reduced supplies, thus threatening Europe and elsewhere with fuel shortages and massive balance of payments problems. Oil which for years had stood at approximately $1.5 a barrel fetched $12 a barrel within months. The shock was enormous, but in a few years Britain was to be self-sufficient in oil with a surplus for export.

The first important North Sea discovery was made in 1969 but it was not until 1975 that the first oil was brought ashore. Britain was lucky in the North Sea carve-up; because of her geography and long coastline she received 46 per cent (for oil and other resource purposes) with the balance going in descending order to Norway, the Netherlands, Denmark, West Germany, Belgium and France. The idea that Britain could be self-sufficient in oil was unthinkable even at the end of the 1960s yet by the mid-1970s BP could say: 'UK national self-sufficiency

North Sea Oil

of around two million barrels per day is expected by 1980 and thereafter a modest surplus at least throughout the '80s.'

The unpredictable nature of oil can be seen from the gaffe of BP's chairman, Sir Eric Drake, who told reporters in April 1970 that he did not rate highly the chances of commercial finds in the North Sea. He said, 'There won't be a major field there,' although he added that BP had an obligation to explore. Six months later they discovered the Forties field and by 1977 this had been upgraded to produce 500,000 barrels a day. Between 1965 and 1975 about 90 discoveries of oil and gas were made in the British and Norwegian sectors of the North Sea. But the government was totally unprepared to deal with the bonanza, which represented the biggest industrial development since the railway boom of the 1840s.

In 1950 coal supplied 90 per cent of primary energy requirements, but from the late 1950s cheap oil captured an increasing share of the market. By 1966 Britain was a two-fuel economy: 60 per cent coal, 40 per cent oil. It was then thought that by 1975 it would be a four-fuel economy: coal (down to 34 per cent), oil (41 per cent), gas (14 per cent) and nuclear power (10 per cent). In fact, oil had by then captured half the market.

The United Kingdom sector, nearly half the 221,000 square miles of the North Sea, was divided into Scottish and English areas along the latitude of 55 degrees 50 north. The Scottish segment is 62,500 square miles and the English 32,800 square miles; most of the prolific finds were in the Scottish area. This allowed the Scottish National Party (SNP) to enjoy a field day claiming Scotland's oil!

The Yom Kippur War added new urgency to the North Sea oil search: for financial and security reasons Britain wanted her own oil as fast as possible. It also revealed that the government was unable to control the activities of the companies (BP and Shell had refused Heath's demand that they should land all their oil in Britain), to tax them adequately or to direct the flow of the oil. As a result, when Labour returned to power in 1974 they set about devising an oil policy although some plans relating to a tax regime had been worked out by the Tories before they went to the polls.

There was a broad belt of gas across the southern North Sea including Leman, which became the world's largest offshore field in production. The first gas finds were in 1965 and by 1967 natural gas was being used in British homes. A number of major fields had been discovered in the period 1969 to 1971 (including Montrose, Forties and Brent), yet the companies held back and were prepared to exploit them fully only after the oil price hike by OPEC. This rise, according to Professor Gaskin of Aberdeen, gave an enormous boost to North Sea exploration 'since it turned an interesting but, in world terms, rather marginal area into a highly attractive prospect, both economically and politically'.

By 1974 constant upward revision of estimates had encouraged a braver govern-

The Economy

ment approach to the companies. A White Paper proposed a state corporation and a special tax regime as well as state participation, as yet undefined. By the end of 1976, when the fifth round of licences for exploitation was offered, the government had worked out the broad outlines of its policy: the new tax regime had been introduced; participation was being negotiated; BNOC (the British National Oil Corporation) had come into being. The oil companies might decry such government activity but the bidding for licences was as intense as ever, for even with greater government involvement the North Sea was a superb oil investment.

By 1977 the British were becoming quite excited about their oil. It was estimated that oil had provided 100,000 jobs in Britain as a whole, (55,000 in Scotland) although up to 75 per cent were part of the production phase and were expected to fall away later. Ten thousand of the jobs were offshore. Little known places in Scotland became household words as sites for the construction of the huge offshore rigs.

The oil boom, with its demands for rapid work, also revealed some of the shortcomings of British work practices. A devastating picture of the construction industry was given in the 1976 NEDO report 'Engineering Construction Performance'. This compared the UK operation with that of EEC, Canadian and US companies – the British came last. The reasons were numerous: inadequate management, bad time-keeping, overrunning on estimates, overmanning, bad industrial relations. The NEDO report said:

> Not only did the UK projects take longer in terms of elapsed years and months, but they also absorbed more man-hours on site; the difference in man-hours was proportionately greater than the difference in elapsed time because of the larger numbers employed on the UK sites.

North Sea gas came on stream before the oil but was largely forgotten in the great excitement which followed, yet by 1976 it had already saved the country an estimated £2250m in a year and was to make an invaluable contribution to the economy thereafter.

The extent of the oil resources became clearer during 1977: in April the Department of Energy announced that half the country's needs would be met out of North Sea resources by the end of the year; eight weeks later it admitted that that target had been passed in May. As Hugh Sandeman wrote in *The Banker* in May: 'After the pessimism that surrounded the long months of official indecision, oilmen are now praising the secure political and economic environment that exists for their operations in the United Kingdom.' By the end of 1977 the pound was rising again, at last; the economy was on the mend; the Labour Party suddenly saw the prospect of winning the next election, something that had looked utterly remote a year earlier; and almost daily the media had something to say about oil and the wealth it would bring.

North Sea oil changed fundamentally the financial and political outlook for the next decades. As a BP briefing paper put it: 'It is difficult to imagine any sector of the UK economy of comparable size which can offer such returns to the nation, or to overstate the relative importance of developing UK oil production in a world of "high" oil prices.' The Treasury estimated that by 1985 oil would be contributing 5 per cent to the GNP. Politicians, though they played down its importance to the economy, were becoming enthusiastic about its possibilities.

The extent of government revenue from oil was at last becoming apparent: their share of royalties and tax was expected to reach £5.5bn in 1980 when the import bill would have been eliminated, and thereafter annual revenue was estimated at approximately £4.5bn. Speaking in Aberdeen in 1977 the Minister of State at the Department of Energy, Dr Mabon, said: 'Within three years Britain will be one of the ten largest oil producers in the world; and one of the very few industrialized countries to be self-sufficient in oil and gas.' When Healey presented his budget in April 1978 he was able to give £2500m in tax relief – made possible by oil. A political oil auction got underway. The Tories favoured a general lowering of taxes. Michael Spicer of South Worcestershire moved in November 1977:

> That this House will use North Sea oil revenues with other measures to reduce income tax on taxable incomes of up to £5000 per annum to 20 per cent, on taxable incomes between £5000 and £10,000 to 25 per cent, on taxable incomes between £10,000 and £15,000 to 35 per cent, on taxable incomes between £15,000 and £20,000 to 40 per cent, on taxable incomes between £20,000 and £25,000 to 45 per cent, and on taxable incomes over £30,000 to 50 per cent.

Public discussion as to the best way to use the oil wealth became a feature of the late 1970s. In a statement to the Wilson Committee 'To Review the Functioning of Financial Institutions' the TUC argued:

> The investment challenge is based on the fact that the benefits of offshore oil are finite. Therefore the key issue is how to use the surplus funds for investment in the regeneration of the UK economy. The objective would be that by the time the oil flow began to lessen, the UK manufacturing and productive sector would have been built up, so that it could meet and beat any international challenge.

The real argument between the Labour and Tory parties, then and later, was about the extent to which oil revenues should be used for interventionist policies or for tax relief. By 1978 the impact upon sterling had been felt with a harder pound (although still only worth $1.93). It continued to rise as the price of oil rose, but fell back when the market weakened. At the end of the 1970s too many hopes were pinned on oil as though its mere possession would bring about a turnaround in British performance. As early as October 1977, Tony Benn, Secretary for Energy, warned against North Sea oil being used as 'a mask which conceals the decline of our economy' and that Britain should not imagine that it could solve her problems.

As it began to flow British concern with OPEC receded noticeably. In 1977 Lord Kearton, chairman of BNOC, said:

> France, for instance, is sweating blood: it imports 75 per cent of its energy. Germany imports 70 per cent. America imports 45 per cent of its oil energy. In 1980 we are going to be the only developed country apart from Russia with an exportable surplus of energy.

Indeed, by 1978, Lord Kearton was arguing that without another OPEC price rise the North Sea bonanza would be over, so quickly had events led to a change in British attitudes.

When Callaghan visited the Forties Field in September 1977, he called for a public debate on how the revenue should be spent and at the Labour Party Conference the following month he declared that thanks to oil, 'the next 20 years will be unlike anything Britain has seen since it first moved to become an industrial power 200 years ago.' There was no lack of suggestions as to how the wealth might be employed. In the Labour Party Denis Healey and Harold Lever favoured tax reductions, while Tony Benn led those who wanted to go for investment in industry, better social services and repayment of external debts. In Washington Sir Geoffrey Howe said: 'Of course the oil funds will not automatically prove to be a cure-all, but they *could* provide an unparalleled opportunity for the regeneration of our economy.'

In *Time and Chance* Callaghan is muted about the effects of oil, almost as though he wished to forget the hopeful words he spoke in the late 1970s. By 1987, when the book was published, oil had become a source of revenue indistinguishable from any other, though what the country would have done without it was another question.

One argument concerned whether Britain should embark upon a policy of conservation: to develop sufficient of her resources to meet only her own needs (foregoing exports) and conserve the balance for the future. The argument was not popular with companies or government, who for once found themselves in agreement. Companies want to maximize profits by extracting all they can as soon as possible, and governments want maximum revenues *now*, not for their political opponents to enjoy in the future. For conservation policies to be effective they had to be initiated as soon as the discoveries were made. Predictably, both industry and government went for maximum production at once. As a senior oilman remarked: 'Posterity! What has posterity ever done for me?'

The biggest impact of the oil, apart from government revenues, was upon Scotland. It had three geographical effects: at the supply bases and ports; in the various, usually remote, fabrication yards; and at the landfall terminals. In each case it made a substantial contribution to employment and prosperity as well as to lifestyles. By 1977 direct employment resulting from the boom had reached 27,000. But as a Church of Scotland study pointed out: 'In Scotland oil developments have created extra jobs and bid up wages to the competitive disadvantage of almost all other Scottish industries. Some time, probably soon, the short-term benefits of the former will be overtaken by the lingering damage to the latter.'

Aberdeen experienced a boom: in office blocks, hotel building, the expansion of the housing sector over a twenty-mile radius from the city. By 1975 it had acquired more than 200 new companies to become the oil capital of the North Sea. It was not surprising that the SNP rode high during this period; in 1977 it was hoping to win as many as 40 seats at the next general election, and was talking of independence. The *Daily Telegraph* of 8 October 1976 had reported the following story: 'Mr Crosland, the Foreign Secretary, asked at a Washington press conference yesterday why Britain refused to give Scotland its independence, said in an aside heard distinctly over the microphone, "because they have got a lot of oil".'

North Sea oil gave a great fillip to Scottish nationalism, even while focusing attention upon Scotland's economic ills. As William Wolfe said: 'Scottish oil can make Scotland the most prosperous country in Europe or it can provide temporary relief for the UK balance of payments. It cannot do both.'

According to Callaghan, Benn thought that if Margaret Thatcher won the election she would export North Sea oil in large quantities to provide herself with large financial surpluses. Benn was to prove accurate. In March 1978 the Labour government produced its White Paper on the use of the revenues and listed four main uses for the money: investing in industry; investing in energy; reduction in the levels of personal taxation; increasing essential public services. In the debate which followed Mrs Thatcher made her view plain when she said, 'We believe that the lion's share could go by cuts in taxation.'

OPEC raised prices again in 1978 and this had the effect during 1979 of pushing up the 'petro pound', as it was then known, well beyond its true worth and making British exports very expensive. As part of the new monetary policy interest rates were also kept high so that by late 1980 the pound went above $2.40. This was also the year when oil production equalled total British requirements; the next year it provided a surplus for export. Arguments about how the wealth should have been spent will probably feature in political debate for years to come.

Writing in *Ruling Performance*, John Vincent argues that in one respect Thatcherite economic liberalism has worked wonders. He says:

> The City has sold British oil at the top and used the proceeds to buy foreign securities at the bottom. Nothing could have worked more neatly. Britain has become per head the largest overseas investor, replenishing the ravages of two wars. British net assets abroad have risen from £2700m in 1975 to £90,000m in 1985.

In the mid-1970s BP estimated that 'the net resources generated and available to the UK economy in the period 1976-85 will be between £20 and £25 billion in 1976 £'s'. Of this, BP estimated that the government would take approximately 83 per cent. Over the same period it estimated that the balance of payments benefit would be between £30 and £35 billion.

In 1987 oil and gas production from the North Sea accounted for approximately 2 per cent of GNP and yielded £9.9bn (oil) and £2bn (gas), with an additional £39m contributed by onshore production. Taxes and royalties taken by government for the years 1978 to 1988 are shown in Table 10.1.

Table 10.1: Government Share – Taxes and Royalties

FINANCIAL YEAR	£m
1978/9	565
1979/80	2313
1980/1	3743
1981/2	6492
1982/3	7822
1983/4	8798
1984/5	12028
1985/6	11343
1986/7	4782
1987/8*	4700

*provisional
Source: 1988 Brown Book of the Department of Energy

By 1987 Britain had become the world's fifth largest producer. It had enjoyed its first surplus on oil trade in 1980, and this continued throughout the decade. It reached a peak in 1985 at £8100m. Exports, mainly to the European Community, were roughly equivalent to half domestic production.

Figures in 1986 illustrate the size of the industry. Output for the year averaged 2.5m barrels (or 332,000 tons) a day. By the end of the year 3062 wells had been drilled or were being drilled in the UKCS (United Kingdom Continental Shelf)

North Sea Oil

divided into 1385 development wells, 1109 exploration wells and 568 appraisal wells. Britain's offshore supplies industry had become the second largest in the world (after the USA) and in 1986 goods and services for oil development were valued at £2231m. Thirty-two offshore fields were producing crude oil and another seven were under development. That was the year of maximum production.

During 1987 the 'one billionth ton of oil' was brought onshore and 123 million tons were produced during the year. Proceeds were £9.9bn (compared with £9.3bn in 1986); comparable figures for gas were £2bn and £1.9bn. Gross capital investment in the industry for 1987 was £2.1bn or one-eighth of total British investment in industry. The offshore workforce was 28,200, of whom 94 per cent were British nationals. Capital investment figures are shown in Table 10.2; production figures in Table 10.3.

Table 10.2: Capital Investment in the Oil and Gas Extraction Industry

	1982	1983	1984	1985	1986	1987
Gross capital investment (£bn)	3.1	2.9	3.2	2.8	2.6	2.1
As per cent of industrial investment	25	22	23	20	17	12
As per cent of gross domestic fixed capital formation	7	6	6	5	4	3

Table 10.3: Oil Production 1975–87
Total production from 1975 to 1987 was 1075.5m tons.

YEAR	TONS (m)
1975 – 1981	353.8
1982	103.2
1983	114.9
1984	125.9
1985	127.5
1986	127.0
1987	123.3

Because of the high quality of North Sea oil Britain exports a high proportion while continuing to import the heavier crudes of the Gulf to mix with it for domestic consumption. Exports are thus balanced in part by continuing imports, but even so her exports in 1986 were 82.1m tons.

In 1976 the managing director of Esso petroleum in Britain, Mr Leslie Pincott, warned that Britain would still face economic collapse when the oil ran out unless the basic performance of the manufacturing industry improved – and that has little to do with oil. If there was any consensus during the great debate at the end of the 1970s it was that its benefits should be used to regenerate industrial structures. Oil is politics and it was Mrs Thatcher's good fortune that it came on full stream when she became Prime Minister. Perhaps the last word should go to one of her backbenchers, Charles Morrison, member for Devizes.

I think if Mrs Thatcher had been Prime Minister without oil – with her sort of determination and energy – that British industry would [still] have become more efficient but the oil has been all important because while on the one hand it has allowed this country to get away with a reduction of its manufacturing base of about a fifth, it has also on the other hand provided the financial wherewithal to cope with the unemployment. . . . I am not one who believes that fundamentally things have changed very much – except that we have got this flood tide of oil.

PART FOUR: THE STRUCTURE OF SOCIETY

11
The Welfare State

'The most civilized achievement of modern government.'
ANEURIN BEVAN

'For its customers it was a godsend, perhaps the most beneficial reform ever enacted in England, given that it relieved so many not merely of pain but also of the awful plight of having to watch the suffering and death of a spouse or a child for lack of enough money to do anything about it. A country in which such a service exists is utterly different from a country without it.'
PETER CALVOCORESSI

The social welfare system provides a range of services which come under three broad headings: the National Health Service, which provides a comprehensive range of medical services to the whole population whatever their means; personal social services, which provide help and advice to the old, the disabled and children in need of care; and the social security system which provides unemployment benefits and is designed to ensure a minimum basic standard of living.

This system, implemented by the post-war Attlee government, was not to be altered in any basic way for 40 years. Then, in the second half of the 1980s, during Mrs Thatcher's second and third terms of office, it came under major scrutiny. The government pushed through reforms which were bitterly resisted by the opposition and caused more questioning in Conservative ranks than anything she had attempted to do in all her years of power. The National Health Service in particular was regarded as an essential part of the fabric of British society, and many who stood to gain from tax reductions in 1988 said they would prefer the money to be spent on the NHS rather than given back in tax relief. Those who took this view were just as likely to be Conservatives (and normal Thatcher supporters) as members of the opposition parties. No other issue raised so much opposition as attacks upon the most lasting monument of the Attlee years.

The NHS was designed to provide a comprehensive range of services covering all aspects of health care – preventive and remedial – for every British citizen. All taxpayers contribute to its costs and by 1988 more than 45 per cent of expenditure went to meet the needs of elderly people. Approximately 86 per cent of its cost is met from general taxation, while the balance comes from National Insurance contributions, charges levied on drugs prescribed by family doctors or charges for dental treatment. The policy of the Conservative government in the 1980s was to encourage the private medical sector in the expectation that more people would turn to this and relieve the pressures on the NHS.

The personal social services are concerned with the elderly, children, families, the mentally and physically handicapped, as well as young offenders and the 'disadvantaged'. The principal facilities provided are residential care, day care, community care and a range of social work. Services for elderly people are designed to help them live at home wherever possible and include domestic help, meals, sitters-in, night attendants and laundry. Local authorities are responsible for special housing for elderly people. Assistance is provided for families in difficulties and covers children needing care away from home, assistance for those who care for the elderly, lone parents and unmarried mothers. Child care is a major part of the whole. Social workers are largely responsible for running these services.

The third area covered by the welfare services concerns social security. This includes pensions for the retired, the unemployed and the sick; for widows and the disabled; compensation for injury or diseases contracted at work or in the armed forces; and child benefits. Contributory social security benefits come from the National Insurance Fund, into which contributions from employers, employees and the self-employed have been paid: these include retirement, sickness and invalid pensions, unemployment benefits and maternity allowances. Non-contributory benefits come from general taxation. Supplementary and housing benefits are income-related but others – child benefits for example – are not.

The social security system changed the fabric of Britain after World War Two. It amounted to a social revolution; any fundamental change to it would constitute another revolution. Its genesis was the wartime Beveridge Plan which was based upon the insurance principle, with everyone contributing and being entitled to receive the benefits for which he or she had paid. The Labour manifesto of 1945, *Let Us Face the Future*, has two sections entitled 'Health of the Nation and its Children' and 'Social Insurance against a Rainy Day', which are short and do not enter into detail. One paragraph covers costs:

> But great national programmes of education, health and social services are costly things. Only an efficient and prosperous nation can afford them in full measure. If, unhappily, bad times were to come, and our opponents were in power, then, running true to form, they would be likely to cut these social provisions on the plea that the nation could not meet the cost. That was the line they adopted on at least three occasions between the wars.

The immediate difficulty facing the Labour government was the bankrupt state of the nation and the urgent need to obtain an American loan, which Maynard Keynes succeeded in doing before his death in 1946. That and the later funds from Marshall Aid were crucial to the effective establishment of the welfare state. The welfare legislation was enacted mainly during the first two years of Labour rule, with the National Health Service coming into operation on 5 July 1948, three years after electoral victory. Conservative opposition to the National Health Service Bill gave the impression that they were against the principle of a health service, an impression they did not fully eradicate until after 1951.

In the debate on the National Insurance Bill of February 1946 Attlee dealt in a memorable passage with the question of whether Britain could afford such sweeping social measures:

> It really means that the sum total of the goods produced and the services rendered by the people of this country is not sufficient to provide for all our people at all times, in sickness, in health, in youth and in age, the very modest standard of life that is represented by the sums of money set out in the Second Schedule to this Bill. I cannot believe that our national productivity is so low, that our willingness to work is so feeble or that we can submit to the world that the masses of our people must be condemned to penury. After all, this is really the payment into a pool of contributions from employers and workers and the products of taxation, and the payment thereout of benefits to various categories of persons. It is a method of distributing purchasing power, and the only validity of the claim that we cannot afford it must rest either on there not being enough in the pool, or on the claim that some sections of society have a priority to take out so much that others must suffer want.

By 1950 Labour's most important contribution to changing British society lay in the mass of social legislation placed upon the statute books. The introduction of the welfare state was Attlee's greatest achievement.

The question of prescription charges was first raised in 1949, for already the costs of running the NHS were escalating alarmingly. Stafford Cripps set an annual spending ceiling of £400m; his successor, Hugh Gaitskell, imposed prescription charges on false teeth and spectacles. Bevan resigned and a split as well as a long-lasting argument emerged in the party. In 1952 the Conservative Minister of Health, Harry Crookshank, introduced further charges including the shilling prescription for medicines.

In opposition during the late 1940s the Conservatives produced their Industrial Charter which accepted the concept of government controls and some measures of nationalization (1947) and then agreed to approve the welfare state in 1949. Even so, Labour expected an assault upon it when the Churchill government was elected in 1951. In fact the Conservatives accepted the entire Attlee social revolution, and initiated the period of post-war consensus. The social services were expanded and the Conservatives quickly outpaced Labour to reach their target of building 300,000 new houses a year. Butskellism, which emerged in the mid-1950s, included full acceptance by both parties of the welfare state.

Iain Macleod took over as Minister of Health (outside the Cabinet) in 1952 and held the post for three and a half years. It was a period of consolidation but as Bevan's widow, Jennie Lee, wrote later: 'When Iain Macleod became Minister of Health he was generous enough to tell Nye how little he found it right, or possible, to change, once he had had a close-up of the Health Service as it was at that time.' Macleod said he wished to be the first Minister of Health not to pass legislation but to make what existed work. He also expressed the hope that he could 'get a complete partnership between voluntary effort and the state.' Macleod's contribution was of major importance: not only did he consolidate what existed and make sure it worked effectively but he removed the Health Service from the political arena and ensured that it was accepted as a national institution.

From its inception the NHS threatened to become a monster consuming whatever funds were available. Less than two years after its creation Bevan said he was shuddering 'to think of the ceaseless cascade of medicine which is pouring down British throats'. Macleod was constantly restrained by lack of money and the need for strict financial controls. It was his job to administer the prescription and other charges introduced by his predecessor, Crookshank, and he defended them when he argued: 'If the charge on prescriptions enables the GP to give more freely of his skill and time to those who really need his care, that will be a great gain.' In his three-year tenure the cost rose from £518m in 1952/3 to £585m for 1955/6.

The Health Service may have been immensely popular but it was a constant cost headache to successive governments. This was partly due to rising costs and inflation over the years; partly to an increase in the size of the population to be cared for; and partly because it was successful. The better it was the more people used it. By the mid-1960s when the full effects of the post-war baby boom became apparent demands upon the welfare services escalated, as did government financial allocations to them. During the Labour government of 1964/70 there was a substantial increase in cash benefits paid under pensions, supplementary benefits and family allowances as well as expenditure on health and education. Then, from 1970 onwards, the steady rise in unemployment placed a major new strain upon the welfare services. Whatever government had come to power at the beginning of the 1980s was bound to face a social spending crisis. Apart from the unemployed, the increase in the numbers of the old both absolutely and proportionately placed an ever-growing strain upon available resources. It was inevitable that the whole system would be re-examined.

The Welfare State

The re-examination came in the Social Security Act 1986, although Heath's 1970 programme had included the idea of greater selectivity. It was the beginning of a logic suggested by the inexorable growth of demand. Broadly the Thatcher approach has been one of a shake-up of administration, greater efficiency and pruning rather than any fundamental cutting back of the programme. That would prove more politically dangerous than most of her backbenchers could stand.

The main reforms were introduced in April 1988 and included the modification of the State Earnings-related Pension Scheme, new arrangements to encourage personal and occupational pension schemes and a shake-up of the system of income-related benefits, which meant a different set of benefits to replace family income supplement, supplementary benefits and housing benefits. These changes, which affected the poorest and often those least able to cope, met with a reaction of great bitterness.

Expenditure on welfare services for 1987/8 broke down as follows: health £23,314m; personal social services £4312m. The two sectors together accounted for 14 per cent of general government expenditure; and social security £46,000m or 26.5 per cent. With welfare services at £71bn approaching one-sixth of GDP, it is not surprising that the government was looking for economies. The search came 40 years after Attlee's defence of such expenditure in 1946 and was instituted by Labour's political opponents, although not in hard financial times.

Nineteen eighty-eight witnessed an acrimonious debate about the welfare services, the state of the NHS and the new benefit regulations. It became all the more bitter following a budget which benefited the country's top earners. Before looking at that debate, it is worth examining some OECD statistics. According to the latest figures Britain has a ratio of 0.5 doctors per 1000 of the population, below that of every other of the 24 OECD countries, none of which has less than 1.3 per 1000 while some are much higher. A comparison of expenditure per head (Table 11.1) reveals that this country again rates low.

Table 11.1: Total Health Expenditure per Head (1985)

	US$
United States	1776
Canada	1282
Sweden	1172
France	1072
Germany	983
Netherlands	938
Denmark	755
Italy	678
United Kingdom	627
Spain	456
Greece	252
OECD average	848

Source: 'No Remedy for Setting the Price of Health', *The Independent*, 7 March 1988.

The Structure of Society

Addressing the Conservative Party Conference in October 1987 the Minister of Health, John Moore, made the point that the more demands for health care are satisfied the more they grow. The longer we are kept alive the more care we need and those who live beyond the age of 70 cost the NHS five times as much as those who do not live that long. Britain has an ageing population and there lies much of the cost-care problem.

Health problems were highlighted at the end of 1987 by the case of a baby boy, David Barber, with a hole in his heart. On five occasions over six weeks a planned operation had to be cancelled because of the closure of one-third of the intensive care beds at the Birmingham Children's Hospital and a shortage of money and nurses trained in aftercare. The parents went to law to insist that the existing facilities should be used effectively. This especially poignant case drew attention to a growing inability of the NHS – through lack of funds – to carry out its proper functions except with delays which are dangerous and sometimes fatal.

In an article in the *Independent* at the beginning of 1988, that most thoughtful of right-wing Tories, John Biffen, said:

> Forty years ago the Conservatives committed the tactical folly of technically voting against the National Health Bill. Patiently in the 1950s and 1960s they restored their reputation for commitment to public health. There is now a danger that the Conservative Party is going to be bundled back into its past, indifferent to hospital closures while promoting tax cuts. It must not happen.

Speaking out against the approach of a government notorious for its insensitivity, he concluded, 'We need the language, the deftness and the vision of Iain Macleod.'

Disquiet with government handling of the NHS (and nurses' pay) surfaced in the Commons Select Committee (Tory-dominated) in Feburary 1988. It concluded that ward closures resulted from uncertainty in health authorities which did not 'have a firm basis on which to plan since they do not know whether the pay settlement which is eventually agreed by the government will be funded in full.' At the same time it was revealed that health authorities were getting deeper into debt by not paying their suppliers because of general shortage of funds. The signs of a major crisis in the NHS were multiplying.

Arguments about costs have to be put into perspective. The Thatcher government has talked a great deal about the high and growing burden of the welfare state, yet public expenditure on health compares badly with that of other countries. (OECD figures, Table 11.2).

Britain's public spending on health is below the OECD average and below that of all major European OECD countries except Greece and Spain.

Table 11.2: Health Spending as per cent of GDP (1985)

COUNTRY	PUBLIC SPENDING	PRIVATE SPENDING
Canada	6.5	2.1
Denmark	5.2	1.0
France	6.7	2.7
Germany	6.3	1.8
Greece	4.1	0.1
Italy	6.2	1.2
Netherlands	6.6	1.7
Spain	4.3	1.7
Sweden	8.4	0.9
United Kingdom	5.2	0.7
United States	4.4	6.4
OECD average	5.7	1.7

Years of parsimony have reduced the country's performance to dangerous levels. In 1948 when the NHS came into being there were 480,000 hospital beds or 10 beds per 1000 of the population; by 1986 this had dropped to 6.7 beds per 1000 while the comparable figure for Western Europe was 9.8 and in Germany, Switzerland and France 11 per 1000. Thus Britain has waiting lists which do not occur in the leading West European countries. This fall in the bed-to-population ratio has been taking place over years and is not ascribable to one government or political party. Estimates suggest that it would now cost £20bn to raise the British ratio to 10 beds per 1000. As the costs of the NHS have risen, so successive governments have cut back on capital expenditure. By comparison with Europe Britain possesses decaying hospital stock and equipment (not a single new hospital was built during the first 15 years of the NHS).

During 1988 the government began to float the idea of an internal market in which health authorities buy and sell services among themselves and with the private sector. The idea may have merits, but it is not a substitute for an adequate state health service. During the budget debate of March 1988 Neil Kinnock pressed the popular view that people wanted the extra revenue which the Chancellor had to go to the NHS. He argued: 'They want it because they know that tax cuts do not buy treatment, that tax cuts do not pay nurses, that tax cuts do not open hospital wards or operating theatres, and that tax cuts do not shorten waiting lists.' Shadow Chancellor, John Smith, argued: 'Behind the facade of tax reform is a major redistribution of tax and income. They took £2bn that could have been given to the NHS and gave it to the rich.'

In a bitter parliamentary exchange with Kinnock in March 1988 Mrs Thatcher claimed that the structural changes were meant to retarget the money spent so that the disabled people, and families with children in low paid work are better off. Cash with transitional protection of income support means that 97 per cent of the sick and disabled, 92 per cent of couples with children, 89 per cent of single parents and 87 per cent of pensioners will get more or the same.

In his riposte Kinnock said: 'You can play the numbers game as much as you like. There are 9 million people in poverty now. There were 6 million reckoned to be in poverty in 1979.'

During the heated public debates many different figures were quoted to prove the government was giving more money, that in real terms it was giving less, that the poor had become poorer while the rich had become very considerably richer, but in the end what was undisputed was that many of the poorest, most dependent members of society were either no better off as a result of the changes or in varying degrees worse off. One estimate suggested that of the 8.5m households which depend in some degree upon social security only 3.2m would gain. That was against a budget background where executives earning £70,000 a year were expected to be about £150 a week better off as a result of the new tax regime.

The 1988 budget, the implementation of the new social welfare regulations, the debate on the poll tax (the conservative CBI pointed out that the poll tax would lead to a 40 per cent increase in taxation on households in deprived areas and a 34 per cent cut in prosperous areas) all pointed to changes whose effects were to widen the differences between the upper and lower economic brackets. So determined was the Thatcher government to cut back on 'welfare dependency' that some measures gave the appearance of being so ill-considered that their implications even for Tory supporters had been overlooked. One such example was the £6000 capital limit which the government was forced by backbench pressure to raise to £8000 so that housing benefits could be obtained.

What appeared to be passed over during the furious public exchanges was the fact that Britain, still one of the wealthiest nations on earth, appeared to have accepted as a fact that 9.4m people were living at or below the poverty line. Most of the debate was about how they were likely to be marginally better or marginally worse off rather than about how quickly and in what manner such poverty could be eliminated. Perhaps more than anything else, that marked the enormous change in public outlook in the late 1980s compared with that which predominated in the 1940s. The earlier years were a time of hope even though many of those hopes may not have been realized. The 1980s appear, at least for the poor, to be a time of despair.

12
Education

'The old pattern of training a small élite has never been broken, though it has been slightly bent.'

C. P. SNOW

'And finally there is that greatest of our social inventions, free, compulsory education. Everyone now knows how to read and everyone consequently is at the mercy of the propagandists, governmental or commercial, who own the pulp factories, the linotype machines and the rotary presses.'

ALDOUS HUXLEY

Until the 1980s British politics were totally male-dominated, and in the period since 1945 the Ministry of Education was given to no less than three of the token women in the Cabinet: Ellen Wilkinson under Attlee, Dame Florence Horsbrugh under Churchill and Margaret Thatcher under Heath, though she turned out to be less of a token than expected. By 1988 some 9.5m children attended 36,000 schools where they received free state-funded education, although about 7 per cent of the school-going population attended independent fee-paying schools. About a third of young people subsequently go on to some form of higher education (the figure in 1965 was one-fifth), although only 14 per cent of the 18-19-year-old bracket enter fulltime courses.

In 1985-6 1.02m students were taking fulltime courses: 310,000 of these were at universities; 290,000 were taking advanced courses outside universities (at colleges of further education or polytechnics), and about 419,000 were taking what are quaintly described as 'non-advanced courses', mainly for vocational or educational qualifications. In addition there are 3.2m part-time students of whom more than half a million are released by their employers for courses during working hours.

The number of universities has increased from 17 in 1945 to 47 (including the Open University) in 1988. Of the 310,000 students attending university in 1985/6 54,000 were post-graduates. Thirty polytechnics have been created in England and Wales since 1967 and these provide a major part of the country's higher education facilities. There were also some 39,000 overseas students attending British universities and 24,000 at polytechnics or other places of higher education. In 1985/6 about £780m was spent by the universities on scientific research.

Other aspects of the system include the youth services; and various forms of adult education, such as courses provided by the extra-mural departments of universities and the Workers' Educational Association, both of which were subject to severe financial cutbacks during the 1980s.

The Butler Education Act of 1944 heralded a new era of education, with its emphasis upon opening grammar schools to clever children and eventually eliminating fees. Ellen Wilkinson fought for the raising of the school-leaving age which she was responsible for seeing on to the statute book. There was no major educational reform during the Churchill-Eden period although Sir David Eccles (who replaced Horsbrugh in 1954) boosted technical schools. Macmillan showed little concern with the question during his first years as Prime Minister, although the late 1950s saw the development of colleges of advanced technology and university institutes of technology. But then, reflecting the rising prosperity, the 1959 Conservative manifesto promised a 'massive enlargement of educational opportunity' and the new University of Sussex was opened in 1961, to be followed through the decade by six more regional universities – York, East Anglia, Essex, Kent, Lancaster and Warwick. The Home government of 1963/4 accepted the report of the Robbins Committee on Higher Education which argued for further expansion.

The two most important advances under the Wilson government of 1964/70 concerned the introduction of comprehensive schools and the beginning of the programme of polytechnics. Thatcher, who was to be accused of every kind of cut in welfare expenditure when she became Prime Minister, was a big spender at Education, where her annual rate of expenditure was greater than during the preceding Labour administration. But there did not appear to be much thought either then or later about the kind of education provided. Indeed, a sad feature of the policies of successive governments was the extent to which reform was seen as expanding existing facilities rather than examining the need to change. Callaghan brought the direct grant schools into the public sector and initiated what he liked to call a great debate on education by a speech at Ruskin College, Oxford. Two questions he raised were why the status of industry was so low in young people's choice of careers and why there was a shortage of mathematics and science teachers.

An examination of the political approach to education during the years since 1945 reveals a lack of any major ideological thrust, an acceptance of what existed and tinkering to make it better, and a general sense that it was accorded low priority in the overall scheme of things. Appointment to the Ministry of Education has rarely been seen as a major advance by ambitious politicians and no govern-

Education

ment since the war has acted as though it believed the country's children were its most valuable resource.

British governments have consistently accorded it less resources than most other comparable countries. UNESCO figures for 1957 show British effort as lamentable in relation to 27 other countries (Table 12.1).

Table 12.1: University Students per Million Population (1957)

COUNTRY	STUDENTS
USA	16,670
USSR	10,000
Argentine	7100
Australia	6190
Czechoslovakia	5960
New Zealand	5570
Poland	5060
Romania	4640
Canada	4550
Finland	4310
Italy	4250
Bulgaria	4080
Spain	4050
Yugoslavia	3930
France	3880
East Germany	3730
Switzerland	3200
West Germany	3000
Austria	2980
Belgium	2810
Egypt	2810
Netherlands	2810
Denmark	2800
Portugal	2480
United Kingdom	1815
Ireland	1790
Turkey	1780
Norway	1690

Source: *UNESCO International Yearbook of Education 1957*, UN.

A comparison with French education at that time (John Vaizey, 'The Tragedy of Being Clever' which appeared in *Suicide of a Nation?*) suggested there was more available and that it was less divisive without the caste divisions of public schools, grammar schools and secondary modern schools and, most of all, that there was an intellectual quality about French education not apparent in Britain. In his *Two Cultures and the Scientific Revolution* (published in 1961), C. P. Snow makes a comparison with the USA and the USSR.

The Structure of Society

Our population is small by the side of either the USA or the USSR. Roughly, if we compare like with like, and put scientists and engineers together, we are training at a professional level per head of the population one Englishman to every one and a half Americans to every two and a half Russians. Someone is wrong.

Most economists and planners accept that there is a clear link between economic performance and education and in the majority of advanced countries the school-leaving age is being steadily advanced to 18 or 19. As usual, we trail along at or near the end. Thus while 90 per cent of 18- and 19-year-olds in Japan remain in fulltime education and nearly the same proportion in West Germany the figure for Britain in 1986 was 30 per cent, a 3 per cent decline from 1983. Table 12.2 shows the numbers of students in higher education per 100,000 of the population and public expenditure on education as a percentage of GNP at the mid-1980s for 17 leading countries.

Table 12.2: Students in Higher Education/Public Expenditure (mid-1980s)

COUNTRY	STUDENTS PER 100,000 POPULATION	EXPENDITURE AS PER CENT OF GNP
Australia	2313	6.0
Belgium	2486	6.0
Canada	4203	7.4
Denmark	2209	6.5
France	2114	5.8
East Germany	2582	5.5
West Germany	2465	4.5
Italy	2065	5.7
Japan	2006	5.7
Netherlands	2737	7.7
Norway	2217	7.0
Spain	2067	2.5
Sweden	2651	8.0
Switzerland	1664	5.1
USSR	1918	6.6
United Kingdom	1600	5.3
United States	5281	6.7

In terms of students per 100,000 of population Britain comes bottom of the list; in terms of expenditure as a proportion of GNP, fourteenth out of seventeen.

Elitism and snobbery are pervasive ingredients, where segregation in various forms is still a major part of the picture. Vaizey says, 'It is the *un*importance of education which is the most striking characteristic of English social history.' Thus, the chances are that arguments about the kind of education most suited to Britain's youth will still resolve themselves into confrontations about different kinds of school and streaming or ability tests which turn into confrontations about class, while other countries argue about how to produce more and better scientists or technologists.

In 1963 Arthur Koestler lambasted the system as

> out-dated in almost every respect – 11-plus, streaming, curriculum, segregation by class and sex – which perpetuates the iniquities of the past. It tears the nation apart and provides, generation after generation, a new crop of unwilling combatants for the cold class war. Equal opportunities for equally gifted children regardless of the status of the parents seems to me the basic axiom of social justice on which a free society must be built.

Studies of the educational system in the 1960s repeatedly come back to questions of snobbery and élitism. In *Educating the Intelligent* the authors (Hutchinson and Young) make the point:

> It is extraordinary that a minor academic matter – the question of whether or not Latin should be a compulsory requirement for entrance to Oxford and Cambridge – should attract more nation-wide publicity than any House of Commons debate on the education of the country.

They point out later much thought goes into the organization of the system but 'surprisingly little is written about what the schools ought ideally to be teaching'.

Another book published at this time was *Education and the Working Class* (Jackson and Marsden) whose title alone says volumes about British attitudes. Parts of it are funny, in a sociological way, but depressing beyond belief as the authors demonstrate how working-class children and their parents want to ape the manners of the children in superior grammar or public schools. The burgeoning of public and fee-paying schools in the 1980s gives little hope that the attitudes described have changed very much since then. A quite different issue is raised in Robin Pedley's book *The Comprehensive School* (also published at that time) where he attacks the churches for insisting upon the segregation of young children in different types of school.

This brings us to the overworked subject of the public schools and whether or not they should be abolished. In the more open culture which came with the swinging sixties, which bred 'loss of deference', it appeared that the snobberies attached to the public school system were being eroded, but by the late 1980s the gains were in reverse as the 'loadsamoney' yuppie culture went on an independent education spending spree.

A great deal of dishonesty informs the topic of public schools. Those who would defend a system of snobbery and purchased advantage insist that they reluctantly send their children to such schools because the state system does not provide an adequate education. Many arguments have been advanced to support their abolition, the most important of which are about social justice: as long as they continue they accentuate unnecessary class divisions in a society which has more than its share.

A principal reason why the state system does not flourish as it ought is precisely because there is an alternative which enables thrusting, ambitious parents to opt out of responsibility for the state system. The freedom-of-choice argument does not bear much examination: in a society which has given up so many, including, incidentally, the freedom not to educate children at all, a freedom essentially divisive ought not to stand in the way of establishing a sounder, more equitable national system. The best argument for the abolition of the fee-paying system is quite simple: if those parents who send their children to private schools were denied that alternative, they would become the most thrusting and effective vanguard of associations determined to ensure that the state system was as good as possible.

Meanwhile the snobberies continue. In 1959 73 per cent of Conservative MPs had been educated at public schools. Susan Crosland tells how Anthony Crosland got her out of bed to say: 'If it's the last thing I do, I'm going to destroy every fucking grammar school in England and Wales. And Northern Ireland.' Why, one wonders, did this zealot on behalf of better education not add the public schools to his death list? By the time Heath became Prime Minister the Conservative Party was seen more as a grammar school party. Yet, when Thatcher came to power, John Vincent could still write (in *Ruling Performance*): 'A party of upper-class public schoolboys changed into a party of middle-class public schoolboys. The non-public-school fringe, if noisy and noticeable, was still a fringe.' Judgements about politics continue to be coloured by class in a society where the 7 per cent who go to fee-paying schools continue to exercise influence out of all proportion to their numbers. It is tragic and absurd.

If educationalists paid as much attention to the teaching of science as they do to class and other segregations, Britain might not so often lag behind. It is not scientific ability which is in question – a high proportion of the best inventions and scientific ideas since the war had their genesis in Britain – but the subsequent exploitation of these ideas and inventions. With monotonous regularity the best scientists are attracted to the United States and others reap the benefits.

The approach to science, as with so many other things, is a question of attitude. In his 1959 Rede Lecture C. P. Snow focused attention upon the need for more scientists and technicians when he argued for professionalism of approach as opposed to the amateurism so beloved of the British élite. The arts versus the sciences has long been a favourite topic of debate in education circles; science and technology have often come second because we remain dominated by snobberies disguised as educational philosophy of the 'rounded person' – which means the arts. When British governments retrench they cut research budgets. We were slow to accept that management could and should be taught at university level. Gentlemen continued to be managers – and we lost one market after another to professionals.

The concept of comprehensive schools was the chief innovation of the 1960s, and its main architect was Robin Pedley. The attraction of comprehensive schools is that they bring together the children of a community and educate them as one, while the tripartite system emphasized and perpetuated differences. One of the ironies of the Thatcherite 1980s is the trend away from comprehensives to division once more despite her claims to egalitarianism.

Given the low political priority accorded to education Britain has done very well on the cheap. In 1947/8 she spent only 2.7 per cent of GDP on it, a figure which had only risen to 4.3 per cent 10 years later in the affluent Macmillan years. A phrase constantly on the lips of educational politicians is that of 'investing in the future' yet the parsimony of the investment has always been notable. Just why this should be so is difficult to say unless we return yet again to a consideration of the effects of the fee-paying system. The majority of our decision-makers have been products of that system: they did very well so why alter it? They forget – if they ever remembered – that the great majority of children cannot benefit from the fee-paying system, yet they do not make the state system as good. The real test of public educators who defend the right of parents to opt out of the state system is simple: leaving aside considerations of class and looking solely at educational-intellectual criteria, are these administrators working to bring the standards of the state schools in line with those of the best private institutions? Only if the answer is an unqualified 'yes' can the continuation of the fee-paying private system be justified.

As with everything else, the test is the end product: how well educated is our population compared with others, what skills do young people possess or lack when they seek employment and what is being done to rectify omissions? A 1987 MORI poll demonstrated that over half the 15 to 19 age group could not understand a simple fire notice; that 44 per cent could not interpret a bus timetable; and that 29 per cent were incapable of deducting £1.80 from £5. The survey also found that problems with reading, spelling and arithmetic were growing rather than declining.

Britain's industrial training has been condemned as inadequate for 100 years. In 1987 the chairman of the Manpower Services Commission, Brian Nicholson, said: 'We had a Royal Commission exactly a century ago on this very subject. The trouble lies in deep-seated, fundamental attitudes in our society and it will not be cured by a quick fix.' All too often, no fix of any kind is on offer.

The Federation of Master Builders reported that up to 39 per cent of building firms experienced manpower difficulties: 59 per cent claimed that they did not have enough carpenters, 47 per cent did not have enough bricklayers, 34 per cent were short of plasterers. The principal reason was given as lack of training. And this was at a time when there were three million unemployed.

In the engineering industry, where the number of workers undergoing training halved between 1978 and 1984, not only is the outlook depressing but Britain again lags behind her European partners. In a report to the House of Commons Employment Committee of 1987, the Engineering Industry Training Board argued: 'The industry has never been faced with the need to retrain adults on the scale and with the urgency now required and the issue is largely unrecognized by the employers. The evidence is clear: there are skill shortages ... at all levels and they are increasingly damaging our productive capacity.' The idea that training of all kinds and at all levels ought to be a constant in any advanced industrial society seems to have little place in British thinking.

After the 1987 election the thrust of Thatcher policy on education was towards central direction at the expense of local council direction, and greater uniformity. The Minister of Education and Science, Kenneth Baker, proposed legislation which would establish the first national curriculum for all pupils of 5 to 16 in England and Wales. Apart from three 'core subjects' – English, mathematics and science – a further group of foundation subjects had to be studied until pupils leave school. For the first time a foreign language would be compulsory for all students, as would technology. Baker's reforms, which included testing at ages 7, 11, 14 and 16 were among the most radical proposals since the war; the debate which followed became one of the most heated of the Thatcher years.

Alas, by 1988 we were back once more to the educational social divide with a vengeance. In the letter columns of the *Independent* (11 February 1988) William Wallace responded to a call from John Rae for the inculcation of national culture in the following terms:

> The social divide in this part of London lies very much between the children who go to state schools and those who go to private schools. I recognize, sadly, that the policy of our present government is to push middle-class parents like me out of the state sector into the private sector; any reasonable person must recognize that the current political and financial squeeze on London's public education will have that effect. We are moving deliberately away from a socially cohesive education system ... towards a sharper divide between good private and poor state schools.

In March 1988 Mrs Thatcher revealed herself to be at odds with Baker over the system of tests at certain ages. The Prime Minister apparently favoured a pass-fail system as opposed to the more sophisticated method of assessment envisaged. Achievement or ranking is her key approach. On balance, but only just, Kenneth Baker appeared to win his argument with her.

In June 1988 Professor Gordon Higginson presented the report of his committee on sixth-form syllabus reform. The report recommended five A-levels which would be 'leaner but tougher', but this was rejected by Baker (at the insistence of the Prime Minister) although he had at first welcomed the recommendations. Professor Higginson said he was disappointed as would be industry and the education world. He said: 'Virtually no one agrees that the sixth-form curriculum is right in its lack of breadth. The evidence was overwhelming. . . . The idea that students can just go on to do a traditional A-level is naive in the extreme.' Despite the 'overwhelming evidence' a government which makes claims to radicalism insisted upon the continuation of outmoded and discredited educational specialization.

According to the *Observer* of 12 June 1988, almost everyone is agreed on the need for reform: 'Education Ministers, industrialists, independent schools, universities and heads want A-level students to follow a broader course.' But not the Prime Minister. A principal purpose of the Higginson proposal was to equip more sixth formers for higher education and to prepare for entry into the world of work the 50 per cent who go straight from school into employment. That argument was lost, at any rate for the time being.

It seemed that élitism had won the battle yet again. The thrusting money culture of the 1980s with the emphasis upon supporting the successful is likely to do more damage to the nation's education than to almost anything else. Ever since the Butler Education Act the thrust of reform has been towards a less élitist, more comprehensive coverage for all the nation's children. Sometimes the impetus towards reform has been barely discernible. And sometimes excessive concern for minority groups has been destructive of more positive education. But the conscious, deliberate move back towards élitism which became apparent in 1988 represented retrogression which, if sustained, will put Britain still further down the league table in comparison with her European neighbours.

13
The Political System

'The whole life of that great party to which I thought I had the honour to belong was nothing but a mere organized hypocrisy.'

SPY

'There are two problems in my life. The political ones are insoluble and the economic ones are incomprehensible.'

SIR ALEC DOUGLAS-HOME

'This party is a moral crusade, or it is nothing.'

HAROLD WILSON

Despite enormous changes in terms of power and Britain's position in the world the Parliamentary system has hardly altered since 1945. The position of the monarchy, the power of the House of Lords, the 650-member House of Commons and the Cabinet operate in 1988 – at least superficially – much as they did in 1945. The power of the Prime Minister has undoubtedly become greater. The addition of life peers has enhanced the influence of the Lords despite legislation which reduced their delaying power from two years to one. And the two-party system operated throughout, although Labour's minority position during the 1970s led to the Lib-Lab Pact.

In 1945 Labour swept to power with the largest majority of the century; in 1951 they lost to the Conservatives who went on to win two more elections and retain power for 13 years. In 1964 Labour returned to power with a tiny majority, which was increased to 100 seats in the 1966 election. In 1970 the Conservatives won again. In 1974 Wilson formed a minority government, then went to the country a second time but won an overall majority of only three seats. These were later whittled away in by-election defeats, so that under Callaghan the government was forced to enter into a pact with the Liberals in order to survive. In 1979 the Conservatives returned to power and won the 1983 and 1987 elections. Between 1945 and 1988 Labour governed for 17 years, the Conservatives for 26.

Despite surges in Liberal and then Liberal and Social Democrat Party support, the majority of voters have continued to favour the two main parties. In historical

The Political System

terms the Conservatives have been the most enduring, emerging from the eighteenth-century Tory party, and continuing to the present. The Liberal Party declined dramatically after the First World War and was replaced by Labour as the alternative ruling party.

The Labour victory of 1945 represented the greatest triumph of the 'Left' in Britain's Parliamentary history. The Conservative Party had yet to adapt to the post-war expectations of the electorate and was tarnished with its image from the inter-war years. If there was to be a brave new world then Labour, so the electorate believed, would provide it. Until that time they had never enjoyed an absolute majority; given a massive one, they used it to put their entire manifesto programme on the statute books.

Tory members who were returned in 1945 were in the main part of the old school; they were shattered by their defeat, they had yet to come to terms with the post-war world. R. A. Butler was the leading Conservative most associated with the idea of modernizing the party and his encouragement of a group of new young men – 'Rab's boys' – such as Macleod, Maudling, Powell and Maude was crucial to changing the Conservative image. In the 1950 election a large number of new Conservatives were returned, eliciting from Aneurin Bevan the description of 'the finest Tory vintage in history'. These new members would be responsible for making the new consensus work in the long period of Conservative rule from 1951 to 1964. But during the 1951 election the notorious *Daily Mirror* heading 'Whose Finger on the Trigger?' represented the perception of what the Conservatives were seen to stand for.

Although Labour regarded the peacetime Churchill with deep suspicion, his 1951 government was what Thatcherites a generation later regarded as the 'wettest' Conservative government since the war. Butler as Chancellor of the Exchequer, Macmillan at Housing and Monckton at Labour were given their heads and presided over policies of consensus social welfare rather than anything which smacked of pre-war Tory attitudes. The Conservatives decided to accept the broad outlines of the Attlee revolution, and ensured the consensus politics of the next twenty years.

Too much should not be made of consensus, however, for political arguments could be long and bitter. Three famous phrases from Labour leaders during the Attlee years – 'We are the masters now', the Tories are 'lower than vermin' and 'I don't care a tinker's cuss' (about non-Labour supporters) – demonstrated the bitterness which could surface from time to time, but on a wide range of issues from NATO and the Cold War through the social welfare services to the end of Empire there was, more often than not, agreement on essentials. Only on one major issue between 1951 and 1970 was there deep and fundamental division and that was over the 1956 Suez crisis. Over the two-year period (1959/61) when Macleod moved at great speed to devolve power in Africa he received welcome support from the Shadow Colonial Secretary Callaghan while fighting off bitter opposition from his own right wing. On the issue of Europe first Macmillan in 1961 and then Wilson in 1966 became converts to British entry and it was only in 1970 with the coming to power of the Tories under Heath that consensus really began to collapse.

Consensus lasted as long as both major parties were prepared to accept the mixed economy, the welfare state and a 'hands off' policy towards the unions. Once those concepts were challenged by both economic circumstances and changing political attitudes during the 1970s it became inevitable that consensus politics would be abandoned.

When ill health forced Eden to resign following the Suez débacle the choice of successor lay between Butler and Macmillan. In the famous consultation of Cabinet colleagues conducted by Lord Kilmuir (the Lord Chancellor) and Lord Salisbury, the question was put to each in turn: 'Well, which is it, Wab or Hawold?' Harold got it. The Conservative Party was not yet ready for elections to the leadership. Macmillan's premiership represented the high water mark of the consensus era. He effected a rapid recovery of morale and presided over a period of prosperity, which enabled him as early as July 1957 to make his famous statement:

> Let's be frank about it. Most of our people have never had it so good. Go around the country, go to the industrial towns, go to the farms, and you will see a state of prosperity such as we have never had in my lifetime, nor indeed ever in the history of this country.

Harold Wilson was an admirer of Macmillan and tried to maintain the middle ground of politics. Michael Fraser describes him: 'A clever tactician rather than a strategist, Wilson spent an undue amount of time and energy in both opposition and government keeping his deeply divided Labour party in one piece, a condition that did not very long outlive his retirement.' The Labour Party captured the centre in 1964 but at a time when the conditions which made consensus work were beginning to disappear: Britain's worldwide power was in rapid decline, the economy was in crisis and the unions were beginning to behave unreasonably.

That much over-rated Labour figure, Hugh Gaitskell, began the process of 'revisionism' which came increasingly to dominate the politics of the party, first in 1959 when he attempted to modify Clause IV (nationalization) and then when he refused to accept the motion in favour of unilateral nuclear disarmament passed at the 1960 Scarborough Conference when he made his famous speech in which he said, 'We shall fight and fight and fight again to save the Party we love.' In his diaries, *Out of the Wilderness*, Tony Benn describes Gaitskell as a divisive leader: 'He had a real civil servant's mind, very little imagination and hardly any understanding of how people worked. His pernickety mind always managed to engineer a confrontation of principles which he would then seek to resolve by brute force.'

Affluence was Labour's worst enemy and following the 1959 defeat an ideological battle developed between the left and right wings of the party. As Anthony Sampson wrote in *The New Anatomy of Britain*, 'Richard Crossman as chief theorist on the left, and Anthony Crosland on the right.' Wilson's managerial genius held the party together from the death of Gaitskell in 1963 until his retirement in 1976. In accomplishing the feat, he inevitably gave the impression that tricks of management were more important than principles, which did lasting damage to British politics and helped create a generation deeply cynical of the entire political process. Neil Kinnock faced identical problems of division between the left and right wings of the party as he, too, faced accusations of revisionism.

The 1960s were an immensely important decade, a watershed in several quite different respects. They are best remembered as the period of the permissive society, when the country became more open and youth appeared to take over. But it was also the decade when Britain's leaders came to terms with the limitations of the country's post-war position. Kennedy's scrapping of the Skybolt missile, de Gaulle's double veto of Britain's application to join the European Community, inability to do anything about UDI in Rhodesia, the retreat from east of Suez each emphasized the country's inexorable decline. These international defeats accompanied a steadily declining economy and the commensurate growth in power and arrogance of the trade unions.

Heath reaped the whirlwind. Although he succeeded in taking Britain into Europe he succeeded in little else. The Industrial Relations Act did not curb union power but heralded a period of growing industrial strife, and when the OPEC crisis occurred in 1973 the fragile consensus began to disintegrate. Following Heath's double election defeat of 1974, the Tory Party began a collective move to the right under its new leader, Margaret Thatcher.

From 1974 to 1976 Wilson tried against increasing odds to hold the Labour Party together but faced growing union intransigence. Holding the middle ground between the revisionists and the left had become an all-absorbing occupation. The key lay with the unions. As Eric Heffer said in 1973: 'Labour is nothing without the trade unions but the trade unions can survive without the Labour Party.' Shocked and battle-scarred by Heath's surrenders to union power, the Conservatives in opposition moved to the right even while Labour supporters were moving to the left. This leftwards progression, which culminated in the 'winter of discontent' and the loss of the 1979 election, led 10 per cent of the most revisionist members of the party to break away altogether under the leadership of the 'Gang of Four' (Roy Jenkins, David Owen, Bill Rodgers and Shirley Williams) to form the Social Democrat Party (SDP).

In his biography James Prior records union anger at the 1978 Brighton TUC Conference with Callaghan's decision not to hold an election that autumn:

> Bill Kendall, the leader of the civil service unions' negotiating committee, said to me that evening: 'You want to thank your lucky stars there's not an election this autumn. You might just have won it, but I can tell you that whichever government is in office this winter is going to have a very rough time. We've had an incomes policy for three years and we're simply not prepared to take it for a fourth. There's going to be a lot of trouble around, and if you had been in office, it would all have been blamed on the fact that the Conservatives simply can't work with the unions.'

The unions did not accept the Callaghan-Healey 5 per cent limit on pay rises that autumn and the country was subjected to the 'winter of discontent'. As Tony Benn said in 1988: 'The strength of the Labour Party has always been ... that there is a single trade union movement – and that the majority of those trade unions have had some affiliation with the political party.' That strength is also the party's weakness.

The Liberals went into terminal decline after 1945 though they have struggled valiantly to make a comeback. Their leader of the 1950s, Jo Grimond, led an elegant team of celebrity figures but the party won only 5.9 per cent of the vote and six seats in the 1959 election. At successive elections they won more votes (around the two million mark) than seats to match, which gave point to their demand for proportional representation. (In the 1987 election the Liberal-Social Democrat Alliance polled 22.6 per cent of the votes cast yet picked up only 22 seats, while Labour, which polled 30.8 per cent of the votes, collected 229 seats.) However, they had surrendered the role of principal alternative party to Labour and through most of these years represented a means of registering protest – as in their spectacular anti-Macmillan by-election victory at Orpington in 1962 – rather than an alternative governing party.

The chances of some form of proportional representation being introduced lie solely in the bargaining that would take place in the event of a hung Parliament. Then, the Liberals and SDP might find themselves in a position to obtain proportional representation as their price for supporting Kinnock and Labour, for example. Otherwise, and certainly in terms of performance in the 1980s when SDP supporters thought they were on the verge of a break-through, the middle parties – the Alliance of the Liberals and SDP – seemed doomed to attract protest votes rather than stand for policies a majority will vote to bring about. During the 1980s when Labour was still trying to determine whether to be left-wing or revisionist and the Conservatives were being unashamedly right-wing, the Liberals and SDP stood for the consensus which the other parties had abandoned.

The 1987 election played havoc with the Liberal-SDP Alliance whose two Davids (Owen and Steel) put on a sort of public Tweedledum and Tweedledee act which fooled very few people. Once the election was over the Alliance fell apart. The hostility and rivalry of the two Davids came into the open, and the SDP split, with Owen leading his splinter off into a wilderness of their own. The Liberal Party under David Steel disbanded itself before Steel resigned and left Paddy Ashdown and Alan Beith to fight for the leadership of the newly formed Social Democrat Liberal Party (SDLP), later renamed the Social and Liberal Democrats. The chief beneficiaries of the bickering in the centre have been the Conservatives who have seen the Alliance rob Labour of much of its centre support. By mid-1988 the antics of the centre parties had become the subject of amusement, disillusion or indifference to many who sought a genuine alternative to either Labour or the Conservatives.

In June 1988 it was revealed that membership of the new Social and Liberal Democrats was lower than the 65,000 Liberal and SDP members who had voted for the March merger. In the heyday of his power Wilson had said: 'You don't need to worry about the outside left – they've got nowhere else to go: it's the inside left that you must worry about.' By 1988 one could paraphrase this in relation to the middle parties: when their 'centre' protests turned out to be of no avail their members could always return to the parties of left or right from which they had defected.

The Conservative Party of 1988 had changed out of all recognition from the patrician party which had excluded Churchill from power for 10 years before the war and uneasily accepted his leadership when the war ended. From 1945 to 1961, though 'Butler's boys' took an increasing number of top jobs, the party remained upper-class and conservative with a small 'c'. When Macleod provoked Lord Salisbury's outburst that he was 'too clever by half' he had goaded the old wing of the party to protest at the growing number of radical policies enacted under Macmillan, whose radicalism had been expressed in his book *The Middle Way*, published in the 1930s.

In the leadership crisis which Macmillan's illness of 1963 precipitated the succession was still decided according to manoeuvres among the party's power brokers, ably orchestrated by Macmillan from his hospital bed. But when Home stood down in 1965 there was a leadership election for the first time and, significantly, this was won by Edward Heath who came from a lower-middle-class background. His successor, Thatcher, came from the same background, and by the late 1980s the old squirearchical Tory Party which Julian Critchley so enjoys writing about had been replaced by many hard-faced men who had done well in the City. There had been another change too. Churchill and

The Structure of Society

Macmillan, for all their style and powerful personalities, had Cabinets who stood up to them and to whom, from time to time, they had to give ground. In 1985 Lord Stockton said of the Thatcher government: 'A brilliant tyrant surrounded by mediocrities'.

The Labour Party was the creation of the unions and that has always been its strength and its weakness. It achieved the apogee of its power and success under Attlee but by the time they came back to power in 1964 Wilson had converted them into an acceptable middle-ground party, the alternative government to the Tories. He had also begun the division between party and union interests which was to haunt Labour thereafter. The problem was raised by George Brown in his memoirs *In My Way* when he asked whether the party should not consider itself a more broadly based party and raise its funds from other sources than the unions so that it was not subject to their veto. An increasing number of Labour revisionists thought the same.

Labour revisionists certainly blame union behaviour for the loss of the 1979 election, but that was not the end of the story. When Neil Kinnock succeeded Michael Foot he set about overhauling the party's image so as to give it an electoral appeal once more, something it failed to demonstrate in the two elections of the 1980s despite the many hostages to fortune presented by the Thatcher government. The emergence of the 'hard' Left at the end of the 1970s and the success of Thatcher economics in capturing working-class supporters during the 1980s convinced Labour that it had to deal with a fundamentally changed political landscape. By the beginning of 1988 they had launched the 'Labour listens' campaign, where leading members of the party went out to see what the people wanted, but whose principal effect was to convince the public that the Labour Party did not know where it was heading.

Then Tony Benn took a hand. His challenge for the leadership (with Eric Heffer challenging Hattersley for the deputy leadership) appeared to have little chance of success. But it did have the immediate effect of forcing Kinnock to begin to define policies, something he had largely avoided. In February 1988 Kinnock and Hattersley produced their revisionist 'statement of democratic socialist aims and values' which embraced the mixed economy and the controlled use of market mechanisms. Yet, all those years after Gaitskell, Kinnock insisted that the party remained committed to Clause IV. Benn was not prepared to accept Kinnock's stratagems. He accused the leadership of trying 'to seize all political power for itself and to force the party to accept elements of what I would call Thatcherite consensus'.

By the middle of 1988, the leadership contest had become bitter in the best tradition of Labour in-fighting, with Benn standing for principles and Kinnock for pragmatism. At first Kinnock attempted to dismiss the challenge as 'divisive, distracting, futile and selfish', but it was to concentrate his mind upon new definitions, something the party badly lacked. Benn and Heffer were challenging the leadership through the machinery of the electoral college which had been established at the insistence of Labour's left wing and from which Kinnock himself had emerged. His greatest problem was simply lack of credibility as an effective party leader and this arose from two broad causes: his apparent inability to match Thatcher in the House of Commons; and his fudging of issues where there should be no fudging. As Peter Kellner wrote in the *Independent* of 28 March 1988: 'Mr Kinnock's enemy, in fact, is not so much Mr Benn but the party's public image. Persuading the party to dump Mr Benn will be easy; persuading the public to dump its view that Labour is an old-fashioned, undemocratic party will be the hard bit.'

Change for a political party is never easy. Margaret Thatcher changed the Conservatives by decimating the ranks of the old guard. David Steel ran the Liberals into the ground in trying to form alliances with other centre forces. And by June 1988 Kinnock found himself at odds with two fundamental Labour totems: The Transport and General Workers' Union led by Ron Todd; and the bomb unilateralists. The TGWU decided to withhold backing for the leadership 'dream ticket' of Kinnock and Hattersley and wait until Conference time in September. And the spectacular manner of Denzil Davies's resignation as Shadow Defence spokesman (because he had not been consulted before the Labour leader repudiated the 'something for nothing' disarmament approach) brought all the old unilateralist sores into the open once more. In the space of a week Kinnock first said he would trade Trident for a reduction of Soviet warheads and then said he would decommission Trident and Polaris on coming to power whether any deal could be secured or not. As Denzil Davies's successor, Martin O'Neill, added: 'Yesterday was an opportunity for Mr Kinnock to set the record straight and the record is that Labour Party policy is not and has not been changed since the general election.' So Labour was back to unilateral nuclear disarmament, a policy which revisionists such as Giles Radice believed had cost them one million votes in 1987.

In 1988 Labour had three years to sort out its policies for the 1990s if it was to have any chance of defeating the Tories at the beginning of the last decade of the century. That it would do so still looked highly doubtful. The Tory Party, as a broad rule, is renewed by realism while the Labour Party is renewed by idealism, which explains why the Tories rather than Labour more often form the government. But in May 1989 Neil Kinnock (like Hugh Gaitskell nearly thirty years before him) staked his leadership on a personal rejection of nuclear unilateralism and obtained a 17–8 majority on the Labour National Executive Committee (NEC) in support of his policy. The next month a newly confident Labour Party which had actually taken the lead in opinion polls fought the Euro-elections to reverse exactly the existing position so that 45 Tory to 32 Labour seats became

45 Labour to 32 Tory. For the first time in many years political commentators (as well as Labour leaders themselves) began to talk of a Labour victory at the next election as a possibility in which they believed.

Perhaps Norman Tebbit, a hate figure for the Left, should be given the last word. In answer to the question (from the author) as to what kind of opposition Labour ought to provide if Mrs Thatcher succeeds in 'burying socialism' he replied that it should adopt a consensus approach: that is, making the Thatcherite reforms work better! Logically he had a point: the Conservatives accepted the Attlee revolution for 20 years after their return to power so why should not Labour (revisionist of course) accept the Thatcher revolution for another 20 years once Thatcher goes?

14
The Monarchy

'The monarchy has become an irrelevant ornament except for those who have a vested interest in its survival.'

WILLIE HAMILTON

'All bunk and bunting'.
STAFFORD CRIPPS

'We're not a family: we're a firm.'
GEORGE VI

In the words of the 1988 Official Handbook 'The British people look to the Queen not only as their head of state, but also as the symbol of their nation's unity.' This is the official line emphasized from Bagehot and Dicey to constitutional writers and other defenders of the status quo in the present age. The Queen's title sounds and is archaic: Elizabeth the Second, by the Grace of God of the United Kingdom of Great Britain and Northern Ireland and of Her other Realms and Territories Queen, Head of the Commonwealth, Defender of the Faith. Even under that centralizing all-powerful Prime Minister of the 1980s, *the other woman*, the pretence is maintained that the Queen is the real ruler of Britain. Whatever the realities of power the forms persist: the state opening of Parliament and the Queen's speech, the state occasions, the deference paid, not least by the Left, all combine to perpetuate the myth. As Richard Crossman wrote in 1963: 'What gives the British monarchy its unique strength is the fact that the court, the aristocracy and the Church – not to mention the middle classes – are just as credulous worshippers of it as the masses.' Such credulity is the stuff of which myths are made.

The Queen's role as 'a super-diplomat' (in Anthony Sampson's phrase) has become one of her most important contributions to the country she 'rules' and this has been of notable importance on Commonwealth occasions. At home, as Bagehot said, she has the right to be consulted, to advise and to warn but usually, in fact, she acts as a rubber stamp. It is with pageantry and ceremonial that the monarchy is now most closely associated and its greatest ally has been television, that ubiquitous presence which has done more than anything to popularize and glamorize at the same time. No show on earth can rival a coronation or royal wedding. The attraction of the coronation, apart from the glitter and pomp, is its age: it has remained essentially the same ceremony for 1000 years and this makes the British feel that they are part of an ancient, enduring continuity. No other monarchy has anything like the ceremonial retained by Britain's and it has to be paid for. Periodically there are questions and rows about its cost when the Civil List is debated or the expenses of one of the numerous princelings is raised in the press but since the British are besotted by ceremonial and snobbery they probably get it reasonably cheaply.

Willie Hamilton MP, that engaging Scottish scourge of the monarchy, persistently asks pertinent questions about its relevance. In his book *My Queen and I* he addresses an open letter to the Queen and one paragraph goes to the heart of the relationship between monarch and people:

> You must surely agree that, by birth and upbringing, by the surroundings in which you live and the company you keep, you cannot possibly understand the feelings and the way of life of the millions of ordinary people it is claimed you keep united in one big happy family. It is a claim you have never contradicted, but in your heart of hearts, deep inside yourself, you must know how absurd it is.

Perhaps the Queen does know how absurd the claim is but supporters of the monarchy will reply that 'it works'.

The Church is today the greatest ally of the monarchy and vice versa. The various ceremonies – principally royal weddings and funerals but also services of thanksgiving – which take place in Westminster Abbey or St Paul's allow the establishment to appear in all its arcane finery, the Queen to wear one of her crowns and the royal males uniforms bedecked with medals they did not win. And the common people can make an appearance along the processional routes or sit at home watching television. Since 1945 television has done well out of the boom in royalty while the Church has given itself relevance by process of mitred association.

The coronation of 1953 was the post-war high point of monarchy: 'All this and Everest too!' as one popular tabloid headlined the event the following day. Otherwise, with the exception of the Queen's silver jubilee of 1977, royal weddings and funerals provide the highlights of the monarchical glamour show. The only event in 40 years to rival these royal parades was the funeral of Sir Winston Churchill and that was a pageant of passing Empire as well as a tribute to the old man.

Such events are occasional and maintaining the popularity of the royal family has been far from easy. Wisely, the Queen has usually kept a low profile, but sometimes her advisers have called on television's help as they did in 1969. The occasion was the investiture of Charles as Prince of Wales; apart from televising the ceremony, the cameras were allowed into royal palaces to screen the film *Royal Family* which showed Britain's first family 'at work'. The effort paid off and the glamour which had been fading through the 1960s was given a new coat of gilt.

Sometimes, of course, the affairs of the royal family get into the hands of the vulgar press. Mark Phillips's horseback courtship of Princess Anne or the less than happy life of Princess Margaret have provided endless copy for 'people's journalists' who go through fantastic contortions to obtain uninteresting copy and boring pictures, for which, none the less, there seems to be a voracious market.

The endless books, the slush articles and the periodic scandals which the foreign press follow with delight, even if the loyal British press are muzzled, have become part of the British way of life. Their image depends upon the stories and Buckingham Palace is adept at the 'no comment' or disdainful silence while harvesting the benefits of the constant media 'hype'. In February 1988 Marion Crawford (Crawfie), royal governess to the Princesses Elizabeth and Margaret, died. Her discreet book of 'revelations' – *The Little Princesses* – had earned her the permanent ostracism of the Palace. In fact, she did the royal family a favour, assisting with the myth that they are both 'royal' and 'just like us'. The extraordinary thing is that such banal writings and uninteresting disclosures are taken seriously. That the monarchy is taken seriously can be seen by the way it is criticized.

There are a number of possible criticisms. The first, that in our modern age the monarchy is simply irrelevant. That is brushed aside by the effective comeback that 'it works'. The second, far more valid, is that the monarchy and its court following perpetuate some of the worst snobberies and class distinctions in British society. The answer to that is that the British like their snobberies and seem determined to maintain them. The third and hardest criticism to refute is the cost. Why should the Duchy of Lancaster and the Duchy of Cornwall, whose revenues are kept secret, go largely untaxed, and why should so many royals have allowances? Direct attacks are hardly ever levelled at the monarchy, and certainly nothing to match the vitriol of the early nineteenth century:

> An old, mad, blind, despised and dying king,
> Princes, the dregs of their dull race, mud from a muddy spring –

Books gloss over or ignore royal weaknesses, sheltering behind the cowardly excuse that they cannot retaliate. When Malcolm Muggeridge dared to criticize the royal family he was dropped from BBC programmes on which he had appeared regularly, while Lord Altrincham, who had commented upon the flat uninteresting tone of the Queen's voice, had his face slapped in public. Prince

Philip has been fair game for press attacks, partly because of the forthright if irritating things he says, and partly because of the 'tradition' dating back to Prince Albert that the Queen's husband should be seen but not heard.

The royal press office is the key instrument in presenting and controlling the public image. On the one hand it must ensure press opportunities to cover and 'present' the Queen and the other royals to the public; on the other it must prevent anything which interferes with 'the dignity or propriety of any formal royal occasion'. Or, as Willie Hamilton will have it, 'To put it crudely, the presentation is "doctored".' Indeed, generally speaking, this is true. Either the press indulges in the sycophancy which attends royal occasions or it is boringly discreet, although the tabloid press muckrakes for scandals.

The monarch's political influence is carefully limited, but can on occasions be important. By 1989 the Queen had been on the throne for 37 years and her influence is likely to grow if only because of her vast accumulation of knowledge. The Prime Minister calls upon her once a week to keep her informed and by 1989 Queen Elizabeth had already been advised by eight Prime Ministers. She is reputed to do her homework, so she must have stored up a formidable understanding of national affairs. As Anthony Sampson puts it: 'The monarch is well furnished with information, and she is well placed to be the best informed person in Britain, since she knows the secrets of past governments, as well as the present one.' Sampson wrote that in 1971, and there have been another 18 years of Cabinet secrets since then.

The Queen's private secretary is the key man whose task it is to translate the monarchy to the outside world. But though the machinery of the various palaces and the Queen's affairs have become extremely sophisticated in the years since 1945, the monarchy really works well only because of the society in which it exists. We may no longer be living in an age of deference, as many people now like to claim, but that is simply not true as far as the royal family is concerned.

Attlee, who presided over a major social and political revolution, was an old-fashioned, unashamed monarchist, impressed by the simple picture of family life presented by George VI and Elizabeth and ready to persuade the Cabinet to increase Princess Elizabeth's personal allowance. He believed that the monarchy had increased its popularity and prestige under George VI and acted as a guardian of royal interests when some of his own party might have expected him to take a more robustly questioning line. He did no such thing. It is claimed that the King influenced Attlee on two occasions: he was opposed to Dalton as Foreign Secretary and pushed for Bevin, though Attlee denied that this influenced him. And in 1951, when the King was embarking on a lengthy tour of Australia and New Zealand and was in poor health, Attlee called the election early to avoid the possibility of a political crisis when the King was abroad.

Winston Churchill was an ardent, sentimental monarchist who had the satisfaction of being Prime Minister when Elizabeth became Queen and could watch benignly over the beginnings of what the press described as the 'new Elizabethan age'. In 1963 there might have been a constitutional crisis, when the departing Macmillan ensured that the Queen sent for Douglas-Home before anyone else persuaded her to send for Butler. Although many ordinary members of the Labour Party are uninterested in the monarchy, this has not applied to their leaders. Wilson was a fervent monarchist, as was Callaghan, but Tony Benn, as Postmaster-General, did his best to remove the Queen's head from the nation's stamps. He failed.

Only over the question of costs, and then only from time to time, do the parsimonious British ask awkward questions. The crown's ownership of land – 182,000 acres in England and 85,000 in Scotland as well as priceless properties in London such as Regent's Park and Carlton House Terrace – provides it with large revenues though the profits from these, after expenses and taxes have been deducted, are handed over to the Exchequer. Occasionally anger about royal secrecy boils over, as it did during the 1971 debate on the Civil List, and if any subject is likely to stir Labour MPs it is royal finances. To quote Willie Hamilton once more:

> The total wealth of the British royal family remains a closed book – one of the most closely guarded secrets of modern times. They resolutely refuse to divulge the real figure. Their investments are clandestine, and no investment is ever made in the name of the Queen herself.

In one area that could hardly have been predicted in 1945 the monarch, or rather the Queen, has come to play an unexpectedly important role and that is as Head of the Commonwealth. The new title was devised in 1949 to accommodate republican India within Commonwealth ranks. The Queen has taken a great interest in it, travelling indefatigably through its member countries and building up personal relations with heads of government which has allowed African leaders, at bitter loggerheads with the British government over its South African policy, to distinguish between Britain (the Queen) and the government (Thatcher). Indeed Mrs Thatcher's disdain for the Commonwealth and the Queen's interest in it has been one of the primary causes of friction between the two women.

Prince Philip, an abrasive arrogant man, has generally been seen as a modernizing influence. His readiness to pronounce upon public issues and inject controversy into them has been a welcome change from the banal level of royal pronouncements. One of the most celebrated occurred in a speech to businessmen in 1961 when he said: 'Just at this moment we are suffering a national defeat comparable to any lost military campaign, and what is more it is self-inflicted ... I think it is about time we pulled our finger out.' But what for

Prince Philip have been carefully selected subjects upon which he could reasonably deviate from controlled impartiality have become more interesting in the case of Prince Charles.

Already in his forties at the end of the 1980s, Prince Charles could well come to the throne in his sixties as did Edward VII after spending a lifetime-in-waiting. Educated at Gordonstoun as opposed to one of the more traditional public schools (the first heir to the throne to have so much public exposure among his peers), Charles has shown none of the usual royal interest in uniforms and things military. Instead, he has worked hard to find areas where he might make a greater impact as Prince of Wales: the Commonwealth, architecture and the plight of the inner cities. Perhaps his most celebrated remark was on the proposed extension to the National Gallery: 'A kind of vast municipal fire station ... like a monstrous carbuncle on the face of a much-loved and elegant friend.'

Unusually sensitive for a royal, Charles is in danger of making an interesting king. His interest in ideas earned him the astonishing back-handed compliment of the *Sun* in August 1987 when it advised: 'Stop that thinking!' It went on to suggest that the best modern rulers have been dim – and by implication should remain so.

The most interesting aspect of his activities has been his insistence upon looking at problems that affect ordinary people during the premiership of one of the most partisan holders of that office since 1945. Prince Charles's concern with the plight of the inner cities at a time of great unemployment and notoriously uncaring attitudes by government towards the plight of the poor has produced an intriguing political paradox. The Tory Party which, until the present era, regarded itself as the monarchist party has found itself increasingly at odds with the Palace. So much has the Prince got under the collective skin of the Tories that in April 1988 their trouble-seeker-and-shooter, Norman Tebbit, publicly warned him not to go too far in his demonstrations of concern since these might impinge on government policy – or lack of policy. Tebbit said that if the Prince 'advocated a socialist solution, a Labour Party solution, that would begin to get dangerous'.

The Prince's sister, Princess Anne, after years of a bad press took on a job as a working royal for the international charity Save the Children, with the result that her reputation recovered and she has been applauded as caring and humanitarian. But if Prince Charles and Princess Anne have problems because they refuse to be the dimwits the *Sun* would prefer, they are the exceptions which prove the rule. As a broad generalization the public, guided by television, expects its royals to provide glamour and leave more serious things to the politicians.

Prince Andrew is a clear media favourite: handsome, dashing, 'randy' and married to the outgoing Duchess of York, he has few intellectual pretensions and can be filmed helicoptering about with the Royal Navy. In June 1988 the *Evening*

Standard carried the headline: 'A royal secret at the top people's pub' and its readers were treated to a gossipy article about the 'Admiral Codrington' pub in Mossop Street, Knightsbridge, which the Duke and Duchess of York frequent along with other top people – Lord Lichfield and assorted MPs. The landlord, Mel Barnett, told the *Standard*: 'The royals may be using the pub but there's not much I can say about it,' and a spokesman for Charringtons brewery added mysteriously: 'We feel it inappropriate to comment.' That is the kind of story the press love: royals using an ordinary pub – even if it is an ordinary top people's pub – and people asked to comment saying sufficiently little that the press keep the pub under surveillance on the off-chance of catching a drunken Duke of York reeling out.

Possibly the least pleasant aspect of the monarchy concerns the archaic system of honours. These are a nonsense beloved by the British. The twice-yearly honours list is notable for the total lack of interest attaching to the recipients. With the exception of a few well-known sporting or show business figures, the great bulk go automatically to civil servants at a certain point in their careers, or to political party hacks. But occasionally the question of honours raises more profound issues.

Lester Piggott, perhaps the greatest British jockey of all time, was awarded the OBE for his services to the sport of kings – the Queen's favourite spectator sport. Later in his career Piggott was found guilty of tax evasion to the tune of £3.5m and sentenced to three years in prison. His OBE was taken from him and many would argue that this was right. Anthony Blunt did not cheat the income tax but betrayed his country. He did so systematically for years and did infinitely greater damage to Britain than did Piggott. Yet every Attorney-General from 1964 to 1979 gave Blunt immunity and he was allowed to keep his honours and continue in public life (looking after the Queen's pictures). He was disgraced only when the establishment was no longer able to cover up on his behalf. The difference of approach to an establishment figure and someone from the ranks is quite nauseating.

Stories and rumours that the Queen and her Prime Minister did not get on with each other circulated for some time before a public row erupted in mid-1986. It was, after all, the first time in Britain's history that the country's two rulers – the constitutional monarch and the Prime Minister – were women. The tensions came to a head in July 1986 over the explosive issue of South Africa. The Queen's sympathies were said to lie with President Kaunda of Zambia and other Commonwealth leaders pressing for sanctions against South Africa, a course to which Mrs Thatcher was and remains implacably opposed. A front page article in *The Sunday Times* of 20 July, suggesting a rift between the Queen and Thatcher and the Queen's support for African Commonwealth leaders, led to an unprecedented row between Palace and press and drew forth a letter from the private secretary to the Queen, William Heseltine, in which he tried to refute what circumstantial evidence suggested overwhelmingly to be true. The funniest paragraph in his letter ran, 'It is equally preposterous to suggest that any member of the Queen's Household, even supposing that he or she knew what Her Majesty's opinions on government policy might be (and the press secretary certainly does not), would reveal them to the press.'

That sentence tells all. The Queen surrounded by neutered, muted paragons who would think it preposterous to murmur any rumour to outsiders; the implication that the Queen's views would not be known to any of her household except by accident, but even then least of all to that hard-working member of her entourage, the press secretary. It is straining credulity very far indeed to believe such rubbish. Of course they know, and one or more were probably delighted to tell the press how little the Queen relishes her Prime Minister. The crisis passed and despite tut-tuttings from constitutionalists and irate Tories it was one of the few breezes of fresh air to blow from the Palace in a long time.

As an anachronism 'that works' the monarchy is assisted unashamedly by the snobberies which surround it. This process is helped by the *bon mots* of Queen Elizabeth, the Queen Mother. Following a meeting with ex-President Carter she is credited with the remark: 'He is the only man since my dear husband died to have the effrontery to kiss me on the lips.'

The monarchy seems set for some years yet.

15
The Church

> '*Outside human desires there
> is no moral standard.*'
> BERTRAND RUSSELL

> '*As for the British churchman, he goes to church as he goes to the bathroom, with the minimum of fuss and no explanation if he can help it.*'
> RONALD BLYTHE

It is a feature of our age that as people become less and less interested in organized religion the Church becomes increasingly concerned with social and political affairs. This growing concern with issues such as the bomb or the plight of the inner cities has brought it into conflict with government and never more so than during the 1980s. There is a particular irony in the growing confrontation between Church and state which has developed during Thatcher's premiership. The Church of England used to be described as the Tory Party at prayer but not any more.

Queen Elizabeth I was parsimonious to a degree and when the ships returned from trailing the Spanish Armada she refused to find the money to pay the exhausted sailors. The Admirals were forced to pay them out of their own pockets while the sick were let go 'little by little'. Later the Queen rode through the City of London 'like a conquering Caesar' to give thanks, and at the service they sang:

> He made the winds and waters rise
> To scatter all mine Enemies

At the thanksgiving service in St Paul's Cathedral following the Falklands War in 1982, where the wounded were carefully screened off from public view, Mrs Thatcher was less than pleased with the Archbishop of Canterbury who condemned all war rather than treat the occasion as though it were the celebration of a glorious victory. In his sermon the Archbishop referred to war as being always detestable though perhaps the line which gave most offence to the Prime Minister was, 'War is a sign of human failure and everything we say and do in this service must be in that context.' No members of the royal family were available to attend, and there was less than harmony between Church and state. It seems that as the Church becomes less relevant it recalls its spiritual message.

There are two established Churches in Britain – the Church of England and the Church of Scotland – and their clergy may work in state institutions such as the forces, prisons or hospitals. The Archbishop of Canterbury is 'Primate of All England'; he is also head of the Anglican Communion with a total estimated world membership of 70m. Lambeth Conferences are held every 10 years when the Archbishop presides over a meeting of the world's Anglican bishops.

Membership of the Church of England has been dropping steadily for years. According to Anthony Sampson in *Anatomy of Britain* (1962) while 60 per cent of Englishmen were baptized (one assumes he meant men and women but he was writing in pre-feminist days), only 30 per cent were confirmed and only 8 per cent attend Easter Communion. Ten years later only an estimated two million Britons fulfilled what is regarded as the minimum condition of membership – attendance at Easter Communion. By 1988 the Official Handbook recorded:

> About one-sixth of the adult population in Britain are members of a Christian church and there are considerable regional variations in church membership: England has the lowest membership with 13 per cent, Wales has 23 per cent, Scotland 37 per cent, and Northern Ireland the highest with 80 per cent.

In 1985 the Church of England recorded average Sunday attendances as 1.18m and at Easter Communion 1.62m. By contrast an estimated 5.7m belong to the Roman Catholic faith, so that four centuries after the Reformation, in so far as people are religious, the greater proportion once more adhere to Rome.

The Church of England is seen as conservative, traditionalist, part of the establishment but as it has become harder and harder to claim more than a small handful of members the Church has felt obliged to modernize its image. During the 1960s when the youth culture predominated some churchmen rendered themselves absurd by becoming 'swinging priests' or turning their crypts into clubs to attract the young, apparently working on the principle that if the young would not join the Church the Church had to swing with the young. The culmination of this nonsense was the helicopter dash in 1967 by Mick Jagger to a rendezvous in Essex where the leading pop star of the day (whose sentence for possessing drugs had just been quashed) could confer with William Rees-Mogg (editor of *The Times*), Sir Frank Soskice (a former Home Secretary), the Bishop of Woolwich and the Jesuit Father Thomas Corbishley. They chatted about the generation gap and the state of Britain. It was a media hype of a high order but also a demonstration of how the establishment was prepared to do anything to recapture control of a situation slipping from its grasp.

The Church also turned its attention to the Third World. The nearest many young people have come to faith in the years since 1945 has been their involvement in aid and Third World development, which allows great scope for 'missionary' ardour. Oxfam, Save the Children, Christian Aid and War on Want or, more

The Church

politically, Anti-Apartheid and Amnesty International have provided many young enthusiasts with a cause which in the nineteenth century they would have found in their churches. The Methodist minister, Colin Morris, produced two popular paperbacks in the 1960s – *Include Me Out!* and *Unyoung Uncoloured Unpoor* – which looked at what later came to be called North-South relations, and crystallized youth's concern with one of the greatest issues of our times. The Church – with certain honourable exceptions like Trevor Huddleston who has spent a lifetime opposing apartheid and trying to make the West angry about this unchristian and appalling system – has hardly been in the van in denouncing iniquities. Ian Ramsey, Bishop of Durham at the beginning of the 1970s, led a deputation to Heath to object to the announced intention of resuming arms sales to South Africa; this mild clerical protest was not regarded with favour by the hierarchy of the Church. The British Council of Churches, cautiously reformist, almost went along with the World Council of Churches in support of South African freedom fighters – but not quite.

Another area of concern was the bomb. This awful weapon has overshadowed our world ever since Nagasaki and Hiroshima, and it was almost inevitable that the Church would become involved in the arguments about nuclear weapons. A working party under the chairmanship of the Bishop of Salisbury produced a report which was published as *The Church and the Bomb* – 'Nuclear weapons and Christian conscience', which was widely disseminated and read. The Church sat on the fence. The analysis – the weapons, distribution, military strategy, the political context, legal and moral restraints – is excellent. But once into sustainable morality we are in trouble. There is a great deal about the 'just war' and the Western ethical tradition, which endlessly circumvents the commandment 'Thou shalt not kill'. As the report says, 'The Just War doctrine implies that war cannot be abolished' which is good for the establishment. The report was published in 1982 (the year of the Falklands War) and contains this gem: 'To give an extreme example, to squander, let us say, thousands of lives in dispute over the possession of a small, unpopulated island of no strategic or economic value could be considered grossly disproportionate.'

Later, the report says:

> According to the Sermon on the Mount ... Jesus is portrayed as advocating the love of enemies by non-resistance, since this is for Christians the only path to the sort of perfection which is shown towards them by the heavenly Father. Such pacifism is not to be confused with *passivity* since it is infused with the positive command to love which does not rule out the use of force, providing, that is, such force is compatible with loving those against whom it is used.

Here indeed is sophistry of a high order; no wonder it has a dwindling membership. Many of the arguments advanced, for example about unilateralism, are excellent material for the Labour Party: 'This would then make renunciation a unilateral stage within a multilateral process,' but they are less than valid coming from a source to which people turn for an absolute lead. At the end, the report takes the popular liberal view when it argues, 'the cause of right cannot be upheld by fighting a nuclear war'.

The third issue which the Church came to grips with in the 1980s was increasing poverty in one of the most affluent societies in the world. Its report *Faith in the City: A Call for Action by Church and Nation* was issued in 1985 following some of the worst urban disturbances in living memory and made recommendations to alleviate the problems of the inner cities. It was on sure ground here if only because Christianity started among the poor for the poor. This also brought conflict with the Thatcher government, because its criticisms were of the harsh uncaring nature of one of the most 'successful' governments of the century.

Morality is the concern of the Church and it is as much its concern when a government is amoral as when an individual is. But the moment that is said we come up against the perennial and ancient historical problem of relations between Church and state. In a wartime Penguin Special (*Christianity and Social Order*) William Temple (later Archbishop of Canterbury) faced the question of social responsibility in his opening paragraph:

> The claim of the Christian Church to make its voice heard in matters of politics and economics is very widely resented, even by those who are Christian in personal belief and in devotional practice. It is commonly assumed that religion is one department of life, like art or science, and that it is playing the part of a busybody when it lays down principles for the guidance of other departments, whether art and science or business and politics.

At the end of the book Temple lays down a six-point programme whose clear social/socialist content did not endear him to the establishment of the time. He concludes, 'The aim of a Christian social order is the fullest possible development of individual personality in the widest and deepest possible fellowship.'

According to the 1988 Official Handbook 'The Church of England's relationship with the state is one of mutual obligation – privileges accorded to the Church balanced by certain duties which it must fulfil.' Those duties, according to some members of the Conservative Party, include an obligation not to criticize when the Conservatives form the government. On the showing of the 1980s the sooner the Church is dis-established so that the Prime Minister does not have a hand in appointing bishops, the better.

The fact that in the 1980s a bitter though decorously handled row was in progress between the Archbishop of Canterbury and the Bishop of London about

The Church

the ordination of women bears testimony to the archaic nature of the Church of England. In 1988 Tony Benn, that most elegant iconoclast of the Left, was proposing an English Church Bill to 'terminate the establishment of the Church of England'. That would mean the dismissal of bishops from the House of Lords, the abolition of any remaining state powers in Church appointments, the deposition of the Queen as Head of the Church and, more important, the recognition that Britain is a secular society in which many people belong to various religions rather than a religious society. Then, perhaps, the Church could get on with its primary function of chasing and caring for souls.

The Church made more headlines of a controversial nature during the 1980s than in the preceding 35 years from the end of World War Two. It has done so, moreover, from a mildly liberal position in a political situation where it has been increasingly difficult *not* to speak out, at least on the effects of goverment policies if not on the policies themselves.

Tory anger has been directed at Archbishop Runcie for his 'wet' views ever since his anti-war sermon at the Falklands service; still more has it been directed at the Bishop of Durham whose forthright attacks included the use of the word 'wicked' to describe the government's favouring of the rich at the expense of the poor. Reacting to the 1988 budget the Bishop said: 'Every political act which is alleged to be targeted on dealing more efficiently with those most in need seems to many who have direct experience to be guaranteed to worsen the lot of very many least able to help themselves.' Later he said: 'Money is for those who can make it. Those who cannot make it must not be allowed to get in the way of its being made.' It was not possible to be much more political than that in 1988.

Like the constitutional monarch, the Church is supposed to be impartial and non-partisan in political matters. This is clearly a nonsense: if it cannot and does not pronounce on the subject of poverty in the most forthright terms, it ought not to be in business. When the Church behaves in an anodyne fashion and avoids controversial 'left-wing' pronouncements, it is patronized; when it speaks out against injustice it is lectured for meddling. That quite extraordinarily pious pillar of the establishment, William Rees-Mogg, recently wrote of the Bishop of Durham: 'The ordinary churchgoer wants bishops to teach faith, not to spread doubt.' Assuming for a moment that this statement is true, one hardly needs to look further for an explanation of why it has become moribund and lacking in appeal. The Bishop of Durham has put some blood into the Church for the first time in generations. When a Conservative MP (in this case Nicholas Fairbairn) calls him a 'fool and an anti-Christ' the bishop must be making an impact.

Less forthright, the Archbishop of Canterbury, Dr Runcie, nevertheless spoke on BBC1's *Panorama* about issues on which the Church might challenge the state. He said: 'It might have a moral duty to oppose some of the immigration policies, policies on South Africa. It might have a duty to question the kind of use of the taxation system to reward success rather than to meet social needs which are urgent and crying.' He hedged later, but what he said was enough to anger a No 10 from which expressions of displeasure have been despatched at an ever widening number of targets.

The argument between Church and Tory Party (rather than Church and state) is elementary: does the Church have the right (and the duty) to comment on political or social issues? A large number of Tories say it should stick to matters of faith. This has always been an extraordinary claim for anyone to make. If it is not prepared to concern itself with moral values – which means political and social values – it will have little impact and deserve less. It is precisely because the Church has been ready to stick to matters of faith for generations that its membership has fallen so drastically. The message of the post-war world has been plain enough: if the Church is to make an impact and have meaning for its constituents, it must speak out on issues which concern people and preferably in forthright fashion.

By mid-1988 there had developed one of those public arguments beloved by the British – the media busy pontificating, the public relishing the discomfiture of one side or other and Church and state battling for 'the moral high ground'. There had been nothing like it for years and it was all the more interesting because the contestants were the Church of England and the Tory Party which had been regarded as natural partners. Welcoming such a debate the Dean of Peterhouse, Cambridge, (Edward Norman) wrote in the *Independent*: 'Confronted with the monolithic secular ethicism of the Marxist states, the West has paraded a confusion of plural values – very many of which disclose a materialism equal to that of the Soviet bloc.'

What was new in 1988 was the sudden political dimension to the debate about morals, with the bishops opposing both the government's poll tax and its education bills in the Lords and the Archbishop of Canterbury saying: 'The Gospel has a pastoral bias towards the weak – and we therefore look upon the protection of the weak as a prime responsibility of government. There is a responsibility to look for the moral and spiritual implications of political issues.' Rarely had the country been subjected to so much media discussion of what the Church and individual members of it stood for. Various leading Conservatives went on to the attack. Douglas Hurd called on the bishops to give a moral lead; Selwyn Gummer attacked the 'condom' culture which he argued the Church helped foster and denounced the Archbishop of York, Dr Habgood, for his liberal stance on homosexuality. At least Mr Hurd admitted the right of the Church to comment on political matters; he then insisted that politicians had an equal right to comment on the role of the Church.

The Church was deep in internal discussion about AIDS, homosexuality and gay clergy. Homosexual Christians accused the Archbishop of Canterbury of hypocrisy following his support for the Bishop of Ripon who had said he would discipline vicars in his diocese who practised homosexuality. There was an openness about the discussions which, in turn, allowed newspapers to run editorials about Church, morality and sex.

On the political front 1988 was also the year when Mrs Thatcher decided to pay public attention to the country's morals. In November 1987 the Prime Minister had seven bishops to Chequers although news of this secret meeting became public only in 1988. In May 1988 the Prime Minister addressed the General Assembly of the Church of Scotland. At the beginning of her speech she said: 'Reading recently, I came across the starkly simple phrase, "Christianity is about spiritual redemption, not social reform".' With that she set forth her parameters. Later she said, 'We are all responsible for our own actions. We cannot blame society if we disobey the law. We simply cannot delegate the exercise of mercy and generosity to others.' The Prime Minister's 'sermon' was widely attacked by political opponents as an effort to mobilize the scriptures in support of her policies, and by clergy as betraying ignorance of Christian ideas of justice.

The Rev Brian Duckworth, general secretary of the Methodist Division of Social Responsibility, said of her speech:

> The issue is not whether people are charitable or courteous, although these are both important. What matters as far as governments are concerned is the stewardship of resources and the justice of the societies they preside over. This has been a central point in both the Jewish and Christian tradition from Leviticus onwards. Our fundamental charge is that we are moving from a relatively just society to a relatively unjust one, and that is something which sticks in the craw of those of us who have to see the consequences.

That riposte certainly went to the heart of the debate. On the day following her address Mrs Thatcher's selective use of texts was savaged. Then one of her own high Tories – another ex-Minister – joined the debate. John Biffen had already spoken of the 'foghorn of conscience'; he now admonished the Prime Minister: 'I would have thought on the whole the public do not really warm to the prospect of politicians in pulpits.' He went on: 'We take a lot of our fashions from North America – monetarism started in Chicago. . . . I do not believe that the politics of this country would be enhanced if we were to try to copy the link that has been established between some of the elements of the Republican Party and some of the elements of the revivalist movement in North America.'

Perhaps Dr Habgood deserved the last word in the debate which followed Mrs Thatcher's sermon. Writing in the *Observer* of 29 May, he went over the references she had used, chided her for her overt simplicities and concluded, 'It is a sign

The Structure of Society

of hope that Mrs Thatcher has so clearly indicated her willingness to talk about fundamentals. If her speech marked the transition to this more constructive relationship, it will have done nothing but good.'

Arguably, one of the most unhealthy aspects of the historical 'bargain' between Church and state was withdrawal by the Church from political questions. Since 1945 it has seen its role in society become more peripheral as older people have drifted away and few young people have joined. It appears to have been trying to redefine its roles. Politicians after 1945 – until Mrs Thatcher – were not greatly concerned with the Church. Attlee took it for granted in an establishment kind of way, Churchill revelled in the pomp of coronations and funerals, Macmillan remarked, 'If people want a sense of purpose they should get it from their archbishop – they should certainly not get it from their politicians.' Wilson, Heath and Callaghan did not see it as a danger to their politics; like them, it stood for consensus. It is Mrs Thatcher who has given the Church a new role, even if it is a political one as an articulate opposition to her policies.

Church uncertainty was demonstrated by the sad and muddled case of Canon Gareth Bennett's suicide. The Canon had written the anonymous preface to the 1987 edition of Crockford's and had attacked the Archbishop of Canterbury. The argument was about 'right' and 'left' or conservative versus liberal churchmen. Basically Bennett was seen as attacking the Archbishop for not endorsing the new moral certainties of the Thatcher era. He was accused of being part of a cabal to force Dr Runcie to retire in 1988, although he denied this. The preface led to a major controversy and, after repeatedly denying that he had written it, Dr Bennett committed suicide. One of the most amazing aspects of the affair was that so many high-ranking traditionalist clergy attended the service for him. Until recently suicide was considered one of the worst of sins and a suicide was buried in unconsecrated ground. The affair was a good illustration of a Church which appears to have lost its way.

16
Justice and the Law

' "When I use a word," Humpty Dumpty said in rather a scornful tone, "it means just what I choose it to mean, neither more or less." "The question is," said Alice, "whether you can make words mean different things." "The question is," said Humpty Dumpty, "which is to be master, that's all." '

LEWIS CARROLL

'Parliament has been the main instrument of our liberties. It has also been, at times, the instrument of oppression.'

LORD HAILSHAM

'To every subject of this land, however powerful, I would use Thomas Fuller's words over three hundred years ago, "Be ye never so high, the law is above you." '

LORD DENNING

Most people are afraid of the law if only in the sense that its obscurities are too complex for them to grasp. When it is equated with justice its workings must baffle all but the most tortuous of minds.

Take the example of the consecutive or the concurrent sentence: why if a man is found guilty of three separate acts of robbery with violence each carrying a sentence of three years does he not have to serve nine years in prison (three three-year sentences to run consecutively)? Instead he is likely to serve only three years (the three three-year sentences to run concurrently) and with remission for good conduct may be out in two? If a man who ought to serve nine years faces only three which may be reduced to two by good conduct, there is an inducement to behave well since he sees an end to his sentence. He is less likely to be a source of trouble in the prison, and will release space that much sooner for someone else. If he has to serve nine years there is less encouragement to behave well and he is more likely to become a 'hard' prisoner who causes problems for the staff. So he is given concurrent sentences. This has a great deal to do with administrative convenience but not much to do with justice.

There are many myths about the law, which are enhanced by its attendant paraphernalia: the wigs and gowns; the ponderous language: the middle-class

Oxbridge accents; the exalted position of judges and the deference accorded to them. As that advocate of the Left, D. N. Pritt, wrote:

> In a country whose leaders boast of its democracy, the very idea of the *demos*, the people, having any say in the selection of judges who may have to deal with their grievances and their misdeeds and send them to prison, fills the establishment with horror – an unconscious revelation of our leaders' deep conviction that only a select, indeed a self-selected, few are fit to exercise any important function.

In the 1980s the myth that violence had increased became part of the public perception, so that the 'law-and-order' movement called for sterner government measures and an end to permissiveness. At the same time the New Right called for greater freedom in the economic sphere in order that those who were able could make more money. A principal British myth is that we are a free society, but as Lewis Namier said in 1930, 'At every stage in social development freedom has to be reconquered' – that has never been more true than at the present time.

We see this especially in the House of Commons where those few who question government or party are treated as cranks or blacklegs. When Tam Dalyell went to see Mrs Thatcher in the course of one of his inquiries and thanked her for making time available she replied that she always made time 'for the awkward squad'. The implications of that reply augur ill for democracy. Raymond Blackburn MP wrote in the 1960s: 'Strong governments generally mean governments which diminish freedom and take extreme actions which party enthusiasts approve but which liberal and independent-minded persons dislike.'

There is a constant battle between the law and those who argue for wider freedom. In 1988, for example, the *Independent* journalist, Jeremy Warner, was fined £20,000 for refusing to reveal his confidential source in an insider-dealing case. Law-and-order enthusiasts would argue he should make the information available for the sake of justice; the liberal lobby would say he should refuse to disclose to safeguard press freedom. The long-drawn-out *Spycatcher* farce with the government pursuing Wright through court after court even when everything in his book had long been public knowledge drew from the Master of the Rolls, Lord Donaldson, 'The existence of a free press ... is an essential element in maintaining Parliamentary democracy and the British way of life as we know it.'

During the Thatcher years the law has come in for a great deal of questioning. Increasing attention has been paid to the practice of justice behind closed doors or in camera. In February 1987, the High Court dealt with 350 cases in camera in one week, and there was a marked increase in the number of secret or semi-secret trials taking place. Where secrecy is applied it usually relates to cases where informers, supergrasses or police spies are part of the evidence or where jury nobbling is deemed likely. In a period when the government has taken a tough line on unions many 'interim' injunctions by employers to prevent strikes have been heard in private, sometimes without a lawyer representing the union concerned.

Britain has always been a secretive society; it is especially disturbing when the law adopts secrecy. Much secrecy concerns cases which have a political content – where government argues that national security is at stake – but there has also been growing misuse of the Contempt of Court Act by which courts can grant anonymity to defendants in certain circumstances. This is often operated in the cases of celebrities who have broken the law, but justice should always be seen to be done, particularly in the case of the powerful or influential.

The rule of law and the sovereignty of Parliament were Dicey's twin pillars of the constitution; both have come under increasing pressure and doubt in the years since 1945 as successive Prime Ministers have assumed greater powers and laws have been replaced by administrative fiat and bypassed in the name of state security. The British judiciary is still one of the most independent in the world, although such a claim must be examined with care when a political case is in question.

There are now three main sources of law: legislation, common law and European Community law, which has added a new dimension. Although broadly similar, different legal systems operate in England and Wales, Scotland and Northern Ireland; some laws have been applied solely in Northern Ireland since the beginning of the latest troubles in 1969.

Although in theory the judiciary is independent of the government and not subject to ministerial direction, in practice this is debatable. Over the last 40 years huge changes have come about in the way the law is conducted, although the structure – judges and courts, the division of the legal profession into barristers and solicitors, the jury, the prison system and the police – appears to be much the same as in 1945.

It is a cardinal rule that where there is a reasonable doubt the benefit must go to the accused. In 1935 the Lord Chancellor, Lord Sankey, laid this down unequivocally:

> Juries are always told that, if conviction there is to be, the prosecution must prove the case beyond reasonable doubt... No matter what the charge or where the trial, the principle that the prosecution must prove this guilt of the prisoner is part of the Common Law of England and no attempt to whittle it down can be entertained.

There are many areas in which the law is far from the impartial process it is portrayed as being. There is the simple matter of money. The rich can afford the services of the best solicitors and barristers available, the poor have to accept those supplied under legal aid. The Bail Act of 1976 lays down the criteria which should govern magistrates in refusing bail. In practice magistrates interpret this very widely, as Patricia Hewitt shows in her book *The Abuse of Power*:

> In the immediate aftermath of the rioting in July 1981 it became apparent that magistrates in some cities were using their power to impose curfews as a condition of bail, and to deny bail altogether even to defendants charged with a first offence.

In the 1970s jury vetting came into the open during an official secrets trial. In 1974 the Home Secretary (Roy Jenkins) and the Attorney-General (Sam Silkin) issued secret instructions to the police and Director of Public Prosecutions to vet juries in serious criminal cases or cases with 'strong political motives'.

Although at the beginning of the 1950s the Tories used the election slogan 'set the people free' this was subsequently described by a Conservative Minister as 'little more than an electoral flourish'. The Conservative Party in office has favoured an authoritarian rather than a democratic approach to questions of law and the Labour Party has hardly been better.

Part of the problem is public indifference and acceptance of breaches of conduct by those in authority. This is given by Tam Dalyell as the reason for writing *Misrule*. His principal thesis is that the Thatcher government has repeatedly used the law to save itself embarrassment by threatening or silencing those who would ask awkward questions about its political motives. As long as a substantial section of the public expects such behaviour from its political leaders it is unlikely to exert pressures for reform.

In 1968 the National Council for Civil Liberties (NCCL) published a study – *Privacy under Attack* – in which it listed the threats to privacy in Britain.

> What we are faced with is not so much a small coterie of evil men seeking to enslave our minds as a large body of opinion which would whittle away our privacy (and thus the very heart of our liberty) in the service of such vague concepts as state security and the national interest.

Few acts have been so insistently used for doubtful purposes in recent years as the Official Secrets Act which has repeatedly been deployed to silence criticism of government failings rather than to keep secret anything which threatened the wellbeing of the state.

The Fulton Committee on the Civil Service, which reported to the Wilson government in 1968, claimed that the administrative process was surrounded by too much secrecy. The Franks Committee set up by the Conservative government in 1971 (to fulfil the election pledge to eliminate too much secrecy) recommended that information obtained (from the police or from medical reports, for example) by crown servants in the course of carrying out their duties should not be subject to special legal protection even though it ought to be kept private. The report recommended that only information 'in the Secret and Defence-Confidential classification' should be legally protected, but the Home Secretary, Robert Carr, generally portrayed as a liberal man, showed little desire to relax government secrecy. He said: 'We believe that, however acquired, personal information about individuals or about private companies and concerns held by a government department requires protection from improper disclosure, by the criminal law.'

Few laws since 1945 have been as anti-libertarian as those relating to immigration. Patricia Hewitt claims in *The Abuse of Power* that not even our vaunted Habeas Corpus has protected black migrants from the arbitrary use of power:

> Under Labour and Conservative governments alike, the Home Office has asserted – and the courts have upheld – a power to arrest without warrant an immigrant settled in this country; the power to imprison him on suspicion of being an illegal entrant; the power to deny him bail, to detain him for an indefinite period and to deport him without ever having laid charges against him or brought him before a court.

In *Misrule* Tam Dalyell examines the police raid upon the Glasgow offices of the BBC to obtain evidence about the banned 'Zircon' programme which was to have been part of the BBC's *Secret Society* series and says: 'It now transpires that not only were legal corners cut, but that what was done was downright illegal.' Civil servants at the Scottish Office and Crown Office were relaxed about the illegal goings-on 'because they were given to understand that it was Downing Street's policy, and therefore no wrath would descend on them or their Ministers'. The local MP, who happened to be Roy Jenkins and a former Home Secretary, said it was the work of 'a second-rate police state.'

The use of the blanket 'reasons of state' to deprive people of liberties and rights has become a feature of British society. As Pritt wrote in 1962:

> The judges, who are the product of their environment – generally a rather narrow 'establishmentarian' one – always tend, often unconsciously, to find ways of so deciding cases as to support government policy and decisions, and to save governments embarrassment. Most laymen take this as a matter of course; many lawyers feel a duty to deny it; and most lawyers know in their hearts that it is true.

Ever since 1945 governments have been taking greater powers which are ever more difficult to challenge in the courts. The 1947 Supplies and Services (Emergency Powers) Act gave the government totalitarian powers to requisition property and direct labour. As Richard Crossman commented, 'It is not a question of dictatorship ... that is inevitable in the modern state.' Governments constantly

The Structure of Society

use emergencies as excuses to enact legislation or to take powers which they say they do not expect to use but want 'just in case'. As a safe principle, a democracy should work to take powers away from its government rather than to confer more upon it.

An admission of another erosion of liberty was made by the Prime Minister in January 1988. The *Independent* revealed how officers of the security services had been told by their MI5 superiors that they could enter, search, burgle and bug private premises under the protection of the Royal Prerogative. This was condemned by the former Master of the Rolls, Lord Denning, and the former Labour Home Secretary, Merlyn Rees, but defended by the current Master of the Rolls, Sir John Donaldson, on the grounds that 'It is silly for us to sit here and say that the security service is obliged to follow the letter of the law; it isn't real.' We know it isn't real to expect such behaviour; it is not silly to do so. Later, replying to a question in the House of Commons from Labour MP Dale Campbell-Savours, as to whether 'alleged offences committed under the auspices of the prerogative right of the crown' could be exempt from prosecution, the Prime Minister merely said: 'Prosecutions are a matter for the Attorney-General and the other prosecuting authorities.' Clearly they were exempt.

The Royal Prerogative is a device to avoid having to legislate or obtain Parliamentary approval. It is profoundly anti-democratic and against the principle of the rule of law. One example of its application was in January 1984 when the Prime Minister altered the terms of service of civil servants at GCHQ, Cheltenham, forbidding them to belong to trade unions. The prohibition was challenged in the courts and when the case eventually reached the House of Lords her action was upheld on the grounds of 'national security', a term which has increasingly covered government decisions not presented to Parliament.

January 1988 was a bad month for the rule of law. While officers of the security services are apparently above it and there was no prosecution of RUC officers in Northern Ireland despite evidence of conspiracy to obstruct the Stalker inquiry, in the High Court Sir Nicolas Browne-Wilkinson, the Vice-Chancellor, told journalist Warner,

> Unless the law is complied with by everybody, the essential cement that binds society together will go. Parliament, in a democratic society, lays down what is the law and what must be done. Journalists are no more entitled to say that they don't comply with it than anyone else.

That splendid admonition ought more properly to have been addressed to the security services or to the RUC, and in an increasing number of cases it is clear that Parliament neither lays down the law nor what should be done.

Civil liberties appear most consistently at risk in issues which embarrass the government – Northern Ireland, immigration control, left-wing protest. The 1968

Bill to deprive Kenya Asians of their British citizenship rights was rushed through Parliament in a week by a Labour government with the full backing and connivance of the Conservative opposition. Following the passage of the Commonwealth Immigrants Act of 1962 the *Sunday Telegraph* reported: 'Magistrates, if not Mr Henry Brooke, appear to regard deportation as an almost automatic penalty for immigrant offenders, to judge from the recommendations which they habitually make to the Home Secretary.' Later the same paper argued: 'Equality before the law is a cardinal principle of British justice. The courts should hesitate to regard immigrants as less equal than others.' Raymond Blackburn commented upon the developments which followed the 1962 Act:

> But the real evil lay in the alacrity with which magistrates operated powers in destruction of the liberty of the subject and the willingness of the Home Office to conform to the will of the judges in breach of assurances given by Ministers in Parliament.

Worse was to come. The 1968 Act was a panic measure which brought no credit to anyone. The 1971 Act created non-patrial citizens, the 1976 Labour Green Paper proposed two citizenships – one with and the other without the right of abode in Britain – and the 1981 Nationality Act created three citizenships: British, citizenship of the British Dependent Territories and British overseas citizenship.

In terms of political protest few groups have been more successful than the women of Greenham Common. Beginning with their march from Cardiff to the USAF Base at Greenham in September 1981, the women have camped, demonstrated, entered the base on repeated occasions and been the subject of sustained legal action to the point where, on 1 April 1985, trespass on common land was made a criminal offence. Between 1981 and June 1986 journalist Janey Hulme recorded 12,000 arrests during the non-violent protests. In 1987 two Greenham women successfully contested the validity of the Military Lands Act Byelaws through the courts, so the case had to be referred to the House of Lords. The Greenham Common women demonstrated the extent to which determination can obtain legal redress against the actions of an arbitrary government.

The phrase law and order is constantly used, especially by the Right, as an appeal for the mainenance of the status quo. Those who protest or demand change are readily equated with disturbers of the peace – meaning the peace of those in possession of power. Ever since the abolition of capital punishment in 1965 the hanging lobby has campaigned for its restoration, and their last attempt was defeated by the House of Commons in June 1988 by 341 to 218 votes: it was the eighteenth such attempt at reversal. Proponents of capital punishment insist that a majority of the people want hanging restored (it is not often that MPs are so concerned with the popular will) and claim that it has a deterrent effect. One of the great ironies of the 'to hang or not to hang' debate is the extent to which it ignores the claims of justice. Capital punishment is not about deterrence but about a just and appropriate punishment for a particular crime. Those in favour of hanging ought to be more honest: they believe in retribution but do not wish to say so.

Britain has always been a brutal society, retaining corporal punishment long after it had been abandoned in most European countries and exporting it throughout the Empire. Whippings and canings were a normal part of colonial administration and the figures for such punishments are horrendous. Back in 1878, for example, 75,223 whippings were administered in British India alone. The notorious brutality of the Black and Tans, following World War 1, has entered the folk legend of Ireland. The long rearguard action of some teachers to retain corporal punishment in schools tells more about the mentality of those in authority than it does about the unruly nature of their charges.

For most of the period since 1945, and especially during the 1980s, there has been constant talk of rising violence. The anti-police riot in Bristol in 1980, the Brixton riots of 1981 which led to the Scarman report, the inner city riots of 1985 each in turn appeared to reinforce the claim that law and order was breaking down. These riots have bred their own myths, and one is the claim that Britain used to be a law-abiding society. Now, so the argument runs, permissiveness, the arrival of Commonwealth immigrants, the relaxation of parental control and a lowering of respect for those in authority have created a more violent society in which people fear to go out at night, where youths use knives where they would previously use their fists, and where soccer hooligans have brought England international disgrace. Statistics are produced to show that violent crime is increasing.

The facts do not bear out the claims. Year after year the Conservative Party Conference debates motions on law and order: in the 1950s it was the Teddy Boys, in the 1960s Mods and Rockers and then the Hippies, and in the 1980s soccer hooligans. In his book *Hooligan* Geoffrey Pearson demonstrates that the same speeches about the rougher elements of society and unruly youth were being made in Victorian Britain and Edwardian Britain. The subject of violence is highly emotive and politically useful as an outlet for frustrations which might otherwise centre upon less safe subjects from the establishment's point of view. Writing in 1860 Matthew Arnold said:

> For a long time, as I have said, the strong feudal habits of subordination and deference continued to tell upon the working class. The modern spirit has now almost entirely dissolved those habits, and the anarchical tendency of our worship of freedom in and for itself . . . is becoming very manifest.

The same sentiments could as easily be expressed in the 1980s. There is little evidence that the soccer riots of the 1980s are any worse than the ugliness of other disturbances at any time over the last two centuries, and there is plenty of evidence to the contrary. Probably the main factor making violence different is affluence. Forty or fifty years ago the average young soccer supporter could not have afforded to travel to Europe. Stories of violence proliferated in the press during 1988; three headlines from one newspaper on the same day emphasize the extent of public concern: 'Violence is the shame of the game', 'Thatcher to press for tougher action on soccer violence' and 'How to tame the terraces'. But in a country where people got into a fever about 'bashing the Argies' in 1982, where for many young people employment prospects are grim, and where the measure of success is a 'loadsamoney' one, soccer violence is unsurprising. Besides, it is not only soccer.

In the midst of the soccer violence stories came the disturbances in the well-to-do stockbroker belt town of Crowborough, Sussex. Nine policemen were attacked by 100 youths outside a wine bar on a Saturday night. Subsequent reports suggested that a rapid rise in rural violence had been occurring, often in places which did not have unemployment problems, whose perpetrators could hardly be classified as the mindless 'oiks' or 'yobboes' so beloved of the press. They were bored affluent youths with nothing to do.

The Minister for Sport, Colin Moynihan, described the 'criminally-minded, so-called (soccer) supporters' who had gone to Dusseldorf and then Frankfurt as 'worse than animals'. Attempts to explain such behaviour always run into difficulties since such violence has occurred in times of unemployment, in times of affluence and as far back as records exist. The summer solstice attracted the annual pilgrimage of hippies to Stonehenge where 1000 policemen were waiting to keep them outside the barbed wire which now rings the stones, while the Druids are allowed inside to celebrate their annual festival. It was in keeping with the Britain of the 1980s where confrontation rather than accommodation is the accepted order of the day. One might ask in passing whose stones they are. Why should the hippies not enjoy them peaceably, like the Druids?

Unlike most Western countries, Britain has no written constitution which can be used to check overpowerful governments, nor does she have a modern Bill of Rights. But the idea was mooted and by the end of the 1960s the Conservative and Labour Parties were at least prepared to discuss the pros and cons of a Bill of Rights.

In 1988, from retirement, Lord Scarman added his powerful voice to pleas for constitutional reforms embodying a Bill of Rights. Having set forth the three principles of the constitution – 'the rule of law, to which all in the kingdom without exception are subject, the independence of the judges, and the supremacy of Parliament' – Lord Scarman highlighted the weakness of constitutional protection against the abuse of political power: 'Magna Carta, Habeas Corpus, trial by jury ... are no different from any other legislation; they can be amended, repealed, or abrogated by the party in control of the House of Commons.' He suggested a Parliament Act and a Bill of Rights which would declare rights and freedoms 'so fundamental that they may not be diminished or taken away save by an Act of Parliament requiring the assent of both Houses of Parliament'. His call was timely.

The period has also witnessed some notable advances in the law and the administration of justice. The general availability of legal aid and a more humane approach to the problems of young offenders represented important improvements in attitude, as have certain key pieces of legislation. The Labour MP, Sidney Silverman, crowned many years of campaigning when his Bill to abolish hanging finally became law in 1965. In 1967 the Criminal Justice Act was passed, dealing with suspended sentences and, on the recommendation of the Wolfenden Committee, the Sexual Offences Act which permitted homosexual acts between consenting adults, while the Abortion Act legalized abortion in certain circumstances. In 1969 the Divorce Reform Act and the Children and Young Persons Act became law. A partial compensation for the Commonwealth Immigration Acts of 1962 and 1965, the Race Relations Act of 1965 was passed. The Lord Chamberlain's powers of censorship in the theatre were ended in 1968.

In June 1988 the Civil Justice Review recommended sweeping changes in the administration of civil justice. In an editorial – 'The case for the consumer rests' – the *Independent* of 8 June 1988 welcomed the proposed reforms, concluding that the main emphasis of the report, correctly, was the rights of consumers as opposed to the interests of judges, magistrates and lawyers. The paper is not noted for pro-Thatcher sentiments and the editorial concluded:

> Having reformed the unions and more recently threatened the professions, it is right that Margaret Thatcher should turn her attention to the law, one of the last great bastions of inefficiency and outdated vested interests. In doing so, she will attract the wrath of some of her natural supporters. She should be bold enough to ignore their special pleading.

The Lord Chancellor, Lord Mackay of Clashfern, came out in favour of the proposed reforms: 'The ultimate goal of all the recommendations is to improve the standard of service provided by the courts to the public. This is a goal which I am determined to achieve.'

Not many talk of freedom as possessively as the British and a foreigner might be pardoned for thinking Britain had invented the concept. Frequent references to the Mother of Parliaments, Magna Carta, Habeas Corpus, freedom of the press and other liberties imply that these are natural for Britons but not for many others, so the British have less excuse than those they criticize for their own shortcomings. It is, therefore, all the more reprehensible when British rulers take away more liberties in the name of national security. The former Lord Chief Justice, Lord Parker said, in the course of the Vassall spy case (1962), that it is one's duty 'in the ordinary way as a citizen to put the interests of the state above everything'. That dictum should be reversed: 'It is the state's duty, in the ordinary way, to put the interests of the individual citizen above everything else.'

Growing official contempt for the ordinary citizen can be seen in what the NCCL describes as 'the subversion of the jury', in their pamphlet 'Justice Deserted'. Before 1949 a juror had to be the occupier of a house with a rateable value of £30 in London and £20 elsewhere, but the Juries Act of that year and the 1972 Criminal Justice Act reformed the law so that almost everyone on the electoral register qualified as a juror.

But other legislation has undermined the jury principle. In 1967 unanimous verdicts were abolished on the grounds that the unanimity rule facilitated intimidation of jurors by criminals, and majority verdicts were allowed. In 1973 the right to question jurors was restricted. This was a result of the 'Angry Brigade' trial when defence barristers tried to discover the political leanings of potential jurors in case they were likely to be biased. A second change that year was the removal of jurors' occupations from the jury list. This was done because the Lord Chancellor, Lord Hailsham, feared that defence lawyers were using occupations as a reason to challenge jurors – which was surely the reason for the occupations being there in the first place. In 1977 a number of cases were taken away from Crown Courts and sent to Magistrates' Courts, which do not have juries. Although the James Committee, responsible for this recommendation, insisted, 'We have approached the issue from the standpoint of principle,' it appeared that the change was made to relieve pressures on the Crown Courts. Efficiency rather than justice seemed to be the primary consideration. The Criminal Law Act of 1977 implemented the recommendations of the James Report and cut down the right of the defence to challenge jurors. Moreover, there is an imbalance: the defence has the right of only three peremptory challenges while the prosecution right is unlimited. In 1978 jury vetting was made legal.

These changes add up to a formidable assault upon the independence of juries, the vetting act in particular allowing the prosecution to pack a jury. The NCCL pamphlet argues: 'The history of jury trial is the history of the struggle to stop the authorities packing the court.' In a Blackstone lecture in 1978 Lord Devlin said of the jury system:

> What makes juries worthwhile is that they see things differently from the judges, that they can water the law, and that the function which they filled two centuries ago as a corrective to the corruption and partiality of the judges

requires essentially the same qualities as the function they perform today as an organ of the disestablishment.

Two other areas deserve special attention: the prisons and the police.

Leaving aside discussion as to which crimes should be punished by a gaol sentence and how long such sentences ought to be, there has been growing disquiet with the prison system for years on grounds of overcrowding, grossly inadequate sanitary arrangements and awful and sometimes brutal conditions. According to the 1988 Official Handbook, 'The government aims to provide a humane, efficient and effective prison service.' Most people who know the system would deny that it does anything of the kind. In 1986 the average daily inmate population was 46,900 for England and Wales, 6000 for Scotland and 1824 for Northern Ireland. By 1988 it had risen in England and Wales to 50,900 and was expected to reach 54,800 by 1990. The present authorized capacity is 43,000 places. Little wonder that prison officers take industrial action. By 1988 prison boards, not noted for aggressive or reforming zeal, were becoming increasingly strident in their criticism of inhuman and degrading conditions, describing Wandsworth's sanitary conditions as 'disgraceful' and Brixton as 'Dickensian'.

In *The Erosion of Freedom* Raymond Blackburn begins one chapter:

> The best way of testing whether a country is really free is to see how it treats its minorities. A good number of these are in prison. So the prisons of a country are a good indication of its standards of liberty. The prisons of Britain today belie its frantic boast to be a pattern of liberty for the world. They are run on the idea that it is a good thing to shut up a large number of people for a long time in a very small space with no work to do other than false or futile work.

More than twenty years later the situation has become worse.

In 1988 the Government was building 26 new gaols at a cost of £1bn to house an additional 22,000 people. Most prisons do not meet even the minimum standards set by their own rules – to provide exercise, work, baths, changes of clothes and adequate medical treatment. Britain now has a higher proportion of the population in gaol than any EEC country except Turkey and it is estimated that 80 per cent of these return at least once. Meanwhile the government has been forced to use the army to run camps as temporary prisons while growing public discussion looked to alternatives to ever more sentences – appropriate community service or tagging and curfew.

A crisis in the system was acknowledged in the 1980s, as was a marked increase in crime during the Thatcher years, averaging 6 per cent a year. Statistics should be treated with great caution since the accounting rules are periodically changed, but one set of figures suggests that the rate of offences rose from 500,000 in the

1950s to 3.5m in the 1980s. But the new policy of crime screening by Scotland Yard – under which officers do not pursue certain minor offences but concentrate on cases they believe they can solve – adds another complication to crime statistics.

In Kent, for example, Detective-Constable Ron Walker made allegations in 1986 about the police practice of write-offs whereby detectives visited petty criminals in prison and persuaded them to confess to unsolved crimes so that these could be written off to improve police statistics. Six per cent of crimes were written off nationally in 1974; by 1984 this had risen to 18 per cent. In June 1988 the annual report of the Metropolitan Police Commissioner suggested that one London household in 30 can expect to be burgled during the year and only 7 per cent of the burglars are likely to be caught.

For a majority of people the 'law' means the police. Their public image has been transformed in the years since 1945 from the 'bobby' on the beat (Dixon of Dock Green) through smart guys Starsky and Hutch to the riot squads facing miners' pickets or the crowds at Wapping.

By no stretch of the imagination is it easy to be a policeman and the less deferential, more 'disordered' society of the 1980s is far less likely to accept their role than was the case in the 1940s. Policemen are better paid, they have become an efficient lobby, and the methods they employ for crime detection and control are far more sophisticated – though whether they detect or prevent more crime is another matter. People are often ambivalent in their feelings; many who denigrate the police and refer to them as 'pigs' or fascists are none the less quick to demand police action if they are attacked, burgled or in trouble. Thus, at the best of times it is a difficult role. Having conceded that, it was also clear by the late 1980s that they no longer enjoyed the public confidence they once expected and received. In 1987 assaults on the police had risen by 20 per cent to 17,000 – an average of 50 a day.

There is an approximate ratio of one policeman to every 400 members of the population. Normally they do not carry firearms, though an increasing number have in recent years. In 1961 an American, George Clark (secretary to Bertrand Russell), was sentenced to nine months in prison for his part in an anti-nuclear demonstration and the magistrate described him as 'a nuisance to the police'. Left-wing political protesters have nearly always received a rough time from both police and courts but the phrase says a good deal about establishment attitudes.

James Callaghan was a Home Secretary who was popular with the police. He had acted as adviser on pay to the Police Federation and so understood many of their problems before being appointed to the Home Office in 1967. In his memoirs he tells a story of how, when *The Times* published a story of CID corruption, the Metropolitan Police Commissioner, Sir John Waldron, went to see him in deep distress at the damage the story would do and angry that the newspaper had not given prior warning. Callaghan says, 'I did not know until later that *The Times* had decided to publish because they feared that unless they did so the Yard would cover up a crime committed by their own men.' The newspaper report was proved correct, and only later when Maudling had become Home Secretary did the new Metropolitan Police Chief, Robert Mark, clean up the CID and put them under the control of the uniformed branch.

The biggest triumph of the police (and Callaghan) during his tenure of the Home Office was the handling of the huge anti-Vietnam demonstration of 1968. This was the year of student unrest and many people had advised cancellation, but Callaghan allowed the demonstration to go ahead. At the end of the evening the remaining police and demonstrators in Grosvenor Square linked arms to sing 'Auld Lang Syne'. Callaghan records smugly:

> The anticipated horrors of the day had been widely reported beforehand in overseas newspapers, and now congratulations flooded in from a number of countries. Newspapers in America, France, Italy and Holland all had kind things to say about Britain's way of handling the affair, and contrasted it with their own experience.

Other police developments were less happy. There have been massive increases in powers of surveillance with little public accountability. Patricia Hewitt (*The Abuse of Power*) listed a number of occasions when the force were responsible for serious assaults on members of the public (the New Zealand teacher Blair Peach, for example, who died as a result of police assault). There is clear need for additional supervision of their actions but 'the police have denied to the public the information about their activities which could make such supervision effective.'

In his book *The Political Police in Britain* Tony Bunyan records the extent of police records (now computerized) in the Police National Computer Unit (PNCU) and quotes from a *Police Review* article a disturbing passage about the information they collect and hold: 'Much of the information is personal details of a suspect, his family associates, way of life, and although it may seem to trespass on the freedom of the individual it is the bread and butter of successful policemanship.' Methods include phone-tapping, the use of bugs, informers, supergrasses and undercover workers.

One of the first actions of the Thatcher government after the 1979 election was to increase police pay by 20 per cent. Since then the police have had a high public profile yet despite good pay and sophisticated methods crime statistics have continued to rise faster than rates of apprehension and conviction. Their reputation did not flourish in 1988. Accusations of corruption centred upon a number of officers of high rank known to be or suspected of being Freemasons. There was the case of Mr Roc Sandford who alleged the police had framed him by planting drugs on him, and that he had been paid hush money to drop a civil case (no action was taken against the officers). It was revealed that the force are breaking the spirit of the European agreement on data protection because in addition to keeping people's names on computer they keep information on cards, which are not subject to the data protection act. A number of criminal prosecutions had to be dropped because exhibits had been tampered with by the police. And in June the Northern Ireland police authority decided to take no action against Sir John Hermon, Chief Constable of the RUC, and two of his senior officers over the long running 'shoot-to-kill' affair (Stalker) although disciplinary measures were taken against more junior members of the force.

It is always possible to fault the police whose job inevitably exposes them, but justice has to be seen to be done and an uncorrupted and incorruptible image is necessary if they are to retain public respect. In the 1980s the police did not enjoy such a reputation. In June 1988 the *Independent* pinpointed four areas of concern. They were writing of the Metropolitan Police, but their criticisms could be more widely applied:

> Over the past quarter of a century there have been four main areas of concern about the Metropolitan Police. They are race relations, law and order, criminal corruption and the growing public perception that the police succumb to the temptation to 'fit up' those they deem guilty if the unembroidered evidence against them is less than adequate to convince a jury. On the first three counts there have been substantial improvements.

There has been a marked loss of public confidence in the police as a whole. This results partly from increasing exposures of corrupt practices; and partly from the changed image which riot gear and confrontation tactics have produced. For the law to be effective the police must be effective, which means that first and foremost they must have the confidence of the public.

PART FIVE: THE MEDIA

17
British Culture and the Media

'There is no expedient to which man will not resort to avoid the real labour of thinking.'
SIR JOSHUA REYNOLDS

'English is the only sensible language, because a knife, for instance, is called by the French couteau, *by the Germans* Messer, *and so on, whereas we English call it a "knife", which is after all what a knife really is. . . .'*
ARTHUR KOESTLER

It is as difficult to define British culture as it is to decide upon the merits and deficiencies of the mass media. Their spread and availability – radio and television, the tabloid press, the cinema and videos, the vast output of pulp magazines and paperbacks – has been matched by public debate about the place of the arts and attempts to make the more élitist aspects of culture available to a wider public.

Writing in the early 1960s Malcolm Muggeridge said:

> The New Towns rise, as do the television aerials, dreaming spires; the streams flow, pellucid, through the comprehensive schools; the BBC lifts up our hearts in the morning, and bids us goodnight in the evening. We wait for Godot, we shall have strip-tease wherever we go. Give us this day our *Daily Express*, each week our Dimbleby. God is mathematics, crieth our preacher. In the name of Algebra, the Son, Trigonometry, the Father, and Thermodynamics, the Holy Ghost, Amen.

The promotion of the arts was taken seriously immediately after the war with government grants going regularly to the Arts Council, the British Film Institute and the Council of Industrial Design. The British Council expanded its overseas operations rapidly to promote wider knowledge of the United Kingdom and the English language. The Local Government Act 1948 empowered local authorities to use part of their rates revenues for encouragement of the arts. The 1951 Festival of Britain was a major government-sponsored act of faith, whose lasting monument is the Festival Hall on the South Bank of the Thames.

The Media

In 1988 the opening paragraph of the chapter 'Promotion of the Arts' in the Official Handbook reads:

> Artistic and cultural activity in Britain ranges from the highest standards of professional performance to the enthusiastic support and participation of amateurs. London is one of the leading world centres for drama, music, opera and dance, and festivals held in towns and cities throughout the country attract much interest. Glasgow, which has developed into an important artistic centre, has been chosen as European City of Culture for 1990. Many British playwrights, composers, film-makers, sculptors, painters, writers, actors, singers, choreographers and dancers enjoy international reputations. Television and radio play an important role in bringing a wide range of artistic events to a large audience.

Reading that description one would imagine that all was in good shape with British culture. Certainly the country is good at selling art; London leads the world in art auctioning, with Christie's and Sotheby's ranking as big business. In the field of architecture, a highly visible expression of a nation's culture, Britain has not done so well, although the rebuilding of Coventry after the war was an exception. In the 1980s the Prince of Wales decided to make architecture a major concern and his strictures, whether acceptable to architects or not, at least ensured a new level of debate.

But the Puritan tradition still permeates much British thinking and for many art remains 'an optional extra' rather than an integral part of life. Culture consists of attitudes as well as end products and if the British insist upon being Philistines that is an integral part of the whole. In *Communications* Raymond Williams asks why we always talk about publics and audiences and cultural systems when the only way to get good culture is to have good artists and performers. He suggests, 'Perhaps the most we can do is to try to create a society in which artists find it worth living.' This is somewhat disingenuous – after all, if we create a society in which everyone finds it worth living, perhaps artists will flourish with everybody else, despite the myth that creativity flourishes in adversity. What does seem essential in a conformist age where the media cater for the lowest common denominator is to ensure outlets for artists who insist upon working on their own terms. This is more difficult than it appears within a system whose purpose, according to Williams, 'is to protect, maintain, or advance a social order based on minority power'. In arguing for greater democratic freedom in the media he said: 'It [the democratic system] is firmly against authoritarian control of what can be said, and against paternal control of what ought to be said. But also it is against commercial control of what can profitably be said, because this also can be a tyranny.'

Rule by mediocracy is a guiding principle of the admass society and there are those who would question why opera should receive state subventions when 'pop' stars do not. The argument is interesting. In a capitalist society, if opera lovers are not prepared to pay for opera, however costly it may be, why should they be subsidized by the state, particularly when the majority come from the more affluent end of the economic spectrum? Part of the answer is that many people at the lower end of the spectrum would go to opera if they could afford to do so, which is a good argument for the sort of subsidy which makes opera so cheap in socialist countries, but it is only part of the answer.

The politics of the period since 1945 have had a major impact upon British culture. The turning of the royal family into elevated 'pop' stars, for example, and a new approach to what is acceptable or not in a democratic admass age – as opposed to automatic acceptance of what middle- and upper-middle-class pundits decreed to be their culture – have altered the parameters of discussion, though not necessarily for the better.

On the credit side has been the rejection of middle-class cultural values, at least in the sense that they alone set the tone. But the debit side has probably been greater. Much of Fleet Street and especially the popular press have abandoned their earlier educational and informational role in favour of vulgarity. One charge levelled against the mass media, especially television, is that it has undermined regional and working-class cultures. In a sense, of course, this must be true: where there is television there is no call for home activities to while away a dull evening. But nostalgia for an idyllic past of working men attending WEA classes to improve themselves should not blur the reality that very many people did little with their spare time, so that television has filled a gap rather than replaced more elevated activities.

Culture, education and leisure are inextricably intertwined and many talk of leisure with little idea of how to employ it. There are sports, of course, and activities which take over for a time, such as the bingo craze of the 1960s, and package holidays have become one of the biggest businesses of all. The British are also noted as hobbyists, and do-it-yourself keeps many people happy as they paint, redecorate, garden, and collect or make just about anything. Indeed, a great deal of British leisure activity consists in doing things rather than reading or watching or listening – except for television, which is far and away the major leisure pursuit among all classes, principally because it is so easy and undemanding.

Another outlet, in one sense peculiar to an affluent society, lies in charitable activities. These extend over a wide range of occupations from overseas voluntary or missionary work to endless societies covering any and every cause imaginable. Britain has a charity to suit every taste but if none exists there is nothing to stop people starting one of their own.

The Media

Whatever the educational system has achieved, it does not appear to have equipped people – at least in the popular political imagination – to cope with abundant leisure time. If this is the case, it is a black mark against British educational culture.

Unlike Germany, which is a consciously cultural-intellectual society, Britain is so anti-intellectual that clever people often go to considerable lengths to disguise their cleverness. The term 'intellectual' is more often than not one of denigration than praise, and the word is even more pejorative when coupled with the political Left, conjuring up dirty, long-haired individuals who, by implication, will argue for sinister, unpatriotic anti-British things. Happily, since 1945, a good many robust intellectuals like Richard Hoggart and Raymond Williams have argued for new approaches to many of Britain's cultural problems. One need not agree with their theses but they have made notable contributions to the debate as to the kind of cultural society she should aspire to achieve. Anthony Hartley is an intellectual of a different kind, who took pleasure in savaging the proposals of such trendsetters of the 1960s as Arnold Wesker. In *A State of England* (1963) he said, 'However, it is impossible not to agree that our national expenditure on culture is something of a scandal, even if we throw in education ...'

In the years since 1945 a great deal of attention has been paid to what the mass of people read or watch or regard as culture. In part this concern grew out of the 'socialist' revolution which followed the end of the war. The expansion of education and the greater opportunities afforded by a period of affluence meant that many people could contemplate new leisure activities. As a consequence, the attitudes of those who purvey culture took on a new significance.

Anyone who examines the tabloids or has watched the more vulgar chat-shows and the degrading giveaway programmes (pioneered by Wilfrid Pickles on sound radio with *Have a Go*), cannot be blamed for a low opinion of their regular audiences. Cecil King who ran the Mirror group and was in a position to know said: 'It is only the people who conduct newspapers and similar organizations who have any idea quite how indifferent, quite how stupid, quite how uninterested in education of any kind the great bulk of the British public are.' But such arguments are always circular; most people take the easiest route to anything and this is as true of a press baron as of his least reader. If there is no obvious demand or pressure to improve the quality of a tabloid newspaper, why bother? In that sense, such a statement is no more than a justification for what King was producing and selling. It takes effort, often of a sophisticated kind, to insist upon improvement or change yet a comparison of the *Daily Mirror* in the years immediately after World War Two, when it presented issues with clarity and simplicity and today's *Mirror* is indicative of a generation of deterioration.

The cinema began as a despised form of popular entertainment for the masses.

It took years of effort by highbrow critics before the intellectual arbiters of culture were prepared to accept it as an art form.

Writing in the mid-1950s Richard Hoggart lists the words used in editorials when the popular press wishes to denigrate. They are: pharisaical, timid, dull, equivocal, snobbish, canting, mealy-mouthed, conventional, hypocritical, ponderous, pompous, humbugging, official and boring. The list stands the test of time yet such words, which have a valid place if correctly employed, are misused in order to attack whatever is the target. Similar words or phrases in the 1980s are 'liberals' or 'the chattering-classes'.

British culture is also firmly divided along class lines. The working or lower classes – to use terms which we like to avoid nowadays – go to soccer matches (and provide the hooligans) or play bingo and read the tabloids; the middle classes go to theatre and opera, read good books and listen to classical music. The working classes go on package holidays to Ibiza and eat fish and chips on the sands, the middle classes sample the cuisine of France. Everybody watches television.

Various post-war writers, some with savage irony, have written of a passing middle- and upper-class world, regretting the replacement of an ordered society with one dominated by the welfare state and admass tastes. In effect they bewail the ending of class privileges. Much of it has been nostalgia, as with John Betjeman:

A game of Grandmother's Steps on the vicarage grass –
Father, a little more sherry. I'll fill your glass.

John Goodall produced a series of elegant little books (published by Macmillan) of pictures of the middle and upper-middle classes – *An Edwardian Season, An Edwardian Holiday, An Edwardian Summer, An Edwardian Christmas* at the end of the 1970s – and one of them was described in the *Sunday Telegraph* as 'a gloriously nostalgic book which depicts the life of a village somewhere in dear, old unadulterated England.' Harmless enough in their way yet part of a nostalgia which often bitterly resented the passing of the middle class's position of dominance. The snobberies of Evelyn Waugh provided television with one of its great series – *Brideshead Revisited* – watched as eagerly by those who did not belong to the class depicted as by those who did.

In Britain, culture has always been used as a mark of class and deep-seated middle-class antagonism to the admass culture is not so much because it is seen as awful, but because everyone can now share what was formerly exclusive. As Anthony Hartley claims, jealousy has played a major part in readjustments to culture:

But the disappointment felt by intellectuals at seeing the working classes reproduce a large number of middle-class characteristics (from an obsession with motor-cars to a fascination with television) was not something that they could easily admit to themselves. . . . Their aesthetic distaste for an increasingly bourgeois society had to be analysed in terms of a scapegoat . . . so now the apparent enjoyment with which the English masses receive the nonsense conveyed by film, television and newspaper can be put down to the account of skilful commercial corruption without any discussion of the real dilemmas of mass culture.

Williams deals with the class aspects of culture in a different way and suggests despite classifications – top people, a Third Programme type, the average reader of the *Daily Mirror* – that there are gradual scales between the different kinds of communications people accept. A particular problem is that an articulate minority tends to obtain most of the limelight in asserting what is good culture and dismiss what it does not like as admass and vulgar. The admass culture has meant the gradual replacement of the Oxbridge accent by the 'mid-Atlantic' voice which increasingly dominates television.

During the 1950s and 1960s, a period of release brought on by affluence and full employment, there was much self-consciously unself-conscious talk of the Working Classes. They were examined in a way that could happen only in a class-conscious country such as Britain. In part it was an attempt to undermine the class system by talking about it openly, admitting that there was a working class which differed so obviously from the middle and upper classes and suggesting that it did not matter, that they could change or be changed. In the educational field we had books such as *Education and the Working Class* by Brian Jackson and Dennis Marsden; and the new wave of theatre and literature brought the 'Angry Young Men' attacking a stuffy, establishment-ridden society with *Look Back in Anger, Lucky Jim, Saturday Night and Sunday Morning, Radcliffe, The Contenders*. The speed of change was especially noticeable during these years.

Richard Hoggart's *The Uses of Literacy* was perhaps the most important book of this period. Its impact was enormous and yet it now seems to have a curiously patronizing air. His constant reproduction of working-class speech – 'There's now't to choose between 'em', 'Well, it brings in the money, dunnit?', 'It doesn't matter what y'believe so long as yer 'eart's in the right place' – was part of the technique of the time, the careful re-examination of British society during a period when change was coming fast.

Discussing the changing availability of reading material Hoggart looks at 'blood-and-guts' sex novelettes and shows how they can not only be purchased from 'magazine shops' but from 'some' railway bookstalls though only from a corner of them: 'But boundaries move so quickly that within the last five or six years many ordinary stations have begun to stock this sort of paperback; they are ceasing to be even slightly furtive reading.' Raymond Williams said more hopefully:

> For the first time ever in Britain we are beginning to get a real range of good cheap books. This may be one of the most important things that has ever happened in our cultural history.... All our old assumptions about 'a tiny minority of serious readers' will have, in practice, to be revised.

Williams was optimistic. Television and escalating book prices killed that dream.

The British press has a relatively massive circulation, greater than any other Western country on a per capita basis. The national character of British newspapers was made possible by the smallness of the country, so that long before the era of electronic transmission of print it was possible to deliver copies of a newspaper anywhere in Britain on the day of publication. This gave owners immense influence and power and imbued quite a few of them with delusions of grandeur.

In 1954 there were 24 national newspapers including three London evenings – *Star*, *Evening News* and *Evening Standard* – and the Sundays. Then as now they divided into the 'quality' newspapers and the popular or tabloid papers. By 1988 the number had dropped to 21 with the *Daily Herald*, *News Chronicle*, *Daily Worker*, *Daily Sketch*, *Star*, *Evening News*, *Sunday Dispatch*, *Reynolds News*, *Sunday Chronicle*, *Sunday Empire News* and *Sunday Graphic* disappearing, and several newspapers changing their titles – the *People* became the *Sunday People* for example – while a number of new names appeared: *Morning Star* (1966), *Star* (1978), *Sun* (1964), *Today* (1986), *Independent* (1986), *Sunday Mirror* (1963), *Mail on Sunday* (1982), *News on Sunday* (1987), *Sunday Telegraph* (1961). Three papers had circulations well in excess of 3m – *Daily Mirror*, *Sun* and *Sunday Mirror* while the *News of the World* maintained its pre-eminence with a 1988 circulation of 4.94m, though this represented a big drop from the 8.13m of the mid-1950s.

The 1980s saw the virtual demise of Fleet Street as a majority of national papers moved editorial and printing facilities out of the centre of London to Wapping or elsewhere when they adopted new technology and fought bitter battles with the unions in the process. In 1988 the national newspapers had a daily circulation of 14.8m and the Sundays 17.5m. Readership is of course considerably greater. Although, to quote *Britain 1988*, 'The press caters for a variety of political views, interests and levels of education,' there has long been argument, especially from the Left, that the newspapers are right-wing and do not give left-wing views a fair airing.

Judgements of the quality of newspapers are biased according to the views of those making them but many people would argue that *The Times* under the ownership of Rupert Murdoch had deteriorated to the point where it could no longer claim to be a national institution – long its proud boast: 'No one can understand *The Times* who does not understand that it is an institution' had been editorialized in 1967 (elsewhere it was described as 'a tribal notice board'). But the justification for such claims had disappeared by the 1980s. The new *Independent*, on the other hand, managed overnight to establish itself on a par with the other 'quality' papers.

A crucial difference in media impact has been the change from what once would have been a commonplace remark – 'Oh, but it was in the papers' to indicate that some current piece of information was true to the present 'Oh, but it was on the television'. That indicates clearly the relative position of television and newspapers as the perceived purveyors of news. As a result many of the popular papers have become purveyors of stories, comment or entertainment rather than hard news, which people now expect from television.

Newspapers are big business and part of the entertainment industry. In 1962 Raymond Williams wrote, 'The organization of communications is then not for use, but for profit, and we seem to have passed the stage in which there has to be any pretence that things are otherwise.' That is even more true now and can be 'verified' by examining the conduct of the press barons.

Press barons have always tended to be larger-than-life figures, from Lords Northcliffe and Rothermere, the obsessive Beaverbrook and the paranoid King, to the relatively gentle figure of Lord Thomson of Fleet through to Rupert Murdoch and Robert Maxwell. Newspaper proprietors regard themselves as naturals for honours; those from the 'colonies' in particular seek elevation to the ranks of the British aristocracy. In the early part of the century the owners of the popular press felt they had an educational duty towards their readership, but little of that tradition seems to have carried over into the television age, when the principal aim of the tabloids would appear to be the provision of sensational stories – crime and sex scandals predominating – as an acceptable alternative to the 'box'.

The Thatcher years have brought the press into conflict with the government. They have also highlighted an ongoing battle – what legitimately ought and ought not to be published. We have seen the growing practice of secret trials and on one day in February 1987 the press were banned from 66 High Court cases. An Old Bailey journalist, Tim Crook, sought to change the law to allow journalists to seek a judicial review of a judge's decision to apply contempt of court orders (which ban publication of proceedings). He said: 'Banned from the courtroom and without the right to challenge the ban, the press cannot fulfil this [reporting] role. Judges in this respect are above the law.'

The 1980s witnessed a revolution. As Rupert Murdoch said of the old system: 'If newspapers can be run so inefficiently and survive, this must potentially be a very profitable business.' He and other owners determined to do what an older generation had shied away from, and confronted the print unions, helped by the anti-union climate of the time. The result was a drastic reduction in labour costs and restrictive practices, the removal to new headquarters, the adoption of new technology and, as a result, bigger profits. It also witnessed some new lows in taste. As Donald Trelford, editor of the *Observer* and therefore an interested party, wrote in an article for the *Independent*:

> Curiously, while standards have improved at one end of the market, on the popular front things are worse than I can remember. Quotations, even whole stories, routinely invented; intrusions into privacy commonplace; political 'angling' blatant. The *Star* is a shameless and shaming new phenomenon that makes even hardened popular journalists blench.

There is nothing quite like the self-righteousness of one journalist when attacking the taste of other journalists, yet Trelford had a point: the standards of the popular press are ghastly. One result was another attempt (one had been tried and failed) to introduce a bill to protect privacy. Predictably the press opposed on the grounds that the public (described as *robust* for these purposes) had a right to know. Their intrusiveness can be shocking, but in a society where official secrecy is a passion and a disease the more freedom there is the better.

Two kinds of attack were made upon the press during the later 1980s: those from official circles, often Downing Street, which were designed to muzzle, often represented as in the national interest; and attacks upon the dishonesty and muckraking or intrusions into privacy and grief generally associated with the tabloids. In 1988 Ann Clwyd, a journalist and a Labour MP, introduced her Unfair Reporting and Right of Reply Bill. The toothless Press Council has condemned some excesses but these are treated like parking fines.

Another problem concerns identification: where does the paper stand on issues and what are its politics? A majority is to the right of centre but a few identify with the moderate Left or liberals, while the *Daily Mirror* is the only tabloid to support the Labour Party. Not to have a clear position is seen as a weakness. Thus Michael Leapman, writing of the *Observer* in 1988 said:

> Many believe that one of the *Observer*'s problems is that its moral conscience has been less apparent since its palmy days in the 1950s and 1960s, when it was the champion of anti-colonialism and Third World issues. 'It's left of centre but it hasn't any great stirring causes,' Mr Worsthorne comments. 'It doesn't have a very identifiable political stance.'

People like their papers to be partisan and to reflect their views rather than to be impartial and objective.

Advertising has always been a key to successful newspapers just as it has been cause of complaint from the Left because capitalist companies were unwilling to advertise in anti-capitalist journals. Any consideration of the media, therefore, must take account of its principal source of revenue – advertising. To obtain the big money papers and television programmes have to go for popular markets and this is where the question of admass entertainment becomes circular and exceptionally difficult to sort out. To quote Anthony Hartley again:

> The apparatus of modern publicity is one of the numerous consequences of the development of industrial mass production, and to attack it in isolation from the process of which it is a symptom is to take a superficial view of its significance. The importance which a number of intellectuals and journalists have attached to it is another example of a tendency to be diverted by irritating detail.

Hartley is saying that you cannot have culture in isolation, in this case isolated from capitalist mass production methods with all the pressures these exert upon any form of mass media.

The British film industry, whose Ealing Studios enjoyed their heyday immediately after the war, has been a major casualty of the television age even though the industry experienced a revival in the early 1980s. Unmistakably middle class in the immediate post-war years – *Brief Encounter, The Best Years of our Lives* – or popular escapist – *The Man in Grey, The Wicked Lady* – or stiff-upper-lip, war nostalgia – *Cockleshell Heroes, The Cruel Sea*, some of these post-war films – *The Third Man* or *Odd Man Out* – were of very high calibre indeed. But cinema went into the doldrums during the 1950s though it experienced something of a revival in terms of quality of output during the 1960s, with *Saturday Night and Sunday Morning, The Prime of Miss Jean Brodie, Accident* and *The Servant*, for example. At the beginning of the 1980s it was again, apparently, on the upswing – *The Elephant Man* and *Chariots of Fire* – though the boom faltered by the late 1980s. In any case it was small-scale, quality output reflecting relatively tiny audiences compared with the 1940s and early 1950s when huge cinemas were filled every night and many changed their programmes twice a week.

Radio too has suffered, taking second place by a long way to the ubiquitous television. Its great days were during and immediately after World War Two when BBC News, Tommy Handley in *ITMA, Housewives' Choice* and then the early and immensely popular sound 'soap operas' such as *Dick Barton, Special Agent* or *Mrs Dale's Diary* were the staple diet of millions of listeners. Broadcasting was then the monopoly of the BBC, and the intrusions of Radio Luxembourg advertisements were regarded as foreign vulgarity. The Home Service, the Light Programme and the Third Programme catered for Britain at home while the external services were divided between the General Overseas Service, special services directed to the Commonwealth and services directed to foreign countries.

Despite enormous changes affecting broadcasting, radio has survived astonishingly well. A Green Paper of February 1987 outlined government proposals for the future of broadcasting including the addition of services run on commercial lines. Meanwhile the three BBC channels had become four – Radio 1 (rock and pop music), Radio 2 (light entertainment and sport), Radio 3 (classical music, drama, poetry, documentaries) and Radio 4 (news, current affairs, drama, comedy, documentaries, panel games, Parliamentary coverage). The BBC had to compete with rivals – Capital Radio, London's LBC and the new night time service Radio Radio, for example – so that proliferation was the most obvious feature of the late 1980s. In January 1988 the Home Secretary, Douglas Hurd, announced the allocation of networks by sealed bid to establish a new national network. What appeared to be the principal objective of the government approach was deregulation in ownership – a privatization of the airwaves.

Even taking television into account, possibly the most spectacular cultural breakthrough has been the emergence of the pop culture. The 1960s saw a boom in popular music epitomized by the rise to fame and wealth of the Beatles. In 1962 came 'From Me To You', 'She Loves You', 'I Want To Hold Your Hand' and by 1963 they had achieved international fame. Between February 1963 and June 1972 their group sales were estimated at 545m in singles equivalents. By 1964 the Rolling Stones were competing in popularity and sales, 'It's All Over Now', 'Little Red Rooster'. They were the symbols of liberated youth. In the 1970s came David Bowie and then in 1977 the punk era got under way with The Sex Pistols, who set a new fashion in outrageousness.

Britain also enjoyed a renaissance of classical music, its orchestras obtaining a new lease of life from the recording industry which the long-playing record revolutionized. Benjamin Britten (*Peter Grimes, Billy Budd, War Requiem*) helped Britain's reputation, which was not outstanding in preceding centuries.

In no field does Britain make so consistently high a contribution as in literature. In the mid-1950s, for example, publishers were producing 13,000 new book titles a year. Thirty years later 58,000 titles were published, of which 44,000 were new titles and the remainder reprints or new editions. In 1982 a much overdue public lending rights scheme was introduced whereby authors received payments from a central fund when their books were borrowed from public libraries (then estimated to hold a stock of 137m books).

Immediately after the war the literary field was dominated by such intellectual critics as F. R. Leavis; or George Orwell whose *Animal Farm* and *1984* had a lasting impact and entered school and university curricula on an apparently permanent basis. The period produced many other literary riches: the novels of Graham Greene, the poems of Dylan Thomas, Anthony Powell's *Dance to the*

Music of Time and C. P. Snow's series *Strangers and Brothers*, Anthony Burgess, William Golding, Iris Murdoch and the Angry Young Men of the John Osborne school who emerged in the mid-1950s and introduced a new realist school in theatre and novels.

Despite its sterilities and the abiding strands of philistine puritanism which are part of the British character, the period since 1945 has been one of rich cultural growth. That is not to say that some things have not been bad. The educational debate – narrow élitist excellence versus broader all-round training – continued unchecked, with some silly and counter-productive additions about race and sex complicating an already complex field. Periodically, debates about grants for the arts surface and successive governments demonstrate their meanness, less perhaps in the sense of how much or how little money they make available than because they give the impression that the arts are peripheral, worth an annual debate but not to be taken seriously.

Occasionally culture is enlivened by scandal, the most notable example being the long-drawn-out obscenity trial of the unexpurgated version of Lawrence's *Lady Chatterley's Lover*, which enlivened the early 1960s. Censorship is another form of cultural philistinism. The Obscene Publications Act of 1959 resulted from a series of prosecutions brought against publishers in 1954; it was altered in 1964 (to allow a publisher to opt for trial by jury) after a magistrate had found against Mayflower Books for publishing *Fanny Hill*. As Donald Thomas, the author of *A Long Time Burning*, asks of censorship:

> The relevant question at any stage of human history is not 'Does censorship exist?' but rather, 'Under what sort of censorship do we now live?' The technology of the later twentieth century offers the means of silencing men – without the danger of making them martyrs – by the most effective method of all, by ignoring them.

Although the arts have always had to contend with the prurience of such self-appointed guardians of morals as Mrs Whitehouse, the 1980s threatened more dangerous government-inspired censorship. It came in several forms. There were attempts to prevent television comment upon the SAS killings of unarmed IRA men in Gibraltar when the Prime Minister talked of 'trial by television'. Her Press Secretary, Bernard Ingham, decided to speak on the record and told the *Observer* that the standards of the media had declined 'to the point of institutionalized hysteria'. It was clear that the Prime Minister, who becomes paranoid when she cannot control attacks on her policies, was trying to create a climate 'which will not tolerate the media overstepping certain bounds'. Ingham's intervention was denounced by Labour's Roy Hattersley, who accused him of usurping the Home Secretary's role as Minister responsible for the media. As the *Observer* said in an editorial on 15 May 1988, with too much truth for comfort: 'Britain was shamefully bracketed with South Africa and India at last week's annual assembly of the International Press Institute as countries where media freedoms are at special risk.' Management of news from Downing Street had become one of the most obvious aspects of the Thatcher years.

18
Television in Every Home

'We are not a nation of intellectuals.'
JOHN PROFUMO

'One dull boy, when asked what was the most important change that television had brought him, said, "I can look at television of an evening instead of sitting at home and doing nothing."'
HILDE HIMMELWEIT

Once the BBC monopoly had been broken in the 1950s there followed competition by independent companies and advertisers to find their way into every home where they have stayed, more or less, ever since. Although it had been around on a small scale since the 1930s it was only in the 1950s that the power of television became apparent and that the 'box' became a permanent part of life, the principal source of entertainment and news and current events, and an arbiter of leisure time as other activities were fitted around the evening's programmes.

By the 1980s its presence in the home was taken for granted, but there was a period during the 1950s and into the 1960s when its programmes seemed to have become the most important focus of life outside work. Acquaintances would remark on how awful the previous day's programming had been: 'nothing worth watching all evening' although it never occurred to them to switch off. That mesmeric attraction has passed and for many people television is the backdrop to some other activities, at any rate until it's time for the favourite soap opera or chat show – *EastEnders* or whatever.

'Broadcasting is based on the tradition that it is a public service accountable to the people through Parliament.' So runs the opening sentence of the chapter on television and radio in *Britain 1988*. Well, yes and no! The tradition of public service is certainly a part of the BBC, while the Independent Broadcasting Authority (IBA) is the body responsible for the provision of non-BBC television and radio services throughout the country. These two authorities are independent but subject to broad control by Parliament, and must ensure that programmes display balance, are accurate with regard to news presentation and show impartiality over controversial subjects. The IBA operates a code of advertising standards. The Home Secretary is responsible for questions of broadcasting policy.

In 1988 there were 15 television programme companies covering the 14 regions (2 cover London) which are subject to regulation by the IBA. Of the 4 television channels in operation 2 belong to the BBC and 2 are controlled by the IBA.

During the second half of the 1950s a television set was the priority consumer durable in a majority of homes. By mid-June 1963 (10 years after the successful campaign to launch independent television) there were 12.75m TV licences in Britain and according to BBC Listener Research time spent viewing by the 'upper middle class' was 11 hours a week and by the 'working class' 13 hours a week. Between 1960 and 1964 the number of households owning a set rose from 82 per cent to 91 per cent. By 1964/5 the daily audience was estimated at 25m or just under half the total population and Britain accounted for more than 1 in 4 of all sets in Europe and one-twelfth of TV sets worldwide.

By 1988 television viewing was by far the most popular leisure pastime, with 95 per cent of the population viewing for an average of 27 hours each week. Moreover, 50 per cent of households now have two or more sets and rent or own video-cassette recorders (VCRs). According to OECD statistics, Britain had 336 sets per 1000 of population (in 1984) – higher than most European countries though lower than Denmark, Finland, Germany and Sweden and considerably lower than Canada or the USA (621 per 1000).

Anthony Sampson argues in *Anatomy of Britain* that commercial television

> was an innovation more sudden and dramatic than the nationalized industries, and like them full of doctrinal implications: while *they* stood as a monument to socialist doctrine, commercial TV is a monument to the free-enterprise lobby of the Conservative party.

Within a few years the commercial companies had become immensely powerful, their programmes more influential than many newspapers, their profits huge. It is the question of profitability which brings us to the core of the culture debate: profit is more likely to be derived from programmes which aim at the lowest common denominator, the admass market, than from those which educate – which makes the claim of public service look somewhat thin. Public service ought to put quality before profit.

In the early 1950s a group of influential figures outside Parliament, including the novelist and former BBC TV controller, Norman Collins, joined with Conservative MPs to lobby for a commercial service. Anthony Seldon says in *Ruling Performance* that Lord Woolton told the Cabinet on 3 April 1952 'the Cabinet committee he was chairing on the issue favoured the introduction of commercial

The Media

television, largely because "a large majority" of the government's supporters favoured the ending of the BBC monopoly.' The populist element of this recommendation was very important, because Churchill and Eden, as well as the Postmaster General (Lord de la Warr) who was responsible for broadcasting, were all against commercial television.

The Television Bill split the old paternalists and the modern free-enterprise Tories but was carried by 296 votes to 269 (the paternalists going along with the free-enterprisers) and the first regular ITV programmes were shown in 1955. A number of powerful new companies – Associated Television, Associated-Rediffusion, Granada, ABC – rapidly became household names. In Edinburgh Roy Thomson, who opened his commercial TV company, Scottish Television, in August 1957, made his celebrated remark: 'You know, it's just like having a licence to print your own money.' Some smaller stations followed and within a decade a new industry was not only firmly established but had created a pantheon of tycoons and stars who were seen to be some of the most influential people in the country. By the second half of the 1980s each of the 14 ITV areas was transmitting over 100 hours of programmes a week.

The instant quality of television, which brings events from all corners of the globe into the sitting room, has revolutionized perceptions of the world in which we live. The Vietnam War, for example, has been described as the 'first sitting-room war'. Famine in Africa, an air disaster, a political coup – all have an immediacy never possible with the printed word. It has also created a form of distortion and a sense of prying possible only with visual media. *The Fog of War* (1987) analysed the media on the battlefield and pinpointed the strength and weakness of television: 'Television has a unique ability to show the events and the people of the day. It has an unrivalled immediacy and impact. But the medium also has its weaknesses and among these is a limited ability to put events in context.'

Being 'there' demands an aggressive pursuit of news which is far more costly than with newspapers, since cameras and equipment have to be where the action is: no picture, no story. When the commander of the 1st British Corps in Germany, Lieutenant-General Martin Farndale, was asked by journalists how much time a commander could allow for getting cameras in position, he replied: 'My job is to win the battle, not to produce a bloody good story about a battle we had just lost.'

Wars since 1945 have been fought mainly in the Third World and from Vietnam onwards it has usually been possible to have the cameras *there*, transmitting instant material. Until, that is, the Falklands – the isolated nature of that war meant that the media could get there only by courtesy of the Royal Navy and could transmit their pictures back by courtesy of channels controlled by the military. Delays between filming and transmission (evidence by ITN to House of Commons defence committee) were 11 days for the surrender and 21 days for the *Sheffield* pictures. *The Fog of War* remarks: 'viewers had to wait longer to see some pictures from the Falklands War than the twenty days which readers of *The Times* had to wait for William Howard Russell's despatch on the Charge of the Light Brigade in 1854.'

The greatest objection to television is an intellectual one: that it trivializes and reduces serious matters to vignettes which all can digest and acts as a drug of the sort envisaged in *Brave New World*. Writing in 1963, when discussion about its impact was taken more seriously (if only because of its relative newness) J. A. C. Brown (in *Techniques of Persuasion*) said:

> The fact is that the mass media are there to be made use of, and what use is made of them depends upon the individual. He can drug himself into insensitivity or use the media selectively – and the ability to do so must begin with education, when it comes to be regarded not as a childhood activity but as a process continuing throughout life.

Unfortunately a majority of people have limited capacity to exercise discrimination in the choices they make. An American professor, Neil Postman (*Amusing Ourselves to Death*), has suggested that television creates a pseudo-reality of its own which in the end reduces everything to one long 'trivialized, sentimentalized stream of entertainment' and that the values of public life – whether political, religious or academic – are reduced to a level of superficiality. The glossy or slick lifestyles projected are always an unattainable cut above actuality; while anybody with a serious message is shown with artificial reverence as though he or she is a superior commercial.

Its impact has to be judged at a number of levels: on our leisure habits, on the cinema as a rival, on children, young people and the old, and on the press and politics.

The 1980s saw the arrival of all-night and breakfast television, with some figures in the industry advocating a round-the-clock service. Writing about the decision to introduce yet more channels in the name of freedom, Richard Ingrams said in the *Observer* of 10 July 1988:

> I have always believed that television is a form of drug in that it induces a vacancy of mind and a mild kind of 'high'. It is certainly addictive, if figures suggesting that the average person watches at least four hours per day are anything to go by.

Its easy availability in the home made it a natural winner in the entertainment stakes: night after night at the turn of a switch, cheap, requiring no effort to go out, it solves problems like keeping the children quiet or providing 'company' for the old. Its faults – among them the low quality of many programmes – are compensated for by its presence: it is always there. Moreover, as John Profumo remarked, the British are not an intellectual people, and many low-brow programmes have huge followings. Although those responsible talk about maintaining high standards, the fact is that many programmes are of mind-boggling banality.

The near demise of the cinema as the leading form of mass entertainment is merely one in a series of casualties in the television age. For a time the English pub was badly hit as habitués watched at home, but there was a partial recovery when pubs installed sets of their own.

More serious debate concerns the effect of television upon children. The Nuffield Foundation sponsored a major study of its effects on the young (published as *Television and the Child* in 1958), whose findings were both disturbing and reassuring. In *Techniques of Persuasion*, Brown is generally sceptical of the harmful effects on children: 'What influences it has for the good are not usually discussed, although talking to children certainly gives the impression that they are better-informed about the world in which they live than formerly ...', and later:

> although many investigators believe that scenes of violence which may leave the average adolescent unharmed might stimulate an emotionally disturbed child or gang and reinforce their delinquent tendencies, others believe on the contrary that such scenes are actually a deterrent to delinquency, permitting youth to work off its aggression vicariously.

Children can be stimulated to explore new things, are capable of being selective and show a robustness in facing unpleasantness on the screen or in real life not always appreciated by those who would regulate cultural tastes. None of this, however, is to suggest that children are not also open to adverse influence from poor television or from too much.

More people have testified to its benefits in relation to the old or sick than in any other field. It is a great comfort to single, lonely and old people – as often as not it acts as a presence in the home where there would otherwise be none.

The impact of television upon journalism is seen principally in the way newspapers have ceased to be the frontline purveyors of news and, in the case of the tabloids, have turned more and more to entertainment or titillation. The 'quality' papers have turned increasingly to comment or 'in depth' analyses and 'insight' articles.

Macmillan was the first leading politician to use the medium and to see how it might be used. His appearance with President Eisenhower, who was on an informal visit to London in 1959, has been described as 'theatre of a very high order'. Television has been one of the most important forces in building party leaders up as presidential figures. As Macmillan told Anthony Sampson: 'Learning to cope with television isn't easy. Either you get involved in a kind of circus act with interviewers or you try solos ... just about the most difficult television technique. How *can* you give a fireside talk to a television camera?'

Ever since politicians have been coming to terms with television. As Max Nicholson said in *The System* (1967), 'We may have reached the point where a poor manner is a worse disqualification for party leadership than membership of the House of Lords, and moreover is one much more difficult to disclaim.' By the 1970s politicians were far more concerned about encounters with the 'heavy' interviewers such as Sir Robin Day than about old-fashioned public meetings – unless the cameras were going to be there.

In February 1988 the House of Commons approved in principle 'an experiment in the public broadcasting of its proceedings by television'. There had long been resistance among MPs to the idea: partly, perhaps, because some guessed how stupid parliamentary proceedings could be made to appear: old habits of lounging with feet up on benches or braying furiously at a speaker could be mercilessly isolated; partly, also, because of the inevitable pressure to play to the audience instead of debating an issue seriously. On the other hand, why should not our Members of Parliament be subjected to the sort of camera scrutiny applied to just about everybody and everything else?

In Thatcher's Britain two contradictory principles appear to motivate the government with regard to the media. On the one hand a move towards more censorship; on the other, greater 'freedom', by which is meant fewer controls. Thus, also in February 1988, the government refused to allow any of its front bench spokesmen to appear on the Channel 4 programme, *How Free to Speak*, which debated the increasing use of legal injunctions to gag the media. They also showed great reluctance to accept European moves for new standards, so that, for example, no programme less than 45 minutes long would contain a commercial break. Mr Hurd told a conference on cable and satellite broadcasting: 'To limit the extent to which programmes could be interrupted would have serious implications for the presentation and scheduling of broadcast advertising in this country.' He went on: 'The system of natural breaks has stood the test of time. To change radically might adversely affect the amount of advertising revenue available to commercial TV.' Britain also opposed European pressures to ban the advertising of tobacco and alcohol.

Then Ulster reared its head, as it does all too frequently. First came the government onslaught on television for not surrendering untransmitted film of the attack on the two soldiers killed at the IRA funeral. In the House of Commons Mrs Thatcher said: 'I believe everyone, the media included, have a bounden duty to ... see that those who perpetrated the terrible crime we saw on television, and which disgusted the whole world, are brought to justice.' Outside the Commons, Norman Tebbit said:

> If, as the TV authorities suggest, there is conflict between their ability to report vicious and sadistic crimes of the kind we saw in Belfast recently, and their obligation to assist the forces of the law to arrest and prosecute those who committed such vile crimes, then there can be no doubt that the obligation to fight crime comes before the privilege of reporting it.

This was typical loaded Tebbit language but the rift between government and television was over a clear principle: while Tory MPs were calling for restrictions on coverage of terrorist events in Northern Ireland (shades of South Africa) the media insisted that the excesses of groups such as the IRA should 'be placed on the public record in direct and graphic form'. The *Independent* argued:

> If it becomes routine for the police to request, and obtain, untransmitted film and unpublished photographs from television stations and newspapers when the law has been broken, then those who gather such material will be regarded, however unfairly, as no more than unpaid police agents. Their independence will be compromised beyond recall.

Hard on the heels of the Belfast killings came the SAS shootings in Gibraltar. This led to the row about 'trial by television' when Geoffrey Howe asked the IBA to postpone a documentary which provided new evidence on the shooting of the three men. The IBA refused and *Death on the Rock* went ahead.

Entertainment may be what most people want from television but the presentation of the news is probably its most influential activity. In a precise sense this is opinion forming: about the country's politics, the Third World, trouble spots such as South Africa or the Middle East, questions of legal or social justice. And the news sensationalizes and trivializes. The formula used gives the game away: presentation by two people who alternately read snippets 'short enough for the most limited attention span', lots of pictures and what in the trade is called a 'soft' item at the end after the more grim bits to relax people into thinking the world is really all right.

The majority of time is devoted to entertainment pure and simple; BBC figures in 1956 showed entertainment 67 per cent, information 24 per cent and orientation or public events 9 per cent. Comparable figures for ITA presentations were 78, 14 and 8 per cent. Some programmes achieve enormous popularity and may run indefinitely, while others, such as *That Was The Week That Was*, are appreciated for their political punch or satire. Norman Collins once said: 'If one gave the public exactly what it wanted it would be a perfectly appalling service ... the overwhelming mass of the letters we get are illiterate.' Unfortunately, far too many programmes do appear to be aimed at the lowest common denominator; Brown quotes the Head of BBC Audience Research as saying: 'You cannot reinforce something that is not there.'

TV personalities have become major public figures – when the television chat-show personality, Russell Harty, spent five weeks fighting hepatitis before he died in June 1988 his struggle was headline news. And when the long-lasting serial *Crossroads* was brought to an end after 23 years its demise was reported in the press as though it were the death of a much-loved human being. But the sting was in the tail. As Sandra Barwick reported in the *Independent*, 'the programme did not change the profile of its viewers sufficiently to attract more advertisements.'

The four staples of popular television are chat shows, quiz shows, soap operas and sport. They occupy the prime slots, have the largest audiences, attract the most lucrative advertisements and provide a large proportion of people with their daily fix of entertainment. And, of course, they have made compères and presenters – David Frost or Terry Wogan, for example – rich and famous.

It is easy to denigrate television from the moral high ground; Lord Reith compared commercial television to the bubonic plague and asked loftily: 'Need we be ashamed of moral values, or of intellectual and ethical objectives?' Periodically its debasing, trivializing nature comes under attack and the medium certainly fuels such onslaughts. But it has been defended by showmen such as Lew Grade, who argue that they are in the entertainment business and will provide what the people want.

Perhaps one of its worst aspects results from those guidelines which insist upon impartiality over controversial subjects. How is it possible not to be biased over Hitler and his gas ovens? And once that question has been posed how not to be biased over Chile, South Africa and many other awful injustices? One of the problems is the opposition of those who run television to the presentation of genuine controversy, because taking sides alienates some of the audience and the last thing ratings-conscious programmers want is to alienate anyone.

In 1988 the Broadcasting Standards Council was set up, with Sir William Rees-Mogg as its first chairman. It was to start as a voluntary organization, though it was far from clear just what role was expected of it. At a time when channels are multiplying (representing the unfettered free enterprise approach favoured at present), the Broadcasting Standards Council seemed more than anything a gesture to demonstrate that the government was a caring one.

Shortly after this the all-party House of Commons Committee on the Future of Broadcasting reported on its findings on the BBC, IBA, ITV and Channel 4. It recommended that the BBC should continue to be funded by an index-linked licence fee, that Channel 4 should remain unchanged, and it expressed concern that either the BBC or ITV should give up regional coverage because of increased

The Media

competition. It recommended that the Broadcasting Standards Council should be confined to research activities and not have powers to vet programmes in advance. It was an altogether refreshing approach given growing government emphasis upon vetting and censorship powers. Those who advocate censorship are mainly vocal minorities out of tune with popular demand and the tradition of freedom which the Conservatives claim to uphold. The Thatcher government took a hammering from the media over the *Spycatcher* affair and there were signs that it wished to impose censorship restrictions, the wish reinforced by the row over the Ulster mob killings and the SAS shootings in Gibraltar.

Meanwhile, major changes were under consideration, including the auction of 16 ITV franchises to the highest bidder when they come up for renewal in 1992. This came after Hurd had announced that three new national commercial radio stations were to be set up in 1989, also to go to the highest bidder provided those bidding could satisfy the licensing authority that they would provide reasonable programming. The independent television companies pledged opposition to the government's plans to switch to competitive tendering (the announcement had wiped millions of pounds off the value of their shares) and the director general of the IBA, John Whitney, expressed concern about the 'guardianship of the audience, who look at television for enjoyment. We must make sure they are not let down by an influx of sub-standard programmes.' As a result of sustained pressures over the government's deregulation plans the Home Secretary, Douglas Hurd, announced major concessions in June 1989, including the provision of substantial fines, if ITV companies failed to meet programme promises; Channel 4 would become a public trust instead of being privatized; although franchise owners will remain subject to takeover.

What was clear was the approaching end of an era. By the early 1990s the number of television channels will have multiplied, offering a far greater number of choices. Whether the quality will be high is another question. Speaking to the Press Association in June 1988, Mrs Thatcher said she did not fear that expansion would drive television down market. At the same time she insisted that if the media failed to exercise self-restraint she would 'strain everything' so that young people were protected from violence and pornography. Few politicians can manage so well combining maximum free enterprise with a high moral tone.

Jeremy Isaacs, who pioneered Channel 4 for the independent producers, has no doubt that television enriches people's lives although he adds the caveat that there are 'soma' elements about it since it can easily take people into a television fantasy world. He suggests that it should provide enough information to help people make judgements and that it should entertain and send people happily to bed – 'It can and should be a boon.'

19
The BBC

'It was in fact the combination of public service motive, sense of moral obligation, assured finance and the brute force of monopoly which enabled the BBC to make of broadcasting what no other country has made of it.'
JOHN REITH

'Wherefore dost thou not bite the tongue of insolence with the tooth of discretion?'
JAMES ELROY FLECKER

'The BBC does itself untold harm by its excessive sensitivity. At the first breath of criticism the Corporation adopts a posture of a hedgehog at bay.'
ANNAN REPORT ON BROADCASTING

There was a time when the BBC was simply there, one of those institutions like the monarchy which were expected to go on for ever. Its pre-eminence after the war when it went its magisterial way as an arbiter of national standards should have alerted its hierarchy to the likelihood of challenge. This came when its monopoly was broken to permit independent commercial television. It came increasingly under attack from the Labour Party for what were seen as right-wing, pro-Conservative views and during the 1960s of the open 'permissive' society and the 1970s when aspects of that society became entrenched in public attitudes the BBC was seen as a pillar of a stuffy and reactionary establishment, even when programmes such as *That Was The Week That Was* took hearty swipes at it. This may not have been fair, but it was part of the public perception.

One of the ironies of the story is that the real onslaught came from the Right rather than the Left, and from the most powerful Conservative government of the century. Neither the BBC nor many other institutions seen as favourable to an 'establishment' status quo had bargained for a right-wing government prepared to undermine the power of any institution regarded as an alternative source of power.

In *The Establishment* (1959) the Corporation was savaged by Henry Fairlie. He mocked the sort of men appointed to its Board of Governors and held up to ridicule the rituals the BBC had perfected in relation to public events. He gave a sarcastically amusing account of how eminent persons were interviewed, care being taken that they are not upset, and he referred to 'the assumption that underlies all the BBC's attitudes to authority: namely, that it *ought* to be on the side of authority.' He claimed that it was opposed to real controversy and argued:

> The BBC remains today as deferential to those in authority and as predisposed in their favour as ever Reith could have wished that it be. It allows fair play only when the two front benches are agreed about a policy, and then only to the front-bench point of view.

Writing at the dawn of the permissive decade, Fairlie suggested that the BBC fostered deference to the accepted order of things:

> It is difficult, in these days, to persuade a majority of people to accept ideas merely because they are advanced by authority or prescribed by custom. It is far easier and more effective to persuade them that there really is no difference between apparently opposing points of view, that there really is no conflict either of ideas or interests with which they need bother their heads, that there really is nothing worth getting excited about.

By the 1980s that line was no longer possible. The age of deference had passed, the ratings battle had forced the BBC into the marketplace, and the logic of such competition meant that sooner or later it would clash with authority. This happened in the 1980s when the Conservative government determined to break its power. The methods chosen were public and brutal.

The BBC, to use a favourite Thatcher phrase, was not regarded in Downing Street as 'one of us'. Reith had understood that independence, as supposedly possessed by the Corporation, could be retained only if it were not exercised too far. Indeed, he went to the other extreme and made it so pompous a pillar of the establishment that many of its subsequent troubles can be traced to his imperious reign.

In *Out of the Wilderness* Tony Benn describes how, as Postmaster-General, he visited the BBC and asked whether it could meet the need for light music 'demonstrated to exist by the audiences which the pirate radios are getting. They said that if you had continuous light music, it would be like keeping the pubs open all day – a real BBC view that it is bad to give people what they want.' It was this assumption, that it knew best what should be purveyed to its listeners, that has earned it many enemies over the years. (Later, as Minister of Technology, Benn was to say: 'Broadcasting is really too important to be left to the broadcasters and somehow we must find some new way of using radio and television to allow us to talk to each other.') But when a Director-General tried to give audiences more of what they wanted he found himself in conflict with a government which argued for greater freedom always provided such freedom did not permit awkward questions about the policies that government pursued. It is a sad irony, and may

The BBC

turn out to be something much worse, that when the BBC appeared to be coming down from its pro-establishment pedestal to give people what they wanted, including real investigative journalism about the workings of our society – the *Secret Society* programmes for example – it was jumped on ruthlessly.

Attitudes die hard and pontificating about the arts by experts personifies even in the 1980s the BBC belief in its cultural role. As Hoggart said, 'The BBC news service is trusted, with the qualifying suspicion that it is the voice of officialdom in the last resort, and the qualifying conviction that it is dull anyway.' And one final quote from Fairlie:

> The mass of a people must find its culture, if it is to be real to them at all, by following their own tastes and their own pleasures. This is what the BBC have always sought to deny them, and what the establishment sought to deny them by resisting the introduction of commercial television.

Future revelations may show Marmaduke Hussey to have been the man deliberately chosen as chairman to get rid of Director-General Milne. He went on record in Feburary 1988 rebuking the BBC for its arrogance and 'reluctance to acknowledge the right of the public to criticize or complain'. Mr Hussey gave a fictitious example of the way the BBC behaved when it received complaints from the public: 'Thank you for your letter which you had no right or reason to send. I have discussed the programme ... with the producer and he tells me, and I agree with him, that the facts were absolutely correct and it was in perfect taste.' He went on to say that the Corporation had shaken up its management and was more commercially minded, but still had some way to go to recapture its reputation for integrity and independence. That last statement was surely twisting the truth. It was because the BBC had attempted to show too much independence that Alasdair Milne had been sacked.

Another of the many ironies surrounding the fall of the BBC from its establishment eminence has been the accusation, levelled against it frequently during the Thatcher years, that its bias was to the *left*. This must be a shock to anyone who has followed its attitudes since 1945. None the less, in March 1988, Ian Curteis wrote in the *Evening Standard* about the play *Airbase* which, according to the *Radio Times*, was an accurate picture of US airmen manning an F–111 nuclear bomb base, that the play was 'quite simply, the most offensively biased programme I've ever seen in its rabid anti-Americanism'.

What was interesting is that the Curteis article appeared at all. Accusing the Corporation of left-wing bias in the 1940s, 1950s, 1960s or even 1970s would have been absurd. What seemed to have happened by the 1980s was that the Corporation realized it was losing ground to an anti-establishment government and to a public which had turned to its more lively rivals. And so it had decided

The Media

that to regain its position it should get closer to the people for whom it had been content over many years to set standards from on high. To do this it moved to the left at the worst possible time, and reaped the Thatcher-Tebbit whirlwind. That this was a departure from historical behaviour may be seen in endless accounts of the BBC's refusal to give equal voice to all political views.

In *Brasshats and Bureaucrats*, D. N. Pritt gives a number of amusing instances of how the BBC did everything in its power to keep him and the views he represented off the air. On the far left of the Labour Party, he was expelled in 1940 for his pro-Russian views. Pritt defeated the official Labour candidate at North Hammersmith in 1945 but although his result was one of the most interesting of the whole election the BBC held back announcing it for four hours. In 1949 he was asked to debate communist political trials with Quintin Hogg (later Lord Hailsham) but had to agree that Hogg would 'spring' the cases on him without his being told in advance which they would be. Pritt won the debate and reduced Hogg to silence. As a result he was blacklisted by the BBC. Lord Simon of Wythenshawe told him, 'Well, that last broadcast you had with Quintin Hogg was planned as a defeat for you, and you won it; so you are never going on again.' Nor did he.

Harold Wilson did not like the media generally and complained of anti-Labour bias by the BBC. In the period before Labour returned to power in 1964, the party had been quite happy to see Douglas-Home mocked and assumed that the 'trendy-left' sympathizers within the BBC would not attack Labour when it came to power. To their astonishment and anger they too were attacked and in private Wilson sought to persuade the Director-General and senior management to lay off. Then, in 1968, in an effort to bring the BBC to heel, he appointed Charles Hill as chairman in succession to Lord Normanbrook, bringing him across from the chairmanship of the Independent Television Authority (ITA). It was a typical Wilson manoeuvre but also indicated the sensitivity of all politicians to the workings of the BBC. Tony Benn said at this time: 'It is the current talking shop, the national town meeting of the air, the village council. But access to it is strictly limited. Admission is by ticket only. It is just not enough . . .'

I had a personal experience of BBC attitudes at the end of the 1960s. I was asked to comment on the Rhodesia crisis in a programme where five people would be questioned, the separate interviews being mixed later. My interviewer had a clipboard upon which our five names were written, and beside each name was a comment. I managed to read the comments upside down: Tory – right-wing view; Liberal – middle of the road; Labour – left-wing view; churchman – God's view; myself – *extreme* left-wing. Now this was indicative not of reasoning but of fashion because what I argued could only have been described as the view of a High Tory: that the government should send the army to Rhodesia, arrest Smith and his Cabinet for treason and hang them.

The government onslaught from Tebbit in 1986 also brought renewed Labour charges of bias and of pro-government presentation. There was nothing new in this but it was interesting that such charges were made so soon after Tebbit had directed his broadsides. Labour charged in particular that coverage of the October 1987 Tory Party Conference had been uncritical. To some extent these accusations were borne out by research which the IBA produced in February 1988 showing that 24 per cent of viewers as opposed to 18 per cent in 1986 believed that BBC1 was biased towards the Conservatives.

The Corporation had shown a post-Reithian political independence in the early 1960s with its hard-hitting show *That Was The Week That Was*, and there was speculation as to whether government pressure had persuaded the BBC to drop the programme. But, as Anthony Sampson reports in *The New Anatomy of Britain* in 1970 the Director-General, Charles Curran, told him that the BBC 'will stand just so much politics, and no more; there's a danger that the politicians, if they don't think about its value, could almost accidentally destroy it.'

In 1988 the BBC televised *Tumbledown*, the story of the young Scots Guards officer, Robert Lawrence, who received terrible head injuries in the Falklands War. Mr Lawrence had complained that he had been kept on the sidelines at the memorial service in St Paul's, out of view as a political embarrassment, and that he was subsequently snubbed by former comrades-in-arms. The play raised important political questions and people complained because it *was* political. Jonathan Powell, controller of BBC1, asked: 'The question is: "what are people complaining about?" They are quite selective about what they make a fuss about. The things that come under fire seem to be those which are deemed anti-establishment.' Such a statement by a senior member of staff showed how the Corporation had made a 180° turn from its pro-establishment image. The BBC was demonstrating a determination to stand up to right-wing attacks, for it had previously dropped a play by Ian Curteis, *The Falklands Play*, which was seen as too right-wing or gung-ho.

Tumbledown attracted a fair amount of comment and editorials in the press as any good programme deserves to do. It also gave rise to a good deal of criticism from the Right. The *Evening Standard* said:

> At bottom, *Tumbledown*'s critics feel instinctively that modern wars in which British soldiers have fought and died should not be exposed to the same dispassionate treatment given any other topic by TV drama. Many Tory MPs find it hard to understand why the BBC should screen *Tumbledown* but reject Ian Curteis's more gung-ho treatment of the same subject, for reasons which have never been satisfactorily explained.

The implication in the *Standard* editorial is that subjects touching upon British patriotism need not be treated impartially and that 'balance' requires a gung-ho as well as an anti-war presentation to cancel out each other's impact. Those are the worst kind of arguments and the BBC rightly rejected them. The most interesting aspect of all was government sensitivity – even if expressed only by its supporters.

Political criticism is reserved for programmes which query the policies of those in power. Periodically, politicians mouth sentiments about standards but on the whole they are content to leave those to the producers. Over the years the BBC has maintained remarkably good if usually 'safe' or 'family' standards: on radio such long-lasting favourites as *The Archers*; on television, inevitably, more exciting fare to compete with independent rivals. Some programmes such as *This is Your Life* (later to move to ITV) stoop to vulgar prying, though people seem to enjoy them, so perhaps they can be excused on the grounds that the BBC is in the marketplace and giving people what they want, which its critics often insist it ought to do.

A great deal was said publicly about standards in 1988. On the one hand a government which had suddenly discovered a puritan streak lectured the media about them, and on the other hand the media stood on the defensive, out to prove their high standards and good moral intentions. The BBC's John Birt mounted an attack on British journalism and the secrecy of official institutions. These targets allowed the Corporation to appear as the guardian of moral standards. Birt has responsibility for news output, which has come in for strong criticisms in recent years for bias or lack of impartiality. Repairing fences with government and 'public' was clearly the order of the day. In a speech 'Decent Media' which he gave to the Royal Television Society Birt delivered himself of a remarkable passage:

> Impartiality in broadcast journalism is a withering plant in need of some sustaining care and attention, and many broadcasters certainly need to have a keener sense of fairness to their contributors. . . . The pursuit of accurate, fair and inquiring journalism of quality on television and elsewhere comes easiest to those who have open minds . . . it comes hardest to those imbued with a disdain for, and not just a healthy suspicion of, established centres of power; and with a preference for pontificating rather than for discovery. Television needs more of the former and fewer of the latter.

He seemed to want to have all things at once: his reference to impartiality as a withering plant was clearly intended as a signal that the BBC was getting back on the straight and narrow; his reference to open minds suggests that no more nonsense is to be allowed from those with closed minds who produce one-sided programmes, and emphasizes this point further by suggesting that those who distrust the establishment are the biased ones who pontificate. It was a 'signal' speech: We are getting our house in order again Mr Tebbit.

In *DG: The Memoirs of a British Broadcaster*, Alasdair Milne devotes a chapter to 'Balance or Fairness' and makes the point: 'Clause Thirteen of the Licence requires that the Corporation should refrain at all times from broadcasting matters expressing the opinion of the Corporation on current affairs or matters of public policy. The BBC cannot entertain an editorial opinion of its own.'

The Corporation has observed that condition of impartiality remarkably well across the years, often to the point of irritating blandness. But in recent years, and especially over such partisan subjects as Ulster and the miners' strike, it has sometimes been difficult to seem genuinely impartial, if only because of what BBC reporters are able to report at any given time. Since even showing more footage of one side of a story than the other may be interpreted as demonstrating a political opinion, it is possible to understand how easily the BBC can be accused of bias. This is even more so in a climate in which a senior political figure (Tebbit) can talk of the *privilege* of reporting as though at any moment that privilege may be withdrawn.

The dangers of the position were highlighted by an extreme article written by William Rees-Mogg (who had been a BBC governor) in the *Independent* of 1 March 1988. Referring first to the campaigning tradition of newspapers as not being among their highest he went on to say:

> These conditions do not apply to television broadcasting in Britain, or to the BBC in particular. It is intolerable and against reason that a public monopoly, funded by a tax on all television viewers, should claim the right to make propaganda rather than truth its standard.

Now that, indeed, is to go too far; the BBC has made mistakes and some programmes – Rees-Mogg specifically complains of *Airbase* – may be faulted for bias or bad taste but that is hardly the same as making 'propaganda rather than truth its standard'. Referring to libel actions brought against the BBC earlier in the decade as a result of 'recklessly inaccurate attacks on individuals' he continues: 'The anti-Birt underground still defends the old excess of zeal which led to the intimidation of witnesses and the sycophantic treatment of terrorists. These evils arise naturally from monopoly advocacy in journalism and from the abuse of producer power.' Given his views, it is amazing Rees-Mogg did not resign from the Board of Governors, on which he sat for several years.

Impartiality is a delicate and difficult principle. It is one thing to argue that the BBC should be impartial as between the Tory and the Labour views on the handling of the economy; it is something quite different to be impartial about solving an international quarrel by means of war as opposed to negotiation. One cannot be impartial as between good and evil (as Rees-Mogg would be the first

The Media

to point out) but the question, as always, is one of interpretation. In the long run it is better that the BBC should come down firmly for justice as it sees it (even if this means mistakes and libel actions) rather than revert to a blandness that forever says 'on the one hand, on the other hand'. The line to be drawn is very fine and that is what much of the argument is about.

The BBC has come a long way since the days of Hugh Greene as Director-General, the first from inside the Corporation. In those days it was still the self-confident establishment institution which had survived from its wartime peak of influence and popularity. In 1964 Greene told Anthony Sampson: 'It's always been my belief that the BBC should not be part of the establishment – or establishments – but that it should be looking at various powers-that-be with an enquiring, a critical, and sometimes a satirical eye.' That sounded suitably lofty at a time when its aura was still eminently high-brow establishment.

Under Greene's generalship the BBC, and especially television, became increasingly identified in drama and *That Was The Week That Was* to anti-establishment forces. Moreover, the notion of balance was altered: balance was looked at over a longer period during which equal prominence would be given to opposing political views. Since then the Corporation has had to fight to maintain its market in relation to the independents and to maintain its independence from a government against any kind of monopoly except its own. This was brought out vividly by the Zircon raid in Glasgow.

Alasdair Milne gives an account of the genesis of the series *Secret Society* and the growing disquiet of the Board of Governors. Milne comes across as a hard-edged man not given to compromise or the subtler nuances which might have made life with a 'conservative' Board easier than he ever managed. He relates how eventually he told the Board that five of the films would be ready for transmission in March 1987 but not 'Zircon': 'the Zircon programme about an alleged British spy satellite, the cost of which the programme claimed had been concealed from the Public Accounts Committee in direct contravention of an agreement made when Joel Barnett was PAC Chairman, was causing anxiety.' By then Barnett was on the BBC Board.

The entire series, proposed by the 'left-wing' journalist Duncan Campbell, was deeply unpopular with the Board for its anti-government, anti-establishment nature and Daphne Park and other governors were demanding to know why Campbell had been employed in the first place: 'He was "a destroyer", he was not the sort of person the BBC should consort with.' So much, one might say, for impartiality. Milne tells how he attended a reception at which the Prime Minister cut him dead. 'The very same evening, after a Board discussion on television. Alwyn Roberts dropped in ... Some Board members, he warned, wanted my "head to roll" because of *Secret Society*. I had no need to ask who.'

Milne was sacked in January 1987. Tam Dalyell devotes a chapter of *Misrule* to 'Making a Secret Society' in which he gives a blow-by-blow account of how the Special Branch raided the BBC's Glasgow headquarters in February on instructions from Downing Street. They had already raided Campbell's home and the offices of the *New Statesman*. They took hundreds of reels of film as well as any paperwork which related to *Secret Society*. The BBC was humiliated in the most public way: its Director-General was forced out and two days later its Glasgow headquarters were raided in a manner which suggested it was a subversive organization rather than the country's premier broadcasting corporation. As Maggie Brown wrote in the *Independent*:

> It is perfectly correct that Alasdair Milne was viewed by Margaret Thatcher as the wrong man in the wrong job. It is also crystal clear that she is taking a detailed interest in the future shape of broadcasting which, if the Conservatives return to power, will be deregulated, and market-led ... The raid does tie in with the reduced respect in which the BBC is held within Whitehall.

Tam Dalyell says of the raid: 'Although their [police] ostensible objective was to find evidence about the banned "Zircon" programme, made by the BBC in Scotland, it was clear even at that early stage that their instructions were to teach the Corporation a lesson.'

The sacking of Milne and the raid represented the full turn of the wheel. The one-time bastion of the establishment had been brutally humiliated, with every indication that its powers were to be reduced and altered. This was done, moreover, under what appeared to be direct orders from Downing Street. That a great public corporation which is deemed to be 'not one of us' can be treated in such a fashion tells a great deal about the change of attitudes between 1945 and 1988. Throughout those years the BBC had been regarded as a principal spokesman for Britain in the world; now it is subjected to treatment associated in British minds with the bullying actions of a police state. What then of its future?

Alasdair Milne's memoirs appear scrupulously fair to those with whom he had little sympathy. Mrs Thatcher may have thought him the wrong man in the wrong job, but that judgement was in her terms. Curiously it may also be an accurate judgement in terms of what Milne and those who sympathized with his view of BBC management most wanted. In the political climate of the 1980s under a government more hostile to media freedom than at any time since 1945 it must have been obvious that the Board – government appointees all – would trim their sails to the winds from Downing Street. Milne does not appear to have seen this and allowed too many programmes whose research or bias could be publicly faulted, in several cases leading to costly libels against the BBC. As William Rees-Mogg (a governor opposed to Milne) wrote in June 1988:

The inherent ambiguity of the BBC's constitution leaves the Corporation permanently under stress. It was his inability to bridge that ambiguity which doomed Alasdair Milne's period as Director-General; with that one can sympathize, for the ambiguity is a fundamental constitutional defect.

In his postscript 'Do We Need The BBC?' Milne poses a question to which the answer is far from clear. It will depend to a great extent on whether the Tories win the election at the beginning of the 1990s. During 1988 there was government-inspired talk of BBC advertising and the Home Secretary's proposal to abolish the television licence in favour of subscription services clearly put its financial future in the melting pot. Once Douglas Hurd had stated publicly that the BBC licence fee is 'not immortal' the question arose: should the fee be abolished, just what kind of BBC would survive? Despite its drawbacks the licence fee does allow the BBC to make programmes not wholly influenced by political considerations; this might cease if the money were a direct government grant. Further, there are several predators in the wings who would be pleased to get their hands on the BBC's radio channels, so that a vested interest exists to attack the Corporation at a time when it faces an especially unsympathetic government.

The real question, however, is not about funding but about whether Britain wants a broadcasting authority which is free to pursue excellence because it is not bound by the market, and that is a very political and ideological question indeed. The BBC's contribution to national life has been immense (those to music and drama perhaps its greatest achievements) but that is not in itself an argument for its continuation. British broadcasting – both BBC and independent – has an enviable worldwide reputation and its standards are the result of the mix between public and commercial competition. This is quite apart from the BBC External Services which transmit 735 hours a week of worldwide radio programmes in English and 36 other languages and are more listened to and highly regarded than those put out by any other major broadcasting nation.

There are two fundamental questions: the first, whether everything in Britain is to be controlled by market forces, in which case there can be no place for the BBC in its present form; the second, whether the British believe in freedom when they say they do. The answer to the first question lies with the electorates of the future. The answer to the second question is very much harder to find. Freedom of dissent has always been relative in Britain and at an earlier stage in its existence the BBC did its share in stifling real dissent by the way it selected who should speak and in what circumstances. As we have seen, it has always been subject to government pressures though for most of its life the complaints of unfairness have been from the Left. When for the first time in its existence it was seen to favour the Left or what might be described as anti-establishment and anti-government views, it came under increasing political and governmental pressures. Its future is precarious under a government of the Right which has demonstrated a greater readiness to assault bastions of the system than any government since 1945, that of Attlee not excluded.

PART SIX: BRITAIN INTO THE 1990s

20
The Thatcher Years

'Mrs Thatcher is incapable of scepticism; a policy is either right or wrong.'

KENNETH HARRIS

'Tory capitalism is a caring capitalism, energetic but never rapacious, and ensures that the citizen who uses his economic freedom to enrich himself will also enrich society at large. We do not forget that the privileges which a free society bestows carry obligations as well.'

MICHAEL HESELTINE

Many young people in Britain cannot now remember a time when Mrs Thatcher had not been Prime Minister; political longevity in office is an achievement and Mrs Thatcher has done better in this respect than any Prime Minister this century. She has also scattered her political enemies. The 'wets', apart from Peter Walker, have been banished to the back benches; would-be rebellions are nipped in the bud; those who fall out of favour or become too powerful are given public signals of displeasure which presage their coming falls; and institutions with lives (and minds) of their own are targets for campaigns the like of which we have not seen in generations. Thatcher has let it be known that she sees herself in office indefinitely and no one says her nay.

It is difficult to assess the achievements of a politician, if only because what some see as achievements others decry as failures or worse. Few, however, would deny that she is one of the most astute politicians to have occupied Downing Street. The essence of a political leader (as of a good general) is the ability to retrieve mistakes. It is recovery after bad times which counts; most politicians can do well enough when the tide is with them. Her reputation was at its nadir in 1982 prior to the Falklands War; with its help she won the 1983 election; 1986 was an awful year for her but she recovered again to win the 1987 election. Her toughness is the kind of which legends are made.

She has changed the face of the Tory Party beyond recognition. The patricians have gone and her Cabinet consists of grey-faced men of the second rank. Despite a decade in which many hostages were given to fortune, the opposition failed to get its act together and as late as 1988 members of the Labour Party talked gloomily of another Thatcher victory in 1991. If politics were about staying power alone, Mrs Thatcher would be among the greats. But they are not.

Her most obvious achievements on the home front have been to get inflation down (though by mid-1989 the signs were not good); to break the power of the trade union movement; to denationalize and privatize not just basic industries but a far wider range of activities; and by a mixture of monetarist policies and privatization to extend people's sense of being part of a money, share and property owning society. On the overseas front her achievement has been to earn a reputation for toughness: that Britain will not be pushed around (though whether the issues she stands firm on are the right ones is another matter).

The term Thatcherism has been used to describe the distinctive aspects of policy most associated with the Prime Minister, such as monetarism and what she herself might describe as good national housekeeping. Her opponents use the term to describe the effects of policies upon the most vulnerable sections of society, making it abuse synonymous with harshness. The word 'uncaring' has been the most effective accusation levelled at Mrs Thatcher and her governments, who have gone to great lengths to explain publicly that they really are caring. Obstinately a large segment of the British people have refused to believe this; another large segment have continued to vote for her and presumably for more Thatcherism.

In the June following her election victory of 1979 Sir Geoffrey Howe presented a budget which included tax reductions (33 per cent to 30 per cent), a raising of thresholds which took 1.3m out of income tax but with a commensurate increase in indirect taxes (VAT up to 15 per cent): more money in your pocket, you choose how to spend it. An early confrontation with the unions took place at the beginning of 1980 with the steel strike. The government sat it out and the steelworkers got settlement below the going rate for the public sector.

Interestingly, the first major clash came not with organized labour but with industry. The abolition of exchange controls in 1979, when the oil price had again been sharply increased by OPEC, meant the pound rose to a rate of $2.40. This had a disastrous effect on exports; industrialists complained loudly that government was not controlling the sterling exchange rate, and that forthright champion of private enterprise, Sir Michael Edwardes, made the astonishing suggestion that we should 'leave the bloody stuff [oil] in the ground'. There is always something amusing in the spectacle of British industrialists who are loud in their insistence upon freedom to control labour protesting when government does not interfere to provide assistance in international competition.

By November 1980 unemployment passed the two million mark and Mrs Thatcher was in deep trouble. The CBI, the most self-interested of all 'wets', called for reflation but she refused this invitation, which would have cost £6bn if CBI figures are accepted. She did, however, draw back from a confrontation with the miners in 1981 over the closure of uneconomic pits. By 1988 the third

Thatcher government had achieved its monetary targets: inflation had been kept to 4 per cent, there had been 6 years of growth at 3 per cent a year and the Public Sector Borrowing Requirement (PSBR) had been eliminated (many would argue that it was only by selling the family silver). The Prime Minister described this 1988 budget as representing 'the defeat of everything Labour thought was permanent in political life. It was the epitaph of socialism.' Brave, arrogant words, hostages to fortune indeed, but justified by the remarkable way her monetarist policies had been applied, not least in face of opposition from many of her own supporters.

As is so often the case in politics, all is not what it seems. Prior to the Tory victory of 1979 Callaghan had been talking of reducing the standard rate of income tax from 33 to 30 per cent while the Liberals had proposed an income tax starting rate of 20 per cent and a top rate of 50 per cent, so the targets which the Thatcher government worked towards were part of the general consensus. Meanwhile, the good housekeeping aspect came out in the government's approach to streamlining Whitehall departments and cutting down the Civil Service. As Michael Heseltine claims boldly in *Where There's A Will*: 'The present Conservative government has begun the task of creating for the first time the essential means of running departments as they should be run.' This claim is debatable although Heseltine was perhaps the best managerial minister to serve in Mrs Thatcher's Cabinets. None the less, by 1988 the Civil Service had been reduced by 130,000 to 600,000, the lowest figure in many years, and Lord Rayner's Cabinet Office Efficiency Unit was reckoned to have made savings in the region of £1bn.

Probably the government's greatest achievements were in creating a new property-owning class. The Tory Party has long regarded home ownership as a key plank of its domestic policies, but a new dimension was added with the sale of council houses. Peter Walker said in 1986:

> One of the great demarcations of our society is that, when the great majority of ordinary people living in council houses die, their children receive nothing. When those that live in middle-class houses die, their families now get a sizeable inheritance. Those with a house and shares can leave an even more sizeable inheritance. But it's quite a big disparity and if, in 10 years' time, virtually everybody owned their own home and everybody had a stake in their own firm or somebody else's firm, over a period of time you would have a situation where, in the middle of their lives, families received an inheritance which enabled them to start new businesses or move to a better house or do more for their children, whatever it may be. That happens now with middle-class families. It doesn't happen with lots of ordinary families in this country. And, if it could happen, it would be a very big transformation.

This went to the nub of the Thatcher revolution: if people own their council houses and own shares, their outlook is likely to be fundamentally different than if they do not own such things. If, as she has boasted, Mrs Thatcher is to bury socialism, this is the way to do so.

But by 1988 Thatcherism faced some of its most damaging confrontations. Bitter rows centred on the Health Service and the application of new social security rules as well as educational reforms. Inflationary wage claims in the first half of the year and angry reactions to the budget suggested that despite a third election mandate Thatcherism had some tough battles ahead.

No other politician since the war has attracted the venom which has been Mrs Thatcher's lot. Others, from Attlee to Callaghan, were lampooned, derided, lambasted for their failings, attacked bitterly in the heat of debate or during a period of controversy yet they were also accorded a degree of acceptance by their opponents. This has not been a feature of the Thatcher years. This is partly the consequence of her brittle and abrasive character, which many of her allies have noted as well as her enemies. It is also because she has visibly presided over the end of consensus even though it was clearly falling apart before she came to power. Perhaps it is because she is a conviction politician and the British do not like conviction politicians, whom they have tended to equate with revolutionary foreigners. More than any of these, it is because she is dictatorial rather than democratic and is seen to be so.

At the Ministry of Education in the Heath government, the only important office she held before becoming Prime Minister, she got an undeserved bad press. People remembered her stopping free school milk; they forget or failed to discover that she was one of the highest spenders who held that portfolio. The image she earned was hard: the *Sun* called her 'the most unpopular woman in England' and years later many continued to feel this despite her achievement in winning three elections in a row.

As any reading of the leadership contest will show, the Tories wanted to get rid of Heath more than they wanted to have Thatcher, so when she obtained the leadership it was without any powerful personal following. A somewhat bemused Tory Party was led into the 1979 election which they won as much as anything in reaction to the 'winter of discontent'. But whatever the reasons for her election as leader, once there she made it plain that she would lead. She expected her Cabinet to agree with her: 'As Prime Minister I couldn't waste time having any internal arguments.' In what had always been an all-male preserve she showed herself tougher than any of the men around her. Her first Cabinet was full of Heathites (minus Heath) for she was cautious; part of the story of the next five years was the elimination of the Heathites – first from key economic posts and then from Cabinet altogether. In his book *Thatcher* Kenneth Harris describes her approach to Cabinet:

> Her treatment of her own colleagues could be just as brusque; the Cabinet of 1979 to 1982 was not only the most divided in modern British history, it was also the most unhappy. Contrary to popular belief, there was a lot of argument around the Cabinet table, some of it quite fierce. This is because Mrs Thatcher likes to argue her case, even though she is determined that her view will prevail: 'You can only get other people in tune with you by being a little evangelical about it.'

To get her way she removed much of the decision-making process from the Cabinet and used a series of committees which she packed as she chose. Nor did she like the old establishment and demonstrated both in government and in her attitudes to the Church or monarchy or BBC that she was prepared to work against such institutions. Only after her September 1981 reshuffle in which Soames and Gilmour were sacked did she achieve a majority of supporters in the Cabinet. By the end of that year she was admired for her toughness if for little else.

Tam Dalyell, no admirer but a man whose questions she fears because he does his homework meticulously, has said of her:

> *De facto*, Mrs Thatcher has stronger reins of patronage than the British political system has witnessed since that eighteenth-century Duke of Newcastle so vividly described by Sir Lewis Namier and Bernard Pares as 'the font of preferment'. And it is this very strength of her Party position which has enabled her to cut corners, with the exercise of government and with the truth.

Later in *Misrule* he discusses Mrs Thatcher's readiness for lively argument:

> She wallows in confrontation in the House of Commons and other places. She will make a public spectacle of seeming to take on Mr Gorbachev. She can put on her fishwife act at whim, haranguing journalists and television interviewers. But does she really like arguing with clever, independent people around her? The answer is that from the day she sacked Reggie Maudling, she revealed her dislike of cleverer people than herself arguing a case at close quarters.

Julian Critchley, the backbench Conservative MP who attracted her wrath when he described her hitting institutions with her handbag, suggests in *Heseltine the unauthorised biography* how Thatcher works when he examines the Westland affair which led to Heseltine's resignation: 'The Prime Minister: imperious, indecisive and belligerent. "Who shall rid me of this turbulent priest?" Over the leak of selected parts of the Mayhew letter, she willed the ends; the responsibility for the means employed is hers.' Later he says that Heseltine found Thatcher 'unpleasant to work with and a bit of a bully'.

Plainly Mrs Thatcher is a ruthless operator, determined to hold on to power at all costs and ready to use any means to ensure she does so. Writing in the *Observer* of 3 January 1988, the day on which she became the longest-serving Prime Minister of the century, Robert Harris said:

> In the words of the former Lord Chancellor, Lord Hailsham: 'You've got to put her in the same category as Bloody Mary, Elizabeth I, Queen Anne and Queen Victoria.' Of the four, he favours Elizabeth I. 'Her handling of men is not altogether dissimilar. If you'd been a courtier of Elizabeth I you would never know whether you were going to get the treatment of an admired male friend or a poke in the eye with an umbrella.'

By mid-1988 there were increasing public signs of her displeasure with her Chancellor, Nigel Lawson, who had become popular with the back benchers as a result of his performance at the Treasury. This public disagreement between Prime Minister and Chancellor, astonishingly, continued into 1989 when in May, Sir Alan Walters returned to Downing Street as Mrs Thatcher's economic adviser. The result was the Prime Minister in Number 10 enunciating one policy, the Chancellor in Number 11 propounding another and the Prime Minister periodically insisting (under pressure) that she had complete confidence in her Chancellor.

No Tory leader since the war has attracted so much criticism in coded and uncoded language from her supporters. Lord Whitelaw, who retired from politics in 1988 following a mild stroke and had been the most loyal of the old Tories in supporting her, finally felt compelled to say publicly of her style:

> A certain hesitancy is not a bad thing, because people prefer it rather than to be told all the time what to do. Hesitancy is not in the Prime Minister's vocabulary. But then she gets away with it because she has been so enormously successful. I don't think she'll ever be described as a popular politician.

Various Tory politicians since 1945 have spoken of 'putting the Great back into Britain' or being 'up at the top table again' as they viewed the apparently unstoppable decline of British power. Finding a new national purpose has certainly been part of the Thatcher ethos; many of her admirers would insist, and some of her opponents would concede, that under her Britain carries more international weight than for many years. Her chance to make this a reality came with the Falklands crisis of 1982.

Prior to the Falklands War there were perhaps five major political developments which demonstrated the way Thatcher was beginning to exert her authority and implement her policies. First came the June 1979 budget which signalled an early start to monetarist policies; in 1980 the steel strike, the first major confrontation with the unions. This lasted thirteen weeks and led to the appointment of Ian MacGregor (brought over from the USA at great expense), who announced that 20,000 jobs would have to go. This despite Jim Prior's opinion: 'From ... low productivity, bad quality and uncertain delivery, it has become one of the best steel producers in the world, and only failed to get back into reasonable profit because of the coal industry dispute.'

Third came the 1981 budget, described as the toughest of all, with its increase in taxes and much lower PSBR; it was 'rigidly deflationary' and Francis Pym argues that it was arrived at unconstitutionally since it was only – deliberately – revealed to the full Cabinet on Budget day. At a time of recession it was the antithesis of Keynesian economics – the touchstone of all British economic policies since the war. The inner city riots were also in 1981: Brixton in April, Toxteth in July. The Scarman Report in November emphasized the national divide which was to be talked of a great deal in the ensuing years though Thatcher could hardly be blamed for the conditions which produced the riots. Despite the initiatives which followed Heseltine's three-week sojourn in Liverpool, it was not until 1987 that Mrs Thatcher paid attention to the plight of the inner cities; on election night she promised she would 'do something' about them. It is still not clear just what is going to be done. Finally, there was the Cabinet reshuffle of September 1981.

The Falklands War has generated a great deal of emotion. There was something anachronistic in the spectacle of a British fleet steaming across the South Atlantic to engage the Argentinians in a sort of World War Two battle. That the Argentinians invaded at all represented the failure of British policy in these islands over many years. Various justifications for the war have been advanced but the principal one is simply that aggression must not be allowed and that the people of the islands wished to remain British. Both came after the event for, despite Foreign Office warnings, the country was taken by surprise and the crisis had all the latent possibilities of division sparked off by Suez in 1956. According to John Vincent, in *Ruling Performance*, Mrs Thatcher did not act as a warlord but followed opinion:

> At Parliamentary level, war fever showed a cross democracy putting its emotions before its interests. If Mrs Thatcher saw it as a test of resolve for the West generally, the only terms in which it made sense, she said little to that effect till after the event. She followed opinion, rather than led it, and very wisely too. She did not play the warlord. The divisions of Suez were not repeated. But why she emerged in triumph, still more why she survived the initial blow, remains a little hard to explain.

The Argentinians invaded the Falkland Islands on 2 April 1982, and at Cabinet that same day when the decision to send a task force was made Mrs Thatcher said: 'Gentlemen, we shall have to fight.' Once the decision had been made she gave unswerving support to the military. Kenneth Harris presents her in the role of patriot, determined to stand up to aggression and to restore British sovereignty to the islands. She was putting the 'Great' back into Britain, and many were happy to take on the Argentinians and defeat them. How the same people would have reacted had a few more Exocet missiles exploded on hitting their targets and had a troopship been sunk is something it is impossible to answer.

If Harris presents Mrs Thatcher in the light of a determined Prime Minister safeguarding Western values, Tam Dalyell thinks differently. His charge is that the war could have been avoided, that with a little more perseverance the Peruvian peace proposals, supported by the USA, would have been accepted by the junta and honour could have been satisfied on both sides. But Dalyell argues, 'Had the Prime Minister accepted them, she ... would be deprived of the "military victory" which is what the Falklands War was all about from an early stage.' His principal argument is:

> given the knowledge of a likely attack on the Falklands, the Prime Minister was quite content to let the situation run and, by seeming inaction, to lure the Argentines on to the punch. A little war, deemed to be righteous by public opinion, might restore the domestic political fortunes of a Prime Minister who sat lower in the opinion polls than any ... had done since political polling began.

There are thus three views: Vincent's, that Mrs Thatcher was reacting to events rather than trying to shape them; the Harris view that she was fighting first and foremost to safeguard Western values, and Dalyell's opinion that she wanted the war because she saw it as a means of restoring her domestic political situation. The British task force performed brilliantly (as well as enjoying great good luck) and did not sustain sufficient losses to cause an alteration of public opinion. The war was won and Thatcher's domestic situation was altered overnight by the 'Falklands factor'. Only in 1988 did it become clear just how much aid in equipment and intelligence Britain had received from the USA, when John Lehman, Secretary of the US Navy at the time, gave an interview on American television. None the less, the success of the war transformed Britain's international image.

Mrs Thatcher called an election for June 1983 and won it with a majority of 144 seats over all other parties (only Attlee had done better with 146 seats in 1945). The Labour opposition led by Michael Foot fared disastrously, winning only 209 seats and a mere 27.6 per cent of the vote, while the Alliance (Liberals and SDP) won 23 seats and 25.4 per cent of the vote, the best possible argument for proportional representation. As Harris says: 'The result of the 1983 general election made Margaret Thatcher the strongest Conservative Prime Minister for a hundred years.'

She has a tendency to lecture people about moral values and on one notable occasion spoke on television about Victorian values though had she known a bit more history she would have been wary of the comparison. In October 1983, just before the Conservative Conference, it was revealed that Cecil Parkinson, then Secretary of State for Trade and Industry and one of Thatcher's bright-eyed boys and closest colleagues, had had a long affair with his secretary, Miss Sara Keays, had told her he would divorce his wife and marry her, and that he was the father of the child she was carrying. It was the sort of scandal the Tories relish. Parkinson resigned and Mrs Thatcher was deeply embarrassed. What makes the Parkinson affair interesting was her subsequent behaviour. Despite her lectures on moral behaviour, she was determined to have Parkinson back in her Cabinet.

She recalled him with what old-fashioned moralists might have thought indecent haste (no shift of penance at Toynbee Hall for Parkinson like his disgraced predecessor John Profumo, whose fall from grace was dismissed by Lord Hailsham in a splendidly self-righteous sentence: 'A great party is not to be brought down because of a squalid affair between a woman of easy virtue and a proved liar.') By 1988 he was not only Secretary of State for Energy and back in the Cabinet but was being tipped to succeed Nigel Lawson as Chancellor of the Exchequer. In view of his behaviour and her well-known addiction to morality it might have been better had the Prime Minister remembered how in another context the late Marquess of Salisbury said, 'The man should be hounded from public life for ever'.

Central to Mrs Thatcher's second ministry was the year-long miners' strike. Although during her first administration she had allowed Jim Prior and caution to prevail, she and the right wing wanted to see the unions' power reduced further and Arthur Scargill insisted upon the classic confrontation which provided the opportunity. Scargill had boasted of his success in organizing flying pickets during the 1972 coal strike and had spoken in class-war terms, 'We were out to defeat Heath and Heath's policies because we were fighting a government.' Mrs Thatcher made it plain to Ian MacGregor, the new chairman of the National Coal Board (moved across from steel), that she regarded Scargill as a Marxist revolutionary. By closing down the Nottinghamshire mines (which did not wish to strike), using his flying pickets, Scargill could not have played into her hands better had he been coached by Mrs Thatcher herself. The level of violence was matched by the heavy police deployment and the confrontation became one which Mrs Thatcher, with her temperament and the powers at her disposal, was not going to lose. She was helped because Scargill had alienated moderate Labour and did not have a united opposition behind him. Despite the bitterness the strike generated, the public on the whole supported the government.

Privatization has been the most visible ideological reversal of the Attlee revolution. Three broad arguments can be advanced to justify such a policy. The first, that privately owned industries are better run than state monopolies. The known inefficiencies of some nationalized industries and their constant need for state subsidies provided plenty of ammunition to support this line. The second, to offer them to the public as shares and encourage a new share-owning class, was very much in line with Thatcherite monetary policies and proved far more popular than had been anticipated. It was as doctrinaire as had been the nationalizations of 40 years earlier. The third was to provide government revenue so as to decrease the PSBR; this is the most questionable of the three justifications. The first two can be supported on the basis of Conservative doctrine, but the third is the opposite of good housekeeping.

The programme began with the sale of 5 per cent of the government-held BP shares, reducing its stake to 46 per cent; then in 1981 British Aerospace and Cable & Wireless were sold; in 1982 and 1983, Amersham International, the National Freight Corporation, Britoil and Associated British Ports. The huge sale of British Telecom for £4bn came in 1984, with 2.3m new shareholders emerging as a result. British Gas, British Airways, Rolls-Royce, the British Airports Authority followed: by 1987 the government had raised about £24bn with more (an estimated further £25bn including water and electricity) to come once the 1987 election was over.

The OECD Economic Survey for the United Kingdom (1986/7) says of the privatization programme:

> The upward momentum of the Government's privatization programme has been maintained and is expected to yield proceeds of £5bn per year (more than 1 per cent of GDP) over the rest of the decade. No enterprise or public utility has in principle been excluded from the scope of the programme. To date, fifteen major companies and some smaller concerns have been transferred to the private sector, involving around 650,000 employees. These transactions have reduced the state-owned sector of industry by more than one-third since 1979.

The programme was sufficiently massive and successful that by 1987 Labour had abandoned talk of renationalization and was suggesting instead that it would convert private shares in British Telecom or British Gas into special new securities. Privatization was also carried into fields few would have thought of when the programme began: municipal refuse collection offered a rich field, while being part of government policy aimed at reducing municipal powers.

One of the most successful aspects of the programme has been the extent to which employees in state enterprises took up and kept their free shares and matching shares. On the face of it, the government seem to have persuaded a new and substantial group to become shareholders: between 1979 and 1988 their number increased from 2 million to 9 million. A principal criticism is that shares have been deliberately under-priced so as to attract small investors to a 'bargain'. Many such rushed to sell at a premium immediately after the issue, leading to a second criticism that the programme was simply a device to allow the government to make a cash handout: this may buy supporters but may not produce a genuine new breed of shareholder.

Many shares, moreover, have been purchased by foreign bidders leading GMBATU's David Williams to ask

> Where is the political justification for removing British Gas from public accountability, for taking an asset owned by the people and placing it into the hands of the highest bidder, be they American oil companies, foreign nationals or shady, unnamed speculators?

The most negative and dangerous aspect of the privatization policy is what the late Lord Stockton referred to as 'selling the family silver'. Sir Geoffrey Howe said at the time of his first budget: 'But it is already clear that the scope for the sale of assets is substantial.' The question then has to be answered: what do you do when all the assets have been sold? Mrs Thatcher ought to recollect that it was a prime Victorian virtue to live off your income; it was profligate to dip into assets or savings which were meant to be kept against a rainy day.

The sale of British Gas is estimated to have yielded the government the equivalent of 4 per cent of 1986/7 public expenditure. For years there has been speculation as to what will happen to the British economy when North Sea oil runs out – to that should be added the new speculation: what happens when there are no more assets to privatize? During the mid-1980s, Nigel Lawson was able to reduce the PSBR almost to vanishing point and make major tax cuts, but these were paid for by the sale of assets. If the Thatcher governments had reduced the PSBR and taxation in terms of annual revenue and expenditure, perhaps they could have claimed a record of good national housekeeping. They have done so only by a massive programme of selling off assets. The government which comes to power in the mid-1990s is likely to find that there are no further assets to sell so that it will be able to meet existing commitments only by higher taxation. At that stage the 'good housekeeping' of the 1980s – and the privatization which made it possible – may well turn out to have been a fool's paradise.

The Westland Affair was not about what to do with a small, ailing helicopter company which dealt in defence contracts. It was about the way Mrs Thatcher runs her Cabinet. The Prime Minister favoured a takeover of Westland by the American firm Sikorsky, while Mr Heseltine, as Minister of Defence, decided to push for a European option. The Cabinet split on the issue. The crux of the problem was that Thatcher thought she would lose the argument and therefore, at a crucial stage in the public row, cancelled a Cabinet meeting to avoid discussion. Parts of a letter from the Attorney-General were leaked to the press. The selective leak was done on the authority of Leon Brittan, Secretary of State for Trade and Industry, who was subsequently made scapegoat and forced to resign. Michael Heseltine's spectacular resignation on 9 January 1986 rid Mrs Thatcher of one of the few figures willing to stand up to her and that, in essence, is what the row was all about.

In June 1987 Mrs Thatcher won the third general election in a row. She had a majority of 101 (still one of the largest of the century) with 13.76m votes (42.3 per cent of the total); Labour obtained 10m votes (30.8 per cent), and the Alliance won 7.35m (22 per cent). Despite Westland, unemployment still above 3m, doubts raised by the American bombing of Libya using bombers based in Britain, and eight years of Thatcherism, the country voted for another dose. Following that election it looked as though the government was finally about to apply some Thatcherite principles to the welfare state and education.

Whatever party had been in power the 1980s would have presented a number of acute questions whose solution was bound to be controversial: growing unemployment, an increasingly elderly population, ever heavier demands upon the welfare system, an economy which had fallen behind, over-powerful unions. Some of these were met head-on during the 1980s; others were ignored. Reducing inflation was made a top priority; so was breaking union power, although circumspection and caution were employed in this until Scargill gave the government the confrontation Thatcher clearly relished. The leaking of a document drawn up by the government's Central Policy Review Staff in September 1986 (which advanced proposals aimed at replacing state by private spending) convinced the opposition that the government intended to dismantle the welfare state; by the 1988 budget, which brought changes in the administration of welfare services, such fears seemed to be correct. The bitter dispute over nurses' pay, the fury at the rich man's budget, the long-drawn-out arguments about education, the inequities of the proposed poll tax and government defeats in the House of Lords on proposed dental check-ups and eye tests all gave point to the claim that radical revision of the welfare system was on the cards.

Heseltine says in *Where There's A Will*: 'There is no convincing evidence to suggest that 10 years hence unemployment will be less than 2m, or that the most vulnerable groups and regions will be less vulnerable.' Nor was there much evidence in 1988 that the government was giving attention to these vulnerable groups who seem to be regarded as a nuisance rather than as part of our society, hence the persistence of the claim that the government, and its Prime Minister most of all, were 'uncaring'. For most of the 1980s unemployment stood at or above 3m, a figure which had come to be accepted in a Britain more affluent in many respects than ever before. In the dry words of the OECD Report

> The rate of unemployment, although decreasing, is still at a high level and the external current balance is projected to deteriorate. A major problem is the stickiness of wages in the face of high unemployment. Given low inflation in other countries, wages need to adjust more if inflation is to decline further and external equilibrium is to be maintained.

Unemployment passed the 2.27m mark in 1981, 2.62m in 1982; it reached 2.9m at the end of 1983 and exceeded 3m in 1984. It stayed above 3m thereafter, although from mid-1986 (with 3.2m unemployed) a downward trend followed. In June 1988 the Secretary of State for Employment hailed another drop (to 2.4m) as part of 'the longest continuous decline (in unemployment) since the war'. In other words, 800,000 fewer were claiming benefit in May 1988 than in July 1986.

Unfortunately, over this time the rules had been changed so that published figures do not reflect accurately the total number of unemployed but only the number who receive benefits. The 1987 Employment Act laid down that people who lost their jobs could not claim benefits for six months (previously the time had been six weeks). A calculation provided by the independent Unemployment Unit suggests that if it were calculated in 1988 as it was when the Conservatives came to power then it would have peaked at 3.64m in June 1986 and been 3.07m in May 1988.

A major battle during the 1980s has been between central government and local authorities. Despite lip-service to freedom and non-intervention the Thatcher government has been consistently interventionist in relation to local authorities. Its main targets were high-spending Labour-controlled councils and first on the list came the Greater London Council (GLC), whose leader Ken Livingstone had earned Mrs Thatcher's ire. The GLC was abolished. Labour militants in other councils made the assault more attractive, but Michael Heseltine was converted to saying 'there is no evidence that central government is more efficient than local.' The Rates Act of 1984 introduced rate-capping and made it illegal for local councils to set rates above certain levels. Much of this attack had little to do with reform and everything to do with destroying the power of left-wing groups opposed to Thatcherite policies. Kenneth Harris admits in *Thatcher*:

> Paradoxically it seemed the Prime Minister, who had most associated herself with the devolution of political and industrial power, was now centralizing

political power on an unparalleled scale. The paradox was explained by the move to eliminate the local Far Left power bases in the inner cities. The government rightly calculated that, although there would be a passing political storm, in the long term its electoral popularity would not be severely harmed, since those people who supported and worked for organizations such as the GLC would always vote Labour whatever the government did.

That explanation, from an unabashed Thatcher admirer, is a clear admission of the purely political motivation in many of the 'reforms' the government has carried out.

Making Britain more competitive has been one of the most persistent claims made through the 1980s. Is the claim true? In the section on 'Industrial Production' in *Britain 1988* there is a summary: industrial production 'fell back by over 14 per cent between 1979 and 1981. It has since averaged an annual rise of a little over 2 per cent but remains below its 1979 level which, in turn, was below the levels of 1973/4.' That is hardly an achievement. Jim Prior observes of the Treasury team in *A Balance of Power*:

> Their attitude to manufacturing industry bordered on the contemptuous. They shared the view of the other monetarists in the Cabinet, that we were better suited as a nation to being a service economy and should no longer worry about production. I could not see how this could be reconciled with the employment of a potential workforce of around 23m people on a small island.

A quite different comment on productivity is to be found in the OECD report: 'The main contribution to growth in 1986 came from *private consumption* [emphasis added]. Consumer spending was supported by both a strong rise in real incomes and a continued fall in the saving ratio.' That fall in the saving ratio hardly represented the Victorian values Mrs Thatcher extols. A leader in the *Standard* during April 1988 had this to say:

> When ancient Athens lost the taste and talent for seafaring which had been the foundation of her greatness, she declined. No part of the British Isles is more than 75 miles from the sea, and Britannia once ruled the waves. Not any more. Within sight of St Paul's, where once the world's trading ships unloaded spices and silks, an ugly converted barge will soon be moored on the Thames for use as a tourist hotel.

A NEDO report of July 1988 claimed that the British electronics industry needs radical updating in its management styles if it is to survive into the 1990s. As the British market for electronics expands the home industry does not keep pace – an increasing proportion of the market is being lost to foreign competitors.

Despite government claims that inflation has been reduced it is still running at a higher level than in competitive countries and

In spite of the high unemployment rate, wages, both nominal and real, have been rising faster than abroad, and the growth in unit labour costs has tended to outpace that in the main trading partner countries. The manufacturing trade balance has shown a trend deterioration and, in 1983, switched into deficit for the first time since World War 2 (OECD report).

It is North Sea oil and gas and invisible exports which keep Britain going. As yet, no Thatcherite economist has answered the question: why, with its stringent monetarist policies has it higher inflation than its principal rivals and much higher (average) base lending rates?

According to Gordon Brown, a Labour Treasury spokesman, people (except those at the top end of the financial scale) paid more in taxes in 1988 than in 1979: 'This year the average family will pay 36.9 per cent of its income in taxes where it paid only 35.6 per cent of its income in 1979.' The basic reason was that the doubling of VAT and a 50 per cent increase in the share taken by national insurance had wiped out the gains from reductions in basic rates of income tax.

Judgements on the Thatcher years will be made for a long time to come, but one thing is certain: the extent to which she has dominated the political scene. In order to do so she has used her powers dictatorially and sometimes unconstitutionally. A leading Tory, now on the backbenches, told the author:

Every so often I have a feeling that the Prime Minister herself thinks her judgement is not only the right one but is so morally unchallengeable that it is near treason to question it. I find this very uncomfortable... It is essential that government should be as subject to the law as Neil Kinnock is subject to the law... in other words the law ought to be a great equalizer and I have watched from No 10 intolerance towards the Church, towards the House of Lords, towards the legal profession, towards the monarchy. In other words towards everything which cannot be run from the Whips' offices... I can't understand *why* because there is such success that has been secured politically and economically that you will look back... upon this as the Tory Attlee years and I can think of no greater accolade. Why then do you have to push it to the point where you want to have all these elements of independence brought under surveillance? It is quite contrary to my concept of the balance as I see it.

21
Two Nations

'The poorest He that is in England hath a life to live as the Greatest He.'
JOHN LILBURNE

'England is the most class-ridden country under the sun. It is a land of snobbery and privilege, ruled largely by the old and silly.'
GEORGE ORWELL

The British are excellent myth-makers and since the 'permissive' sixties have increasingly persuaded themselves that class is a thing of the past and that deference disappeared as the mid-Atlantic Newspeak replaced the Oxbridge accent. If this is true, class has given way to poverty as the dividing factor and deference has been replaced by envy.

There are many appalling divisions in the Britain of the late 1980s: the growing regional divide between the steadily deindustrializing North and the rich Euro-centric South; the class war in such London boroughs as Hackney, where the local people resist 'gentrification' of property; the money divisions representative of Thatcher's Britain; and others which emphasize that their minorities remain minorities. It is an age of silly money-oriented divisions – yuppies (young upwardly mobile professionals), dinkies (dual income, no children), bobos (burnt out, but opulent); in 1988 they discovered woopies (well-off, older people) and jollies (jet-setting older people with lots of loot). It's all about who has money and who does not. Mrs Thatcher, who likes to extol Victorian values, might consider reading some Dickens – *Little Dorrit* or *Hard Times* perhaps.

Despite government attempts to deny it, the North-South differences are becoming sharper. A study published in 1987, *Local Prosperity and the North-South Divide*, revealed that all the highest scoring towns (in terms of development and prosperity) were in the southern half of the country and highlighted the 'London factor', which is leading the economic recovery. In February 1988, on a political tour of the North, Mrs Thatcher talked of exciting vistas if only people would take advantage of them. Her audiences were less than impressed. Edward Heath used the occasion of his first Harold Macmillan Memorial Lecture to attack her for presiding over the most divided Britain in history. He suggested that the Thatcher government would end in disaster 'if it persists in the application of policies and in behaviour which are widely seen by the public as authoritarian, unfair or beneficial only to a narrow sector of the population.'

An estimate produced in the Department of Social and Economic Research at Glasgow University suggests that one million jobs have been lost in the North since 1979 while half a million have been created in the South. The indications are growing that the south-east will attract the great majority of all new jobs and development while the North continues to decline in production industries. Skills in short supply in the South remain unused in the North.

Increasing inequities in the system of taxation have been criticized by Mrs Thatcher's followers. Michael Mates, Conservative MP for Hampshire East, attempted to amend the proposed poll tax. He said; 'The government is proposing a tax which will not only hit the poor harder than the rich but which will manifestly be perceived to be unfair.' As an example of its unfairness he cited the case of a young nurse who is 'going to pay around £200 of her £6250 salary, while her senior consultant contributes the same £200 from his salary of £40,000 or £50,000.'

Attacking Thatcher for using private medicine, Roy Hattersley suggested that the poor are 'more likely to die under Thatcher policies'. This was good robust political knockabout, but he made a fundamental point about the choice argument so persistently advanced by Thatcherites. He said: 'It is important to realize that while Mrs Thatcher is demanding a doctor of her choice on the day of her choice, she is implementing policies which make that privilege unobtainable to millions.'

Attitudes towards minorities are a good guide to any society. In 1988 the National Association for the Care and Resettlement of Offenders reported that black prisoners with fewer previous convictions than white prisoners are less likely to obtain bail on similar charges. Some 14 per cent of prisoners in England and Wales are from ethnic minorities (7050 out of 50,270 on 30 June 1987), which is double the proportion of minorities in the population as a whole. The director of the association, Vivien Stern, argued, 'These figures do not show that black people are more prone to crime than white people, but they do suggest that black people who offend are more likely to go to prison.'

'Rich Scum Out of Hackney' was the headline of an article in Class War's newspaper in March 1988. It is possible to argue that such extremism is not representative of attitudes as a whole, but there are sufficient reactions of that kind by the poor to the new rich that they can neither be discounted nor dismissed as exceptions. Ian Bone, founder of the Class War movement, says of yuppies coming into Hackney:

Just because people have a lot of dosh doesn't mean they have the right to come into areas like this and push the working class out. It's not right for them to take homes away and push up prices so the working class don't have a hope of staying in the area they were brought up in.

What comes across again and again in the Britain of the 1980s is an increase of harshness. Those at the bottom of the heap show growing bitterness and resentment against those who are better off. The better off are harder, more arrogant, less caring about those who have failed to make it in material terms. These hardening attitudes are taking place against an economic background in which income tax has been reduced from 35p basic to 25p and top rate from 98p to 40p under a government whose philosophy appears to be that you can assist the poor by letting the rich become richer.

In an age dominated by Thatcherism plenty of Tories are, none the less, exhibiting growing unease at the divisions in society. Lord Whitelaw, long Thatcher's most loyal lieutenant, said in an interview with the author in 1988

> There is probably a greater division, certainly in terms of wealth, between the richest and the poorest in the country (the poor are less poor, the rich very much richer). Purely in social terms divisions are less, in terms of wealth greater. Many more people have moved in the middle upwards but that has left the poorest in the community more isolated than they were.

Another Tory, Charles Morrison MP, makes a different point about money when he argues:

> The relative extremism which exists now, the ending of consensus which happens to be true at the moment, is a luxury in which a country may be able to indulge if it has got lots of money coming in to keep the machinery going. . . . The Thatcher revolution has been financed by the flood of oil.

'Money goes before a fall' – in August 1986 the *Observer* published some comparisons of pay rises among the country's top bosses. Ernest Saunders, shortly to be disgraced over the Guinness scandal, received a pay rise of 59 per cent; Lord Hanson, a major backer of the Tory Party and chairman of Hanson Trust, received a 70 per cent increase, while averages for workforces in the different companies his trust controlled were between 6 and 7.5 per cent. After the 'Big Bang', the *Sunday Times* reckoned it could provide the names of more than 200 people in the City with annual incomes in excess of £1m. Speaking to business students in 1985, American Ivan Boesky said: 'Greed is all right, by the way. I want you to know that. You can be greedy and still feel good about yourself.' Mr Boesky came a cropper in a New York financial scandal, but the sentiments he expressed had clearly been taken to heart by trendsetters in the City.

In December 1986, measures came into effect to free the financial service sector from restraints. They included allowing the building society movement (£125bn worth) to move beyond its traditional business (mortgages) into a range of activities such as property ownership, investment management, unsecured lending. This could prove in retrospect to be one of those turning points – not perhaps obvious at the time – when an institution whose rectitude had become proverbial (the Man from the Pru) entered the 'free-for-all' and became less. Their shackles were removed at a time when the Department of Trade and Industry was overwhelmed with inquiries into illicit dealings in the City, whose once proud boast was that a man's word was his bond.

There have always been City scandals and in fairness one should recall the 'Stanley Affair' of the late 1940s which led to the Lynskey Tribunal. But not in living memory have there been so many big company names associated with scandals (mainly insider dealing) which did not 'rock' the City but appeared to be natural – that ordinariness, the expectation that they would occur, tells a good deal more about the moral climate of the time than any particular scandal.

When Tory MP Keith Best was found to have made illegal multiple applications for shares in British Telecom, he was reluctant to resign though he was obliged to do so in the end, announcing that he would quit his seat 'to uphold the high standards of those in public life'. Had he not been found out upholding high standards in public life would presumably not have bothered him. He was representative of a trend and a philosophy: everyone wants more money, it is *only* money and getting more doesn't hurt anyone, so you are wrong only if you are found out. As Alan Sugar of Amstrad said in 1986: 'If there was a market in mass-produced portable nuclear weapons, we'd market them too.'

By 1988 the average salaries of the 100 best paid executives were in excess of £270,000, but a survey suggested that that figure could be increased by at least two-thirds when account was taken of the perks which go with the job. Many are so extravagant and so valuable – daily allowances for lunch as great as some people's weekly earnings, chauffeur-driven company cars, seats at Covent Garden or Wimbledon – that they make a mockery of published salary details.

The takeover has become a symbol of the money-grabbing ethos. Although they are presented in grave City language, many are about asset stripping and quick profits. In the summer of 1988, when the Swiss firms Nestlé and Suchard bid for the famous Quaker chocolate firm Rowntree, there was a public outcry. Swiss law prevents a comparable bid from outside for a Swiss company so City predators could not move in the reverse direction. The Nestlé bid was successful, and City solicitor Andrew Phillips pointed out:

> That Great Britain plc is up for grabs is no longer in any doubt. Although takeovers – foreign and indigenous – have been an increasing feature of the

British scene in recent years, culminating in overwhelming foreign domination of the City (the clearing banks apart), the Rowntree affair really rubs it in.

This is one of the many ironies of the Tory claim that under Thatcher Britain has moved to the top again in business – even in so far as the claim may be true, more and more of the companies doing well are no longer British owned or controlled.

Almost every observer of Britain in the 1980s who does not belong to the Conservative Party (and many who do) accepts that greed, envy and an amoral attitude towards the making of money have become central to our business life and culture. When the long Thatcher political ascendancy is finally assessed, her 'greatest' achievement may well be viewed as making greed respectable. It is hard to think of a worse indictment than that.

Accompanying money greed is vulgar and conspicuous consumption. Occasions such as Ascot exist to permit the rich to show off; newspapers point out with a certain relish that those now wearing top hats and being admitted to the royal enclosure often have little idea of correct behaviour, but their children will be expensively educated to become the Sloane Rangers and Hooray Henrys of tomorrow. That kind of transformation is indeed Victorian – it happened throughout that period of thrust and advancement.

The other side of this equation is growing poverty. In November 1987, it became apparent from a Green Paper outlining the poll tax proposals that charities could find themselves responsible for collecting poll tax for government. The Salvation Army would have to levy a daily tax on those using their hostels; so would women's refuges or halfway houses for the handicapped, which would drive the most needy away from the organizations where they could normally expect to receive help.

Cutting benefits for unemployed young people, ending benefit entitlement for those under 18 not in employment or on a Youth Training Scheme, the abolition of emergency one-off payments under the Social Fund – all have been defended as ending the 'dependency culture'. What is most likely to come in its place is an alienation culture. When there is constant reference to growing crime rates, many government measures in the social sphere seem likely to lead to an increase in teenage crime.

A phenomenon of the late 1980s has been the amount of public discussion about *the poor* as a class to be analysed, dissected and morally probed. The poor may always be with us, but in the 1980s their plight in Britain has become glaringly apparent – and that in a society where new wealth is also glaringly apparent: the plight of one being highlighted by the ostentatious consumption and harsh indifference of the other. Part of the conventional wisdom advanced

– in the year when changes in social welfare adversely affected the incomes of the country's poorest and tax concessions increased markedly the incomes of the most wealthy – was that tax or benefit reforms are always unpopular with the losers. This argument was advanced as though it explained everything and the inequitable results could be accepted without more discussion. Articles appeared with titles such as 'The mood of the poor'; what was most depressing about them was the fact that we appeared to have accepted that this new class of 'the poor' from nineteenth-century Dickensian Britain was back with us and here to stay.

A survey of childcare services in Europe reveals that Britain comes bottom. A report on 'The Health Divide' (from the Health Education Council) highlights two nations and shows that major diseases affect the poorest more than the rich. To read in 1988 that working-class people are shorter, more liable to obesity, more prone to illness and have lower survival rates for cancer or heart disease is like delving into reports of nineteenth-century slum conditions. What has happened to the brave promise of post-war Britain? A distressing revelation is the extent to which sweated labour is now carried out in the home. More than one million homeworkers, the majority women, are paid an average of 50 to 60 pence an hour and have no protection under the Health and Safety Acts.

The inner city riots during the first half of the 1980s drew national attention to the slums which disgrace some of our major cities. Neglect, deindustrialization, huge grey derelict housing estates whose planners must have been thinking of controllable housing for the 'proles' of Huxley's *Brave New World* provide all the explanation needed to understand the rise of political militants.

It seems that at some point during the 1960s and 1970s the public just assumed that institutions which were in place would continue to answer all the calls made upon them without any commensurate effort to ensure that they were constantly updated. By the time Thatcher's radical government achieved power the rot had already set in, but the remedies applied were all monetarist – economic measures rather than assessments of how to make existing institutions do a different job from the one they had been created to perform decades earlier. That would appear to be a major part of the 1980s problem. It also helps to explain the uncaring image the government has earned: it concerns itself with institutions and returns on investment rather than with people and their needs.

A growing lack of civility is another aspect of Britain in the late 1980s: it is rare to see an old person given a seat in a crowded underground train, while brusqueness and indifference are likely attitudes to be met with in public. A unique phenomenon is young people begging: they sidle up in a casual, friendly way and murmur something about not having a job and needing lunch.

Perhaps nothing illustrates the new harshness as much as the greater visibility of the police. They race through the London streets with their sirens wailing; they are out in force with riot gear; their leaders appear on television to explain how they are dealing with crime or hooligans – they have become a powerful lobby. It is a long time since the British have referred to their police as being 'wonderful'. Too often the individual who takes a problem to the police finds they simply 'do not want to know'. Complaints against the police are almost always handled by the police and, long after the event, the complainant has often obtained no satisfaction; instead, an internal cover-up takes place. In 1988 Chief Inspector Brian Woollard alleged that a clique of Freemasons was operating at the heart of the Metropolitan Police; rather than investigating to see whether his allegations were true, Scotland Yard began the process that would lead to his dismissal. He faced allegations that he had failed to report for duty and had made unauthorized communication with the media. These charges had all the appearances of another career-busting exercise comparable to the Stalker affair. Despite the high public profile, the police appear to be coping less ably with law and order than their humbler, less arrogant predecessors of a generation ago.

A buoyant youth culture indicates a vibrant and exciting society. During the 1960s we heard a great deal about youth and its new freedoms. In 1986 *The Times* carried out a survey of what it called 'Thatcher's Children', young people who had reached voting age since she came to power. The survey found a basic indifference to the country's politicians, and if these young people had opinions of political leaders they were almost always negative: 61 per cent thought the Prime Minister was out of touch with young people, 60 per cent that she talked down to people, 56 per cent that she was out of touch with ordinary people and 45 per cent felt she was narrow-minded. The best rating any politician obtained was Neil Kinnock with a 36 per cent vote saying he was down to earth. As *The Times* said on 4 September, the Prime Minister 'has created a political culture in which cost-cutting and efficiency are prized. Can she adapt it into a culture in which to take on a new workforce is as admired as to slim down an old one?'

Two years later another study of 'Thatcher's generation' (15-24-year-olds) by Mintel market research found that young people were marrying later, were obsessed with fashion, watched television for much of their time and were sensible and responsible. The Mintel report sounds remarkably like Tory Party propaganda: 'Ten years of Tory rule', it claims, had produced a generation of young people with well balanced and mature attitudes, very different from those of 'the confused, misunderstood, alienated rebels associated with previous generations'. A number of comparisons were made in 1988 with 1968, the year of student revolt, the apogee of the youth decade. What comes across most forcibly is that while youthful aspirations are much the same as they were, 1968 was a time of hope while 1988 is a time of sober concern about the future.

A major change in most British lives since 1945 is in the approach to credit. During the austere post-war 1940s and early 1950s people made an effort to live within their means; to do so was a kind of moral imperative, a leftover from the Victorian age. Hire purchase or buying on the 'never-never' was frowned upon and resorted to only for special items such as washing machines or refrigerators. The affluent 1950s altered this but the process was gradual. Today we carry card wallets which unfurl like concertinas to show a range of credit cards and the status conscious vie to see how many different cards they can collect. Young spenders are encouraged by banks to accept credit cards and given spending limits that bear little relationship to their earnings or experience of managing money. Few people realize the interest they are paying, and one estimate suggested that the average adult was in debt to the equivalent of a year's salary or earnings. The pattern has changed: just about anything can be purchased on credit – holidays, furniture, hardware, travel, entertainment, meals, clothes. Alluring advertising campaigns suggest that credit will ease a difficult period and make planning easier. The credit card has become a potent symbol of the consumer society and for many people represents an immediate affluence whose cost need be met only at a later date. If the Thatcher economic 'miracle' goes bust in the 1990s, the credit card will be partly responsible for the collapse; no other factor has done so much to promote profligate spending.

Social and ethical values are never absolute; each generation determines what is central to its lifestyle, what is peripheral and what is outmoded or meaningless. Speaking in the USA at the beginning of 1988 the Archbishop of Canterbury said: 'To turn one's back on pluralism and to attempt to re-establish the positive society in the shape of old values could be achieved, but only under an oppressive and totalitarian regime.'

The Hitler years and the fight against fascism destroyed faith in the sanctity of authority which may explain why subsequent generations do not show deference to their leaders even when they would like a firm moral lead. It is a dilemma which the churches have found as hard to deal with as the politicians. The Archbishop also said,

> However the silent majority may cry out for authority, as they cry to the churches for a firm moral line, and yet decline to take the medicine which authority prescribes. The moral free-for-all simply continues...

In the end a society's morality is determined by the attitudes of the majority. The outlook for curtailing greed is not good. At the beginning of 1987, during the height of the City scandals, an article by Bob Beckman 'Honestly, wouldn't you do the same?' appeared in the *Standard*. Its main thrust was that since there was little to indicate that the public suffers as a result of insider dealings, why bother? This attitude is also frequently aired when people are caught cheating on their tax declarations: 'Everyone does it, so what's the fuss, I have just been unfortunate to be caught.'

Few subjects illustrate better than pollution and the environment how determined are those making money not to be held back by considerations of public welfare. Britain lags behind most of Europe in pollution control. Green issues do not rate the attention that they do in Germany or Scandinavia and though the government argues that sulphur dioxide emissions from power stations or car exhausts are declining the figures contradict them: between 1984 and 1986 sulphur dioxide emissions increased by more than 5.5 per cent and nitrogen oxides by almost 15 per cent.

It is perhaps a British paradox that while evidence suggests that in any contest between morality and money it is the latter which will win, in other areas there are signs of a prudish and repressive morality coming once more to the fore in public life. Its leading proponent is Mrs Mary Whitehouse who has for many years campaigned through her National Viewers and Listeners Association to restrict and control programmes shown on television. She framed the draft of the Obscene Publications Bill 1987, which Thatcher helped through to the committee stage by imposing a whip on ministers. Michael Tracey, author of *Whitehouse* says, 'Her aim is to impose a specific morality. I don't think you can do that within a democracy. Mrs Whitehouse believes in protecting people against themselves.' That goes to the heart of any moral argument: who has the right to protect people when they do not wish to be protected? Mrs Thatcher certainly gives the impression that she has such a duty, but the Britain of the late 1980s was a place of moral uncertainties rather than convictions.

Tolerance, or its absence, provides a guide to society and, on paper, Britain is one of the most tolerant. She is a democracy wherein almost any political view can be aired. Religious freedom is present and those who choose not to have religion are free to do so. There is relative sexual freedom and individuals are at liberty to marry or cohabit. A 'free' press exists, as does a broadcasting system purveying a wide spectrum of views. The legal system is open to all and, in theory, treats the highest and the lowest in the same way. Britain has free public education and an almost free health service: and is one of the richest societies on earth. In terms of capacity, she ought to be able to put right most of the things which are wrong, at least in a material sense. The reality is different.

The 1980s have seen a rise in levels of intolerance, something which is always a bad sign in a democracy. The key to this intolerance is wealth: its division between those who have it and those who do not. Lord Whitelaw explains the intolerance which has come with new wealth:

> I think we are a less tolerant society. I think those people who have acquired a new position, new resources, better opportunities are in fact less tolerant of

those from whom in some way, you might say, they have escaped than were the older generation who had always known the better position and therefore were extremely tolerant of those who were less well off than they were. People [now] who make their way in the world and get a new position don't see why the people from whom they emerged should not do the same for themselves.

Lord Whitelaw has described the classic situation which arises when a great deal of new wealth is created, which has happened during the Thatcher years. The 'get on your bike' syndrome does not mean only that those who do not get on their bikes get left behind, but that they are despised for being left behind. But the depth of the two-nation divide is not simply economic; if it were a future government could redress the inequalities by economic measures. The divide affects other aspects of our national life, many of which cannot be changed by legislation: these include that between the prurient and the permissive, the secretive and the open in government, the censors and the advocates of free speech (in its widest sense), the majority and the ethnic minorities.

We have examined most of these in the course of this book; what has all too frequently emerged is a sense of harshness. Clause 28 of the Local Government Bill, which bans the 'promotion' of homosexuality through local authority funding, is an invitation to narrow-minded councils to exercise a form of censorship which could be used to ban from public libraries some of the world's great literature. The debate surrounding the clause brought out much latent intolerance, often in high places, and the AIDS scare resulted in increased attacks on gays and lesbians.

The government's obsession with secrecy and the gagging powers it proposed in the summer of 1988 were more symptomatic of narrow tyranny than of concern for the national interest. This may not appear to have much to do with tolerance but a government which favours secrecy and finds reasons not to debate its actions is profoundly anti-democratic. Those who argue that restrictions should be placed upon the press (because it abuses its freedom), television (standards are deemed offensive), football fans (some behave badly), the BBC (no longer supports the establishment line), churchmen (for discussing political issues), homosexuals (they might spread AIDS), Prince Charles (shows concern for the plight of the inner cities) are supporting intolerance and creating divisions. There will always be divisions but what Britain requires, perhaps more than anything else, is the spirit of Voltaire: those with whom one disagrees must have the same liberty within the law as those with whom one agrees.

Tolerance becomes important only when disagreements are profound and when the capacity to suppress resides with the one side. Profound disagreements now exist in Britain; the instincts of the Thatcher government and of far too many others lean towards suppression and nothing is more calculated to perpetuate divisions than suppression, in whatever form it comes.

22
Britain in 2000

'We know nothing of tomorrow; our business is to be good and happy today.'
SYDNEY SMITH

'Government is a contrivance of human wisdom to provide for human wants. Men have a right that these wants should be provided for by this wisdom.'
EDMUND BURKE

From 1945 to the present Britain has experienced changes which have been revolutionary in scope. On the international scene she has seen the inexorable diminution of her power: she has joined the European Community and divested herself of a huge Empire. On the economic front she has done less well than her principal trade rivals or partners; at the same time most of her people have achieved economic goals – home ownership, holidays abroad, a family car and a range of household goods – unthinkable except for a tiny minority in the austerity of the 1940s.

It is on the social front, however, that the changes have been greatest. The welfare revolution implemented by the Attlee government took away fear: fear of the poverty that came with unemployment, of the misery of ill health and an old age which could be a burden. Then in the 1960s, when affluence had changed outlooks fundamentally, the British came out of the closet. We refer to the period as the permissive decade, but a better description would be the 'open' years. Affluence released inhibitions so that people were prepared to do their 'thing' – whatever it was – and do it openly. The youth culture symbolized by the Beatles and the Rolling Stones, the disappearance of deference, the denim revolution, the sexual revolution, and the liberation of women: these transformed the Britain of the 1960s and 1970s from the society which had emerged at the end of World War Two.

Judgements of the period of one's lifetime are bound to be subjective and are also likely to be erroneous, but an examination of this era (1945 to 1989) would suggest that three Prime Ministers exercised a special, possibly profound, influence on the way Britain has developed. The first was Clement Attlee: the social revolution over which he presided altered our lives for the better and laid down parameters of compassion which have remained yardsticks to the present day. He did this, moreover, at a time of almost unbearable international pressures. His government behaved with a certainty, a sense of purpose and a determination to overcome odds which we have not witnessed often in our political history.

The second outstanding Prime Minister was Harold Macmillan. This urbane, subtle, brilliant man made the British accept their declining power by suggesting that they were like the Ancient Greeks alongside the American Romans. It was no mean feat and, given the British aversion to intellectuals, Macmillan's performance was masterly.

The third is the present incumbent of Downing Street, Margaret Thatcher. Brittle, abrasive, narrow and brutally determined to get her way, she is quite remarkably successful. Of all Britain's post-war leaders she is the one who earns least affection. Yet she has changed the parameters of the society in such a way that for the next 40 years we will be coming to terms with or undoing the changes over which she has presided.

To get any age into perspective is not easy. This period, for example, has seen the protest movement develop into something of a fine art, dominated by the bomb, Vietnam and South Africa. The Campaign for Nuclear Disarmament (CND), whose first march to Aldermaston took place in 1958, became a symbol for protest against the tyranny of organized government. Over five years it developed into the largest public protest movement in a century, and it became *de rigueur* for those on the Left to wear CND badges. Only the Anti-Apartheid Movement has had a comparable impact. With *glasnost* defusing the nuclear debate, it is likely that CND will decline during the 1990s while Anti-Apartheid will reach a climax as the denouement in South Africa unfolds.

When most people feel remote from government, protest movements are an outlet; often the subject of the protest is less important than the act of protesting. Much of this has been in relation to events in the Third World: the huge response to Bob Geldof – Band Aid and Sport Aid – was spontaneous and generous. It was also a response in the sense that here was something that could be done at once, which would bear immediate fruit, and that is a feeling people do not often have with regard to their governments.

There is every indication that the 1990s will see government in Britain become more authoritarian, more centrist, more remote and with a greater capacity to interfere in the public's lives than ever before. The ingrained habit of official secrecy has long been with us but leaks during the Thatcher period (other than inspired ones) have produced a government almost paranoid on the subject. As the *Observer* pointed out on 3 July 1988, the new censorship powers the government is seeking will mean that journalists would face jail for revealing serious abuses by the state. According to the White Paper on reform of Official Secrets it would no longer be necessary to prove that a civil servant was responsible for a leak. Newspapers would simply be prosecuted for printing facts deemed 'harmful'. If such regulations receive the force of law, Britain will have achieved a level of state censorship which for years we have persuaded ourselves belongs only to totalitarian regimes.

The rapid growth of data storage means that increasing information about individuals is available to an ever-widening range of organizations. The Data Protection Act gives everyone the right to see personal records, but it does not prevent these records being stored, and there are wide-ranging statutory exceptions so that an individual may not have access to information stored for national security or crime detection or taxation purposes. These exceptions give the state immense power, because it will decide what information can be withheld. There are growing pressures upon the medical profession to reveal information about patients to third parties – for example, whether they are AIDS infected – without the knowledge or consent of the patient. The old idea that the doctor-patient reationship is strictly confidential is on the way out.

Old concepts of privacy are beginning to disappear in an age when so much information is stored and where such phrases as 'in the national interest' are used far too frequently. Most governments hide their misdemeanours when they can and one has only to look in the official records to discover how much all our governments have deceived us over the years. Only at the beginning of 1988 did we discover, under the 30-year-rule, that the 1957 fire at Windscale was the worst nuclear disaster until Chernobyl in 1987.

The Thatcher government has insisted that its monetarist policies are the key to its other achievements, so will it be judged upon the durability of those policies. By the summer of 1989 there were signs that the Thatcher economic miracle was falling into deepening disarray. The rate of inflation had passed 8 per cent and nearly a dozen increases in the bank rate over a year had raised it to 14 per cent. The economic strategy was clearly in deep trouble, a situation that was not helped by the overt split between Prime Minister and Chancellor over the argument as to whether or not Britain should join the Exchange-rate Mechanism of the EMS. These differences raised fundamental questions about the entire monetarist policy whose successes have been based upon two sources of income: oil, which was the government's good fortune; and privatization, which is a wasting asset. Without these the economic performance would look very thin indeed. Some time in the 1990s the present monetarist policies will be shown up for what they are: extremely successful sleight of hand rather than 'good housekeeping'. No government since the war has used assets so irresponsibly to pay for its policies.

One of our most acute political commentators, Neal Ascherson, drew attention to a fundamental cause of the malaise in British society in an *Observer* article in March 1988. It was in reaction to the Home Secretary's speech at Tamworth of a month earlier, when Hurd asked what would have distressed Peel in the Britain of 1988 and had answered his own question:

> As a good Victorian, he would be surprised and disturbed that this rise in the general standard of living should have been accompanied by a decline in religion, in discipline, and in respect for the law, rather than by the rise in standards of behaviour which accompanied Victorian prosperity.

He went on to suggest that we have lost 'social cohesion' and asked where are the teachers, the churches and the parents whose task it is to maintain cohesion. Neal Ascherson's rejoinder was:

> There is, I suspect, one other question which he [Mr Hurd] felt it prudent not to ask. Where are the mothers? There is an answer. They are in low-paid, under-organized, underclass jobs. They are there not because they have understood the feminist revolution – although most have – but because they need the money. They are there because government policy over the last nine years has been to replace organized male labour with young people on cheap 'work experience' rates and with low-paid women.

There are now three million people in Britain who take tranquillizers daily. An ever-growing number resort to psychiatrists – a habit the British used to deride as an American excess – and an increasing number of men are subject to anorexia (self-starvation) as a reaction to the stress of making money. The successful middle classes have become so un-British as to relish talking about their psychiatrists: therapy has become the third favourite conversation topic at some dinner parties after house prices and schools. It is sad that making money and being successful should cause increasing illness, but that has become the pattern.

The 1960s, which constituted a turning point in so many ways, produced a reaction to welfare statism, which was taken for granted, and brought about a surge of individualism. By the 1980s individualism had hardened into the yuppie culture: a frenetic money-making philosophy which damned the hindmost to their place in the new poor. But the 'Black Monday' crisis of 1987 demonstrated those who rise fast in the frantic free-for-all of the City are liable to fall just as fast. No doubt there will be a reaction to the greed of the 1980s, most likely when assets available to government have run out in the 1990s, but it looks as though the City is about to draw the line at the size of golden handshakes to directors. A major row developed over Rothman International's decision to give outgoing chairman Robert Crichton-Brown a gift of £750,000. There is an obscenity about a society which allows that kind of hand-out while admitting so much poverty and talking of the new poor.

The pendulum of change swings inexorably and if we look back to 1945 and try to predict the 1990s it is possible to perceive a pattern: 1945 to 1955 was the period of post-war recovery and austerity; 1955 to 1965 saw affluence, full employment, 'you've never had it so good' and a sense of release, not just from the war years and rationing but from a much longer period stretching back to the depression and the dole queues of the 1930s. The 1960s were the high point; inevitably, such openness was not to last and the 1970s saw a reaction: battles between organized labour and the government, with the unions winning more often than not; the rise in unemployment and a realization that affluence for everybody had been a temporary phenomenon; the end of consensus. And so to the Thatcher years: the consolidation of the end of consensus, an economic free-for-all which has made many rich at the price of a steady increase in those who are poor, and an attitude of harshness between the new rich and those they have left behind and in the attitudes of government to the poor. This brings us to the 1990s.

Norman Tebbit has suggested that a new period of consensus could follow as Labour, when it forms the government, makes the Thatcher reforms work. The question to ask about the 1990s is which Thatcher reforms will be durable? AIDS (a heaven-sent ally for Thatcher and Whitehouse) and reaction against permissiveness are likely to mean a more prurient society which parades the virtues of family life but merely reverts to the repressive and hypocritical behaviour of an earlier age. It is unrealistic to imagine that we shall abandon the greater freedoms we have learned to enjoy although the new climate might make us more wary of demonstrating our enjoyment of them: back to the closet.

But there are some ugly pointers to growing state powers, which should be resisted. Organ transplants illustrate the point: in June 1988 the government backed away from requiring doctors to ask next-of-kin if patients' organs could be used for transplants because a working party of the Royal College of Physicians came down against 'required request' yet the junior Health Minister at the time (Edwina Currie) and others favour such a law and it may well be introduced in the future. It is one more example of the way lives, and in this case bodies, are being controlled by legislation.

Under the Education Reform Bill 1988 the Minister was given 415 new powers which the government claims will free schools from professional and bureaucratic straitjackets and create an educational service which responds to consumer needs. Opponents see it as a major shift of power to the centre and as one of the biggest onslaughts on local democracy this century. It has been a feature of the Thatcher years to lessen local authority power and the 1990s are likely to see a central government stronger and with more power at its disposal than at any time since the seventeenth century. And, despite what politicians say in opposition, there are few instances of governments which inherit great powers dispossessing themselves by handing them back to the people or to local authorities.

Curiously, this increased centralization of power is being harnessed with the dangerous Conservative doctrine of privatization. The idea of privatizing the prison system is one of the most bizarre put forward by any government this century. If you can privatize the prisons, why not the police and the legal system? It all opens up Kafka possibilities of an individual bringing a case against another individual through a private justice company (paying for the service, of course) which will send its private police to arrest the individual who will be charged in a privately-run court and be sent to a privately-run prison. It says a good deal about the climate at the end of the 1980s that there could be serious discussion of private prisons and that, as usual in Thatcher's Britain, the principal point of departure is how cost effective they might be.

For years now, but increasingly so during the 1980s, a demand has been growing for a Bill of Rights. It has long been a British boast that the country has no written constitution; it is not a boast worth making any more, and the sooner rights are enshrined in a Bill which cannot be overriden, no matter how, the better. Lord Scarman has become the most eloquent advocate of this though others (including Lord Hailsham) have shown an increasing inclination towards the idea.

Britain also needs a Freedom of Information Act. It has always been an inexplicable anomaly that a country which has so often and so persistently put itself forward as a champion of freedom seems determined to prevent its subjects from knowing what the government is up to and why.

Thirdly, we need a return to an earlier and more robust Parliamentary tradition where backbenchers cease to be party hacks and insist upon questioning and demanding explanations which at present they are neither given nor expected to request. But perhaps that is to ask too much of our rigid party system.

Tony Benn, whom many dismiss as an extremist of the Left, has an excellent historical sense in relation to matters pertaining to the constitution. Speaking of the Thatcher years he has said:

> My opinion is that Mrs Thatcher has actually destroyed public confidence in the institutions under which we are governed and put back on the political agenda every issue that has ever been discussed over our history: the role of the Lords, the role of the crown, the role of inquests in Ireland, the rights of women, the rights of unions, the democratic argument, the Combination Acts and so on.

What is certainly true of these years is that Britain has become one of the most highly regulated systems imaginable, despite claims to the contrary. The entrenchment of goverment secrecy, the attacks upon alternative centres of power including local government and the GLC, the unions, the Church, the BBC and the monarchy have all contributed to the enhancement of a forbiddingly powerful centrist state. This has been the most dangerous achievement of the Thatcher years and principally the achievement of the Prime Minister herself. She has often spoken of liberty, especially when directing her remarks at the communist world, but the restraints she has placed upon British liberties make it pertinent to ask whether she understands what liberty means.

It does not mean muzzling the press or attacking centres of power which advance different views. It does not mean constant expressions of disapproval from Downing Street for anyone or any institution which dares to differ. 'Not one of us' is possibly the most appalling of the pronouncements attributed to her, for by virtue of her office she has become more than a partisan politician who divides her supporters into acceptable 'drys' and unacceptable 'wets'. She is, or ought to be, the guardian of all our liberties and should listen to those who disagree without dubbing them the 'awkward squad'. She has the right to disagree but should do so like Voltaire: 'I disapprove of what you say, but I will defend to the death your right to say it'.

The principal political question for the 1990s must be what kind of system is to be established once Thatcher has gone. Whoever succeeds her will, in the pendulum nature of politics, move back towards a more central, consensus approach. The principal economic question will be how to manage an economy whose oil is running out, whose assets for privatization no longer exist and whose deindustrialization has reduced her further in the world league. The principal social task will be to create 'one nation' again.

These three problems will require political leadership of genius.

Bibliography

A comprehensive bibliography covering the subject matter of this period would require a volume of its own. The bibliography that follows, therefore, is largely confined to those books which I have quoted in the text.

An official handbook *Britain 1988*, HMSO, 1988.
ARNOLD, Bruce, *Margaret Thatcher: A Study in Power*, Hamish Hamilton, 1984.
– *What Kind of Country*, Jonathan Cape, 1984.
ARNOLD, Guy, *Britain's Oil*, Hamish Hamilton, 1978.
– *The Unions*, Hamish Hamilton, 1981.
– *Towards Peace and a Multiracial Commonwealth*, Chapman & Hall, 1964.
ATTLEE, Clement, *As It Happened*
– *Empire into Commonwealth*, OUP, 1961.
BENN, Tony, *Out of the Wilderness: Diaries 1963–67*, Hutchinson, 1987.
BLACKBURN, Raymond, *The Erosion of Freedom*, Times Press, 1964.
BROWN, George, *In My Way*, Penguin, 1972.
BROWN, J. A. C., *Techniques of Persuasion*, Penguin, 1963.
BUCKMAN, Peter, *The Limits of Protest*, Victor Gollancz, 1970.
BULLOCK, Alan, *Ernest Bevin, Foreign Secretary*, Heinemann, 1983.
BUNYAN, Tony, *The Political Police in Britain*, Julian Friedmann, 1976.
BURRIDGE, Trevor, *Clement Attlee*, Jonathan Cape, 1985.
CALLAGHAN, James, *Time and Chance*, Collins, 1987.
CARVEL, John, *Citizen Ken*, Chatto & Windus, 1984.
CHURCH OF ENGLAND, *The Church and the Bomb*, Hodder & Stoughton, 1982.
– *Faith in the City: A Call for Action by Church and Nation*.
CHURCHILL, Winston S., *Europe Unite: Speeches 1947 and 1948*, Cassell, 1950.
– *The Unwritten Alliance: Speeches 1953–1959*, Cassell, 1961.
CLARK, Colin, *British Trade in the Common Market*, Stevens & Sons, 1962.
COLEMAN, Terry, *Thatcher's Britain*, Bantam Press, 1987.

Bibliography

CRITCHLEY, Julian, *Heseltine: the unauthorised biography*, André Deutsch, 1987.
DALYELL, Tam, *Misrule*, Hamish Hamilton, 1987.
DANIEL, W. W., *Racial Discrimination in England*, Penguin, 1968.
DEPARTMENT OF ENERGY, *Development of the Oil and Gas resources of the United Kingdom* (Brown Book), 1988.
EDEN, Sir Anthony, *Full Circle*, Cassell, 1960.
ELLIOTT, John, *Conflict or Coooperation, The Growth of Industrial Democracy*, Kogan Page, 1978.
FAIRLIE, Henry, *The Establishment*, 1959.
FISHER, Nigel, *Iain Macleod*, André Deutsch, 1973.
FOOT, Paul, *Immigration and Race in British Politics*, Penguin, 1965.
– *The Rise of Enoch Powell*, Penguin, 1969.
GELBER, Lionel, *America in Britain's Place*, Praeger, 1961.
– *The Alliance of Necessity*, Robert Hale, 1966.
HAMILTON, Willie, *My Queen and I*, Quartet, 1975.
HARRIS, Kenneth, *Thatcher*, Weidenfeld & Nicolson, 1988.
HARTLEY, Anthony, *A State of England*, Hutchinson, 1963.
HENNESSY, Peter & SELDON, Anthony (eds.), *Ruling Performance*, Basil Blackwell, 1987.
HESELTINE, Michael, *Where There's A Will*, Hutchinson, 1987.
HEWITT, Patricia, *The Abuse of Power*, Martin Robertson, 1982.
HIMMELWEIT, Hilde T., OPPENHEIM, A. N. and VINCE, Pamela, *Television and the Child*, OUP for Nuffield Foundation, 1958.
HOGGART, Richard, *The Uses of Literacy*, Penguin, 1957.
HUTCHINSON, Michael and YOUNG, Christopher, *Educating the Intelligent*, Penguin, 1962.
INGLIS, Brian, *Private Conscience and Public Morality*, Four Square, 1964.
JACKSON, Brian and MARSDEN, Dennis, *Education and the Working Class*, Penguin, 1962.
KEE, Robert, *1945: The World We Fought For*, Hamish Hamilton, 1985.
KING-HALL, Stephen, *Power Politics in the Nuclear Age*, Victor Gollancz, 1962.
KOESTLER, Arthur, (ed.), *Suicide of a Nation?* Hutchinson, 1963.
LETWIN, Oliver, *Privatising the World*, Cassell, 1988.
MACMILLAN, Harold, *The Middle Way*.
MARQUAND, David, *The Unprincipled Society*, Jonathan Cape, 1988.

Bibliography

MAYNE, Richard, *The Community of Europe*, Victor Gollancz, 1962.

MERCER, Derrik, MUNGHAM, Geoff and WILLIAMS, Kevin, *The Fog of War*, Heinemann, 1987.

MILNE, Alasdair, *DG: The Memoirs of a British Broadcaster*, Hodder & Stoughton, 1988.

MORGAN, Kenneth, *Labour in Power*, OUP, 1984.

MORRIS, Colin, *Unyoung Uncoloured Unpoor*, Epworth Press, 1969.

– *Include Me Out!*

MORRIS, James, *Farewell The Trumpets*, Faber & Faber, 1978.

NICHOLSON, Max, *The System*, Hodder & Stoughton, 1967.

NUTTING, Anthony, *Europe Will Not Wait*, Hollis & Carter, 1960.

OECD, *Economic Surveys 1986/1987: United Kingdom*, OECD, 1987.

PEARSON, Geoffrey, *Hooligan*, Macmillan Press, 1983.

PEDLEY, Robin, *The Comprehensive School*, Penguin, 1963.

PONTING, Clive, *Whitehall: Tragedy and Farce*, Hamish Hamilton, 1986.

POSTMAN, Neil, *Amusing Ourselves to Death*, Methuen, 1985.

PRIOR, James, *A Balance of Power*, Hamish Hamilton, 1986.

PRITT, D. N., *Brasshats and Bureaucrats*, Lawrence & Wishart, 1966.

– *Law, Class and Society* (Bk 111) *Law and Politics and Law in the Colonies*, Lawrence and Wishart, 1971.

RADICE, Giles, *The Industrial Democrats*, George Allen & Unwin, 1978.

SAMPSON, Anthony, *Anatomy of Britain*, Hodder & Stoughton, 1962.

– *The New Anatomy of Britain*, Hodder & Stoughton, 1971.

SHANKS, Michael, *The Stagnant Society*, Penguin, 1961.

SHANKS, Michael and LAMBERT, John, *Britain and the New Europe*, Chatto & Windus, 1962.

SHONFIELD, Andrew, *British Economic Policy since the War*, Penguin, 1958.

SMITH, Trevor, *Anti-Politics Consensus, Reform and Protest in Britain*, Charles Knight, 1972.

SNOW, C. P., *The Two Cultures and the Scientific Revolution*, CUP, 1961.

STALKER, John, *Stalker*, Harrap, 1988.

STRACHEY, John, *The End of Empire*, Victor Gollancz, 1959.

TAYLOR, Robert, *The Fifth Estate*, Routledge & Kegan Paul, 1978.

TEMPLE, William, *Christianity and Social Order*, Penguin, 1942.

THOMAS, Donald, *A Long Time Burning*, Routledge & Kegan Paul, 1969.

Bibliography

THOMAS, Hugh (ed.), *The Establishment*, New English Library, 1959.
WHITAKER, Ben, *The Police*, Penguin, 1964.
WILLIAMS, Raymond, *Communications*, Penguin, 1962.
WILSON, Harold, *The Relevance of British Socialism*, Weidenfeld & Nicolson, 1964.

Index

Acheson, D. 1, 10, 33
Altrincham, Lord 135
Andrew, Prince 138
Anne, Princess 135, 138
Arnold, M. 156
Ascherson, N. 231–2
Ashdown, P. 129
Attlee, C. 1, 7
  achievements 17–18, 22, 229
  and BBC 199
  and Commonwealth and Empire 43, 51
  consensus politics 10, 125
  contrasts with Thatcher 29
  and economy 80–1
  government of 15, 21
  and monarchy 136
  and nationalization 27, 212
  1945 election 16, 210
  and social security 107, 109, 111
  and unions 89, 130

Baker, K. 86, 122–3
Barnes, J. 82
Barnett, J. 196
Barnett, M. 139
Barwick, S. 187
BBC 189–99
  and authority 189–90
  and bias 191–2
  criticism of 189, 193–4
  funding 198–9
  impartiality 194–7
  standards 194
  and Zircon programme 196–7
  see also television
Beaverbrook, Lord 174
Beckman, R. 225

Beith, A. 129
Benn, A. 3, 49, 145, 234
  and economy 100, 101
  Labour Party 126, 128
  leadership challenge 28, 130–1
  and Northern Ireland 73
  as Postmaster General 137, 190, 192
Bennett, G. 148
Best, K. 221
Betjeman, J. 171
Bevan, A. 25, 125
  and National Health Service 110
Bevin, E. 11, 92, 136
  and Cold War 9
  in government 21–2
  international power 34
  nuclear weapons 38
  relationship with USA 18
  and unions 20, 77, 81, 88–9
Biffen, J. 24, 49, 112, 147
Birt, J. 194
Blackburn, R. 150, 155, 160
Blunt, A. 139
Bone, I. 219
Boothby, R. 35
Borges, J. L. 48
Bowie, D. 177
Brittan, L. 214
Britten, B. 177
Brooke, H. 155
Brookeborough, Lord 66
Brown, George 62, 130
Brown, Gordon 217
Brown, J. A. C. 183–4, 187
Brown, M. 197
Browne-Wilkinson, Sir N. 154

Index

budget
  1979 204
  1988 3, 24
Bullock, A. 35, 81
Bunyan, T. 162
Burgess, A. 178
Bush, G. 1, 2
Butler, R. A. B. 52–3, 82, 125–6, 137
Byrnes, J. 34

Caldwell, A. 20
Callaghan, J.
  as Chancellor 79–80, 205
  and Church 148
  and Commonwealth and Empire 126
  and education 116
  and Europe 63, 85
  as Home Secretary 161–2
  and immigration 52, 54
  and monarchy 137
  and North Sea oil 100–1
  and Northern Ireland 67–8, 70
  pact with Liberals 124
  as Prime Minister 128
  relationship with USA 40
  and unions 90, 92–3
Campbell, D. 196, 197
Campbell-Savours, D. 154
Carr, R. 89–90, 152
Carrington, Lord 11
Castle, B. 53, 90
Charles, Prince of Wales 135, 138, 168, 227
Church 141–8
  and Conservative Party 146–7
  membership 142
  and nuclear weapons 143–4
  poverty 144, 145
  relations with state 144–5, 147–8
  and Third World 142–3
Churchill, W. S.
  and BBC 182
  Britain's declining role 8, 9
  and British Petroleum 27
  and Cabinet 130

consensus politics 87–8
and emigration 21
and Empire 41–2
and Europe 58–9
funeral of 134
and immigration 52
and monarchy 136
and nuclear weapons 38
post-war government 125
relationship with USA 35–6, 39
resignation as Prime Minister 16, 82
and social security 18
Clark, G. 161
Clwyd, A. 175
coal
  nationalization of 18–20
  in 1988 25
  and North Sea oil 97
  strike (1984) 211–12
Collins, N. 181, 186
Commonwealth 9, 43, 45
  growth of 47–9
  immigration from 51–2
  and monarchy 137–8
competitiveness 216–17
consensus politics 10–11, 125–6
  and economic decline 80, 84–5
  end of 206
  and unions 87–90
Conservative Party
  changes in 129–30
  and Church 146–7
  and law and order 156–7
  leadership of 206
  in 1980s 23–4
  and Thatcher 203–4
Cook, R. 27
Cousins, F. 87, 89
Craig, W. 67
Crawford, M. 135
credit 224–5
Crichton-Brown, R. 232
Cripps, Sir S. 21–2, 81, 88, 109
Critchley, J. 129, 207

Index

Crook, T. 174
Crookshank, H. 109–10
Crosland, A. 101, 120, 127
Crossman, R. 127, 133, 153
Cuban missile crisis 10
culture
  and affluence 172
  and censorship 178–9
  and class 171–2
  and education 172–3
  growth of 178
  and politics 169
  pop 177
  youth 224
Curran, C. 193
Currie, E. 233
Curteis, I. 191, 193

Dalton, Dr H. 18, 20–2, 136
Dalyell, T. 94, 150, 152–3, 196–7, 207, 210
Daniel, W. W. 52
Davies, D. 131
Day, Sir R. 185
De Gaulle, C. 10, 39, 59–62, 83, 127
decline in power 7–8, 9–20, 28
  economic 77–86
  reaction to 11–12
defense expenditure
  1950 17
  1980s 37–8
Denning, Lord 154
Devlin, B. 66
Devlin, Lord 159
Donaldson, Lord 150, 154
Douglas-Home, A. 45, 52, 129, 137, 192, 198
Drake, Sir E. 97
Duckworth, B. 147
Dulles, J. F. 36

Eccles, Sir D. 116
economic decline 77–86
  growth rates (1959–64) 83
  and inflation 86
  in 1950s 82–3
  post-war recovery 78–9, 81–2
  sterling crises 79–80, 84
  and Thatcher 85–6
  and unions 81, 84–5
economic policy
  and entry to European Community 63–4
  foreign investments 25–6, 27–8
  monetarism 231–2
  Thatcherite 24–7
Ede, C. 51
Eden, A.
  and broadcasting 182
  and economy 82
  Egyptian policy 9
  relationship with USA 36–7
  resignation 126
education 4, 115–23
  central direction of 122–3
  and comprehensive schools 116, 121
  and economic performance 118–19
  higher 115–16, 117, 118
  industrial training 121–2
  and media 170
  and public schools 119–20
  Reform Bill (1988) 233
  science teaching 120–1
Edward VII 137
Edwardes, Sir M. 204
Eisenhower, D. D. 36, 37, 39, 184
elections
  1945 16
  1950 22
  1983 210
  1987 214
  European 5
Elizabeth I, Queen 141
Elizabeth II, Queen 133, 137
Elizabeth, Queen Mother 136, 140
emigration 20–1
Empire
  end of 9, 41–9
  and immigration 52–4
  and India 41, 43–4

243

Index

and nationalism 42–3
  phases of 43–5
Ennals, D. 54
Europe 57–64
  and economic decline 83, 84
  and EFTA 61
  and European Community 1, 2, 58–9, 61–2
Evans, M. 92

Fairbairn, N. 145
Fairlie, H. 189–91
Falklands War 48, 208–10
Farndale, M. 182
Farrell, M. 72
Faulkner, B. 66, 67
Festival of Britain (1951) 10
financial services industry 220–1
Fisher, N. 61–2
Fitzgerald, G. 3, 69
Foot, M. 130, 210
Fraser, M. 126

Gaitskill, H. 22, 53, 82, 109, 126–7, 130
Gardiner, Lord 71
Gaskin, Professor 97
George VI, King 16, 136
Gibraltar killings 72
Gilmour, I. 207
Glass, R. 55
Golding, W. 178
Goodall, J. 171
Gorbachev, M. 1, 10, 40, 207
Gore-Booth, Sir P. 28
Gormley, J. 91
Gorst, J. 93
Gow, I. 69
Grade, L. 187
Greene, G. 177
Greene, H. 196
Griffiths, P. 53
Grimond, J. 128
Gruenther, General 35
Gummer, S. 146

Habgood, Dr 146, 147
Hailsham, Lord 3, 159, 192, 208, 234
Hallstein, Professor 58
Hamilton, W. 134, 136, 137
Hammond, E. 95
Hanson, Lord 220
Harris, K. 207, 210, 215
Harris, R. 208
Hart, D. 94
Hartley, A. 170–1, 176
Hattersley, R. 130, 178, 219
Haughey, C. 68, 70
Healey, D. 10, 85, 93, 99, 100
Heath, E.
  and Church 148
  consensus politics 80
  defeat as party leader 90
  election as Prime Minister 129
  and Europe 40, 62–3, 84, 127
  and North Sea oil 97
  and race relations 54–5
  relationship with USA 39–40
  and social security 111
  and Thatcher 206–18
  and unions 211
Heffer, E. 28, 127, 130–1
Hermon, Sir J. 163
Heseltine, M. 24, 140, 205, 207–9, 214–15
Hewitt, P. 152–3, 162
Higginston, G. 123
Hill, C. 192
Hitler, A. 41
Hoggart, R. 170–2, 191
home ownership 205–6
Hong Kong 2, 48, 49
Horsbrugh, Dame F. 115
Howe, Sir G. 2, 56, 91, 100, 186, 204, 213
Huddleston, T. 143
Hurd, D. 56, 146, 177, 185, 188, 232
Hussein, King 44
Hussey, M. 191

Index

immigration 2, 50–6
  1953–61 51
  see also racism
industry 204
inflation, reduced 205, 214
Ingham, B. 178
Ingrams, R. 183
Isaacs, J. 89, 188

Jenkins, C. 27
Jenkins, R. 85, 127, 152–3
Johnson, L. B. 40
Jones, C. 51
Jones, J. 87, 92
Joseph, Sir K. 23

Kaufman, G. 2
Kaunda, K. 139
Kearton, Lord 100
Keays, S. 211
Kellner, P. 83, 131
Kendall, W. 128
Kennedy, J. F. 10, 39, 59, 127
Keynes, J. M. 35, 109
Kilmuir, Lord 126
King, C. 170, 174
Kinnock, N. 113–14, 127–8, 130–1, 217, 224
Koestler, A. 119
Khrushchev, N. 36

Labour Party
  government (1945) 15–17, 124–5
    achievements of 17–18
    election results 16
    legislation 21–2
    nationalization of coal 18–20
    social policies 18–21
  in 1980s 28
  and unions 130–1
law 149–63
  capital punishment 155
  Emergency Powers Act (1947) 153
  and freedom 3, 150–1, 153–4, 158–9
  juries 152, 159

  legal aid 158
  and Northern Ireland 154–5
  Official Secrets Act (1968) 152
  police 161–3
  prison system 160–1
  and protest 155
  secrecy 227, 230–1
  sources 151–2
  and violence 150, 156–7
Lawrence, R. 193
Lawson, N. 3, 23–4, 208, 211, 213
Leapman, M. 175
Leavis, F. R. 177
Lee, J. 110
Lehman, J. 210
Lemass, S. 66
Lennox Boyd, A. 45, 52
Lever, H. 100
Liberal Party 128–9
Lichfield, Lord 139
Linlithgow, Lord 43
Livingstone, K. 215
Lloyd George, D. 24
Lloyd, S. 83
local authorities 215–16
Lynch, J. 68

Mabon, Dr 99
McCann, D. 72
MacGregor, I. 209, 211
Mackay, Lord 158
Macleod, I. 45–6, 52, 61, 110, 112, 125, 129
Macmilllan, H. 4
  and cabinet 125, 130
  and Commonwealth and Empire 9, 45, 48, 60
  consensus politics 83, 126
  and economy 82
  and education 121
  and Europe 61–2, 84, 126
  and immigration 52
  and monarchy 137
  and nuclear weapons 38

Index

as Prime Minister 230
and privatization 213
radicalism of 129
relationship with USA 38–9, 59
and television 184–5
Macnamara, R. 39
Margaret, Princess 135
Mark, Sir R. 162
Marquand, D. 77
Marshall, General G. 34
Mates, M. 219
Maude, A. 125
Maudling, R. 46, 66, 125, 162, 207
Maxwell, R. 174
Mayhew, Sir P. 169
media 167–79
  the arts 167–8
  censorship 178–9
  cinema 170–1, 176–7
  and education 170
  literature 177–8
  press 169, 173–6
Messina Conference (1955) 60
Milne, A. 191, 195–8
monarchy 133–40
  and Commonwealth 137–8
  costs of 137
  criticisms of 135–7
  Queen's role 133–5
  system of honours 139–40
Monckton, Sir W. 87, 125
Morgan, K. 22
Morris, C. 143
Morrison, C. 104, 220
Morrison, H. 17, 20, 22, 43
Mountbatten, Earl 44
Moynihan, C. 157
Mugabe, R. 47
Muggeridge, M. 135, 167
Murdoch, I. 178
Murdoch, R. 173–4
Murumbi, J. 48

Namier, Sir L. 150, 207

Nasser, Colonel A. 36, 44
National Health Service
  government handling of 112–14
  implementation of 18
  in welfare state 107–8, 109–10
Neave, A. 68
Nehru, P. 47
Nicholson, B. 121
Nicholson, M. 185
Norman, E. 146
Normanbrook, Lord 152
North Sea oil 96–104
  and energy requirements 97
  exports 217
  government policies 100–1
  investment in 103
  jobs 98
  production 103
  revenue from 99–100, 102
Northcliffe, Lord 174
Northern Ireland 3, 65–73
  Anglo-Irish Agreement 69
  Catholics' rights campaign 66
  power sharing 69
  Stalker affair 71–2, 154, 163
  Sunningdale Conference 63
  troops despatched to 66
  violence in 66, 70–1
nuclear weapons 38–9

O'Neil, M. 131
O'Neill, T. 66
Orwell, G. 177
Osborne, Sir C. 51, 53
Osborne, J. 178
Owen, D. 127, 129

Paisley, I. 66, 67
Pares, B. 207
Park, D. 196
Parker, Lord 159
Parkinson, C. 211
Peach, B. 162
Pearson, G. 156
Pedley, R. 119, 121

Index

Philip, Prince 136, 137
Phillips, A. 221
Phillips, M. 135
Pickles, W. 170
Piggott, L. 139
police 223–4
Pompidou, G. 62
Postman, N. 183
poverty 222–3
Powell, A. 177
Powell, E. 52, 54–6, 62, 68, 125
Powell, J. 193
Prior, J. 68–9, 83, 91, 93–4, 128, 209, 211, 216
Pritt, D. N. 150, 153, 192
privatization 4, 27, 212–13
Proetta, C. 72
Profumo, J. 184, 211
protest movement 2, 230
Pym, F. 209

racism 50–6
  riots 52
  Smethwick election 53
  see also immigration
Radice, G. 94, 131
Rae, J. 122
Ramsey, I. 143
Rayner, Lord 205
Reagan, R. 2, 40
Rees, M. 154
Rees-Mogg, W. 142, 145, 187, 195, 197
Reith, Lord 187, 190
Rhodesia 46–7, 55
Ridley, N. 5
Roberts, A. 196
Rodgers, B. 127
Rome, Treaty of 60
Rothermere, Lord 174
Royal Family *see* Monarchy
Runcie, Archbishop 145
Rushdie, S. 2

Salisbury, Lord 46, 52, 126, 129, 211
Salmond, A. 24

Sampson, A.
  on Church 142
  on Labour Party 127
  on monarchy 133, 136
  on television 181, 185, 193, 196
Sampson, C. 72
Sandeman, H. 98
Sandford, R. 162
Sandys, D. 48, 54
Sankey, Lord, 151
Saunders, E. 220
Savage, S. 72
Scanlon, H. 92
Scargill, A. 91–2, 94, 211–12, 214
Scarman, Lord 3, 72, 157
secrecy 227, 230–1, 234
Seldon, A. 181
Shanks, M. 78
Shonfield, A. 79
Silkin, S. 152
Silverman, S. 158
Simon, Lord 192
Smith, I. 46–7, 55
Smith, J. 113
Smuts, J. C. 41
Snow, C. P. 11, 117, 120, 178
Soames, C. 207
Social Democratic Party 128–9
social services
  attack on 27–8
  and welfare state 108
South Africa 55–6
Spicer, M. 99
Stalker, J. 71–2
Stanley, O. 20
Steel, D. 129, 131
steel industry 25
Stern, V. 219
Strachey, J. 42
Suez Crisis (1956) 36, 44
Sugar, A. 221

takeovers 221–2
Tebbit, N. 24, 138

Philip, Prince 136, 137
Phillips, A. 221
Phillips, M. 135
Pickles, W. 170
Piggott, L. 139
police 223–4
Pompidou, G. 62
Postman, N. 183
poverty 222–3
Powell, A. 177
Powell, E. 52, 54–6, 62, 68, 125
Powell, J. 193
Prior, J. 68–9, 83, 91, 93–4, 128, 209, 211, 216
Pritt, D. N. 150, 153, 192
privatization 4, 27, 212–13
Proetta, C. 72
Profumo, J. 184, 211
protest movement 2, 230
Pym, F. 209

racism 50–6
  riots 52
  Smethwick election 53
  see also immigration
Radice, G. 94, 131
Rae, J. 122
Ramsey, I. 143
Rayner, Lord 205
Reagan, R. 2, 40
Rees, M. 154
Rees-Mogg, W. 142, 145, 187, 195, 197
Reith, Lord 187, 190
Rhodesia 46–7, 55
Ridley, N. 5
Roberts, A. 196
Rodgers, B. 127
Rome, Treaty of 60
Rothermere, Lord 174
Royal Family *see* Monarchy
Runcie, Archbishop 145
Rushdie, S. 2

Salisbury, Lord 46, 52, 126, 129, 211
Salmond, A. 24

Sampson, A.
  on Church 142
  on Labour Party 127
  on monarchy 133, 136
  on television 181, 185, 193, 196
Sampson, C. 72
Sandeman, H. 98
Sandford, R. 162
Sandys, D. 48, 54
Sankey, Lord, 151
Saunders, E. 220
Savage, S. 72
Scanlon, H. 92
Scargill, A. 91–2, 94, 211–12, 214
Scarman, Lord 3, 72, 157
secrecy 227, 230–1, 234
Seldon, A. 181
Shanks, M. 78
Shonfield, A. 79
Silkin, S. 152
Silverman, S. 158
Simon, Lord 192
Smith, I. 46–7, 55
Smith, J. 113
Smuts, J. C. 41
Snow, C. P. 11, 117, 120, 178
Soames, C. 207
Social Democratic Party 128–9
social services
  attack on 27–8
  and welfare state 108
South Africa 55–6
Spicer, M. 99
Stalker, J. 71–2
Stanley, O. 20
Steel, D. 129, 131
steel industry 25
Stern, V. 219
Strachey, J. 42
Suez Crisis (1956) 36, 44
Sugar, A. 221

takeovers 221–2
Tebbit, N. 24, 138

Index

and media 186, 193, 195, 233
and socialism 132, 133
and unions 92–3
television
  BBC 189–99
  changes 188
  commercial 181–2
  entertainment 186–7
  in the home 180–8
  impact of 183–4
  news 182–3, 186
  and politics 184–6
Temple, W. 144
Thatcher, M. 7
  and Church 141, 147–8
  and Commonwealth 137
  consensus politics 80, 88
  and education 115–16, 122
  and law 150, 158
  and National Health Service 107
  in 1988 3, 23, 218
  and North Sea oil 101
  and Northern Ireland 67, 72
  and poll tax 219
  as Prime Minister 11, 129, 203–17, 230, 234
  relationship with USA 40
  reputation of 28
  and Rhodesia 47
  and South Africa 139
  and television 185, 188, 197
  and Tory Party 127, 131–2
  and unions 93–4
  and welfare state 114
Thatcherism 204, 207
Thomas, J. H. 66
Thomas, Donald 178
Thomas, Dylan 177
Thompson, Lord 174, 182
Thorneycroft, P. 83
Todd, R. 26, 131
tolerance in society 226–8
Tracey, M. 226
Trelford, D. 175

Truman, H. 7, 17, 33
two-nations concept 218–28
  and minorities 219–20
  and North-South divide 218–9

Ulster *see* Northern Ireland
unemployment 204–5, 214–15
unions 81, 84–5, 87–95
  coal miners' strike
    1972 91–2
    1984 211–12
  and consensus 10–11, 80, 84–5, 87–90, 127–8
  decline of 88
  and Donovan Report (1968) 88, 90
  and Heath's government 90–1
  social contract 92–3
  and Thatcher 93–5
United States of America, relations with 1, 2, 33–40
  advantages to Britain 39–40
  and Churchill 35–6
  in World War Two 33–4

Vaizey, J. 117–18
de Valera, E. 66
values, social and ethical 225–6
Vincent, J. 102, 120, 209–10
violence 150, 156–7, 223

Waldron, Sir J. 161
Walker, P. G. 53
Walker, Peter 203, 205
Walker, R. 161
Wallace, W. 122
Walters, Sir A. 4, 208
Warner, J. 150, 154
de la Warr, Lord 182
Waugh, E. 171
welfare state 107–14, 108
  expenditure on (1985) 111–13
  National Health Service 107–8, 109–10, 112–14
  prescription charges 109
  reaction to 232

Index

social services 108, 114
Wesker, A. 170
Westland Affair 213–14
Whitehead, P. 67
Whitehouse, M. 178, 226, 233
Whitelaw, W. 56, 64, 67, 87, 208, 220, 226–7
Whitney, J. 188
Wilberforce, Lord 91
Wilkinson, E. 115–16
Williams, D. 213
Williams, R. 168, 170, 172–4
Williams, S. 127
Wilson, H.
  and BBC 192
  and Church 148
  and Commonwealth and Empire 47
  consensus politics 80, 89, 126
  and education 116
  and Europe 63, 84–5, 126
  as leader of party 83–4, 130
  and monarchy 137
  and Northern Ireland 67
  and political parties 129
  and race relations 54
  relationship with USA 40
  and Rhodesia 47–8, 62
  secrecy in government 152
  and unions 10, 92
'Winter of Discontent' 11, 128
Wolfe, W. 101
Woollard, B. 224
Woolton, Lord 81, 181

Yamazaki, T. 25
Younger, G. 26
youth 224

Zedong, Mao 34
Zimbabwe *see* Rhodesia